STUDENT'S SOLUTIONS MANUAL TO ACCOMPANY MULTIPLE-CHOICE & FREE-RESPONSE QUESTIONS IN PREPARATION FOR THE AP CHEMISTRY EXAMINATION

(FOURTH EDITION)

Peter E. Demmin
Amherst Central High School, Retired
Amherst, New York

Copyright © 2000 by D & S Marketing Systems, Inc.

All rights reserved.

No part of this book may be reproduced or transmitted in any form or by any means, electronic or mechanical, including photocopying and recording, or by any information storage or retrieval systems, without written permission from the publisher.

Printed in the U.S.A.

Preface

This Student's Solutions Manual is designed as a supplement to MULTIPLE-CHOICE & FREE-RESPONSE QUESTIONS IN PREPARATION FOR THE AP CHEMISTRY EXAMINATION, FOURTH EDITION.

The solutions provided are designed to give thorough and convincing explanations to the questions. Where appropriate, explanations are also provided to account for reasons why the distractors are not correct. The explanations provided are not necessarily the only correct or plausible explanations. Many problems in chemistry can be solved using alternate routes to satisfactory answers. The multiple-choice questions were written with the expectation that there is only one correct (or best) response. The free-response questions allow for a broad range of "correct" or partially correct answers.

The explanations were chosen for presentation based upon their clarity and persuasiveness. Another important criterion for inclusion was the extent to which a given explanation could be extended to other problems. The general directions for the multiple-choice section of the examination often ask for the "best" answer. The explanations provided in this MANUAL are intended to help students identify the "best" answer for the multiple-choice questions and a strong, thorough answer to each free-response question.

Dimensional analysis – also known as "the factor-label method" – was chosen as the method to solve most quantitative problems. Frequently, the available responses in the question book provide a mathematical expression containing numbers only. The SOLUTIONS MANUAL includes labels for these numbers as part of the explanation. Application of simple algebra then leads to the correct response. Estimation arithmetic is also presented as a useful tool as an efficient, time-saving method for solving some quantitative problems. Because calculators are permitted only in part A of the free response section of the examination, both dimensional analysis and estimation arithmetic become very useful problem-solving stategies.

As with the question book, whatever quality is found in this work is due primarily to my observations of the learning and study skills used by my students over the years. Especially useful to me was the large number of attractive (but incorrect) responses that seemed plausible to my students. Reflecting upon the thinking – even it was "incorrect" – of some three thousand youthful, vigorous minds has provided much of the substance of the explanations offered as solutions in this MANUAL. To those minds must go my greatest thanks.

Sincere thanks also go to my colleagues, Jerry Mullins, of Plano (Texas) Senior High School and Patsy Mueller of Highland Park (Illinois) High School whose frank and careful review of the manuscript helped prevent some poor questions from getting any ink. Their insightful knowledge of chemistry and, especially, of how students perceive chemistry, provided significant input to the quality, level and clarity of the questions and their solutions. The experience of their years as active leaders and consultants in Advanced Placement Chemistry has made a major contribution to the credibility of this work offered for the preparation of students.

A large measure of gratitude goes to my wife, Ruth, whose understanding and support helped carry me through many hours of writing and revising a few hundred questions – only to find more of the same waiting their turn to be served.

Peter E. Demmin
Amherst Central High School, Retired
Amherst, New York

This book was typeset by CHK Associates, Inc. New York City. All communications concerning this book should be addressed to the publisher and distributor:

D & S Marketing Systems, Inc.
1205 38th Street
Brooklyn, New York 11218

Table of Contents

Chapter 1: Atomic Structure 1

Chapter 2: Chemical Bonding 9

Chapter 3: The Phases of Matter – Solid, Liquid and Gas 19

Chapter 4: Solutions 27

Chapter 5: Stoichiometry 39

Chapter 6: Chemical Kinetics 48

Chapter 7: Chemical Equilibrium 59

Chapter 8: Thermodynamics 70

Chapter 9: Acid-Base Systems 82

Chapter 10: Electrochemistry 94

Chapter 11: Organic Chemistry 105

Chapter 12: Descriptive Chemistry 118

Sample Examination I 127

Sample Examination II 157

Sample Examination III 192

Chapter 1
Atomic Structure

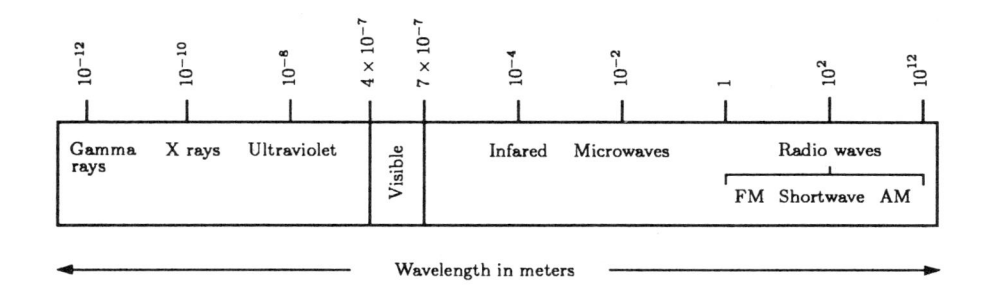

1. Energy is directly proportional to frequency; energy is inversely proportional to wave length. The highest energy is that radiation with the greatest frequency and shortest wave length; that is, x-rays.

   The correct choice is (E).

2. Absorption of energy in the visible region can be used to determine identity and concentration of colored solutions.

   The correct choice is (D).

3. Microwave energy such as that provided by an ordinary kitchen microwave oven emits radiation that could pass through ordinary glass but is blocked by treated glass.

   The correct choice is (B).

4. Radiation with the shortest wave length and greatest frequency is used to analyze the structure of metallic crystals.

   The correct choice is (E).

5. Such a beam must be harmless to people. It must have low energy and high wave length.

   The correct choice is (A).

6. Within a period, metallic character (the ability to lose electrons rapidly) increases as atomic number decreases. Within a group, metallic character increases as atomic number increases. The Br, Se, As, list matches the "period" criterion. The other choices do not match either criterion.

   The correct choice is (D).

7. The electron configurations of the nitride ion and the oxide ion are the same, both with 10 electrons: $1s^2, 2s^2, 2p^6$. The other choices have different electron configurations.

   The correct choice is (B).

2 Chapter 1   Atomic Structure

8. Potassium atoms give off one electron each to become positive ions. No protons are taken on. When electrons are given off, the radius decreases. Only option I is true.

   The correct choice is (A).

9. Kernel electrons are those located in inner energy levels. Fluorine atoms have 2 kernel electrons and 7 valence electrons. Beryllium has 2 kernel electrons and 2 valence electrons. Na, P, and Ar atoms have 10 kernel electrons each. The number of valence electrons is 1, 5, and 8 respectively.

   The correct choice is (B).

10. Using the formula $E = h\nu$ and substituting 6.63×10^{-34} J·sec for h and 8×10^{15} sec^{-1} for ν, the value for E is closest to 5×10^{-18} J, (actually, at two significant figures, 5.3×10^{-18} J). The other choices are various incorrect combinations of given values.

    The correct choice is (C).

11. Using the formula $c = \nu\lambda$ and substituting 3.0×10^8 m·sec^{-1} for c and 6×10^{15} sec^{-1} for ν, the value of λ is closest to 5×10^1 nanometers, (actually, at two significant figures, 50 nm). Note that 1 meter = 10^9 nanometers. The other choices are various incorrect combinations of given values.

    The correct choice is (B).

12. The electron configuration for a chromium atom is [Ar core] $4s^1$, $3d^5$. This is a variation from the usual *aufbau* rule. The outer six electrons are located in half-filled orbitals, hence unpaired.

    The correct choice is (D).

13. Most members of the lanthanide series have electron configurations that include [Xe core] $6s^2\ 5d^1\ 4f^n$ where n varies from 1 to 14. Within this series, the number of $4f$ electrons shows the greatest variation.

    The correct choice is (A).

14. Both the ion and the atom have the same number of kernel electrons, 10. The electrons in the valence shells are shown in the Lewis dot diagrams below. The phosphide ion has three more electrons but no unpaired electrons.

    The phosphorus atom has three unpaired electrons. Thus, only I and II are true.

    The correct choice is (B).

15. The ℓ quantum number of 1 corresponds to the p-sublevel. In scandium, the $2p$ and $3p$ sublevels are filled with six electrons each. Thus the number of electrons with ℓ quantum number of 1 is 12.

    The correct choice is (E).

16. The given electron configuration represents a transition element, specifically the element with atomic number of 30 $\left(18(\text{Ar core}) + 2(4s^2) + 10(3d^{10}) = 30 \text{ electrons}\right)$. This atom has two valence electrons accounting for an expected ionic charge of 2+ as its most common ion. The corresponding formula for the oxide is XO since the oxide ion has the charge of 2−.

    The correct choice is (A).

17. The possible combinations for H_2O are: (molar mass given)

    ^1_1H ^1_1H $^{16}_8O$ (18 g); ^1_1H ^2_1H $^{16}_8O$ (19 g); ^2_1H ^2_1H $^{16}_8O$ (20 g)

    ^1_1H ^1_1H $^{17}_8O$ (19 g); ^1_1H ^2_1H $^{17}_8O$ (20 g); ^2_1H ^2_1H $^{17}_8O$ (21 g)

    accounting for four different numerical values for the molar mass of water.

    The correct choice is (C).

18. The Law of Multiple Proportions addresses the ratio of masses of one element per fixed mass of a second element. Assuming 100 g of each compound, the given information places masses of manganese in the numerators of the complex fraction. Placing the masses of oxygen (36.81 and 22.50) in the corresponding denominators permits calculation of mass of manganese per (one) gram of oxygen. The Law of Multiple Proportions will be illustrated if that fraction is a simple whole number ratio. In this case, the fraction is 1.74/3.44 or simply 1/2. The other choices are various incorrect combinations of values. Calculation of moles of each element does not provide mass ratio information as specified in the Law of Multiple Proportions. Such calculations do not support the Law of Multiple Proportions.

    The correct choice is (E).

19. The dot diagram shows six electrons – two pairs of electrons and two unpaired electrons. This matches the valence electron structure of the atoms of elements in the oxygen family. The two unpaired electrons are from the p-sublevel. The two half-empty orbitals accommodate two additional electrons. Atoms of every element in the oxygen family have four electrons in the outermost p-sublevel accounting for the ℓ quantum number of 1. This atom could be oxygen, itself, with only 2 kernel electrons; thus, choice (C) cannot be inferred from this diagram.

    The correct choice is (C).

4 Chapter 1 Atomic Structure

20. The quantum numbers

$$2, 0, 0, +\tfrac{1}{2}; \quad 2, 0, 0, -\tfrac{1}{2}$$

correspond to the two electrons permitted in the *s*-sublevel of the second energy level. The next electrons permitted will be placed in the *p*-sublevel of the second level. The corresponding n and ℓ quantum numbers are 2 and 1, respectively.

The correct choice is (E).

21. The electron configuration of sulfur is $1s^2$ (one filled orbital), $2s^2$ (one filled orbital), $2p^6$ (three filled orbitals), $3s^2$ (one filled orbital), $3p^4$ (one filled and two half-filled orbitals), giving a total of seven filled orbitals.

The correct choice is (D).

22. The series S^{2-}, Cl^-, K^+ has members with the same number of electrons (18) and which must, therefore, have the same electron configuration. The series Mg, Ca, Sr has members with the same number of valence electrons only. The series Mg^{2+}, Ca^{2+}, Sr^{2+} has members that have the same charge and the same number of valence electrons. The series Fe, Co, Ni are members of the "iron triad" but have different numbers of electrons. There is no relationship between the electron configurations of the members of the series, F^-, S^{2-}, As^{3-}.

The correct choice is (C).

23. One good way to remember the relationship between color of visible light and the corresponding wavelength, frequency and energy is to learn the mnemonic ROY G BIV -

<u>R</u>ed/<u>O</u>range/<u>Y</u>ellow   <u>G</u>reen   <u>B</u>lue/<u>I</u>ndigo/<u>V</u>iolet

Red is the color of light that has the greatest wave length, lowest frequency and lowest energy. Violet light has the lowest wave length, highest frequency and highest energy. Another way to help keep track of the relationship is to recall that ultraviolet (*"more" violet than violet*) light is the high energy radiation that causes sunburn.

The correct choice is (C).

24. Information about electron population is given by the quantity, $2n^2$, where n is the principal quantum number associated with the energy level in question. Where $n = 4$ (fourth energy level), the number of sublevels permitted is $n(4)$, the number of orbitals is $n^2(16)$ and the number of electrons is $2n^2(32)$.

The correct choice is (E).

25. To calculate the number of neutrons, the atomic number is subtracted from the mass number (given). The atomic numbers for Mn, Fe, Co, and Ni are 25, 26, 27 and 28, respectively. Thus, only the nuclei ^{58}Ni and ^{57}Co have the same number of neutrons (30).

The correct choice is (D).

Atomic Structure Chapter 1

Free-Response Questions

26. Overall Strategy: Use the Periodic Table and principles relating structure of atoms to chemical properties. Especially useful is the relationship between location on the Periodic Table and configuration (arrangement) of electrons. Energy changes related to changes in this electron configuration are often related to various chemical properties.

   (A) The presence of color is due to energy absorption associated with the movement of unpaired d electrons from lower to higher energy levels. The Ti^{3+} ion has one unpaired electron in the $3d$ sublevel, allowing for such movement. The Sc^{3+} ion has no electrons in its $3d$ sublevel.

   (B) An oxidizing agent gains electrons. Atoms of both chlorine and iodine have one electron vacancy in the outer energy level. The unfilled outer energy level of chlorine is closer to the nucleus than is the corresponding outer energy level of iodine. In addition, a "shielding effect" is established in which inner (kernel) energy levels decrease the attraction of the positive nucleus for the outer energy levels. Therefore, due to both factors, compared to the nucleus of the iodine atom, the nucleus of the chlorine atom exerts a greater attractive force for the electron to be added to the outer energy level vacancy during an oxidation/reduction process.

   (C) A reducing agent loses electrons. The outer electrons of the barium atom are farther from the nucleus than the outer electrons of the magnesium atom. At this greater distance, there is less attractive force on the outer electrons of barium. The "shielding effect" plays a role here as well. With the greater number of filled energy levels in the barium atom, there is less attraction between the nucleus and electrons in the valence energy level. Thus, the electrons of barium, a reducing agent, are lost more easily to the oxidizing agent during an oxidation/reduction process. Compared to magnesium, barium is a better reducing agent because of this weaker attraction between the barium nucleus and its valence electrons.

   (D) The sulfide ion has 16 protons in its nucleus. The chloride ion has 17 protons in its nucleus. Both sulfide and chloride ions have the same number of electrons, but the species with the greater nuclear charge holds the electrons with greater force, hence closer to the nucleus. Thus, the radius of the sulfide ion, S^{2-}, is greater than the radius of the chloride ion, Cl^-, due to the lower nuclear charge on S^{2-}. From another perspective, the radius is smaller when the proton-to-electron ratio, p/e, is greater. Comparing p/e- ratios: Cl^-: 17p/18e$^-$ is higher, hence nuclear attraction is stronger in Cl^- than in S^{2-}: 16 p/18 e$^-$.

27. **Overall Strategy:** Refer to the Periodic Table to locate magnesium. Note that it is a member of the group of Alkaline Earth Metals. (Group numbers are not used on the Periodic Table that is provided with the AP examination.) Use principles relating the chemical properties of magnesium to its atomic structure. Its electron configuration as a ground state atom is $1s^2\ 2s^2\ 2p^6\ 3s^2$.

- (A) The radius of the Mg^{2+} ion is smaller. The electron configuration of $Mg°$ includes two electrons in its $3s$ sublevel. Those electrons are missing from the Mg^{2+} ion. Both species have the same nuclear charge; therefore, the species with fewer electrons and fewer occupied energy levels, Mg^{2+}, is smaller.

- (B) $^{27}_{12}Mg \rightarrow\ ^{0}_{-1}e\ +\ ^{27}_{13}Al$

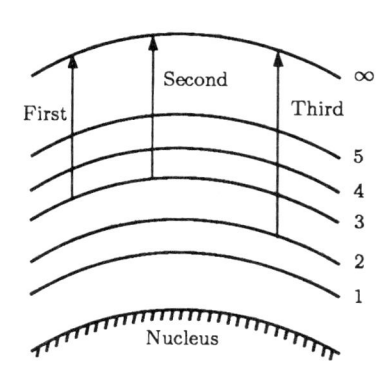

- (C) (1)

    [Diagram showing energy levels labeled 1, 2, 3, 4, 5, ∞ above Nucleus, with arrows marked First (to level 2), Second (to higher level), Third (to ∞).]

    (2) The difference between ^{24}Mg and ^{27}Mg is in the number of neutrons: ^{24}Mg has 12 neutrons; ^{27}Mg has 15 neutrons. The number of neutrons does not affect the strength of attraction between the nucleus and the valence electrons. Therefore their ionization energies are the same.

    (3) With the first ionization energy, one electron is removed from a neutral atom. With the second ionization energy, one additional electron is to be removed from a particle that has become a +1 ion. Both the neutral atom and the +1 ion have the same nuclear charge. The higher ratio of protons to electrons and the smaller size of the ion places the outer electron of the +1 ion closer to the nucleus. More energy is needed to remove that second electron (from a +1 ion) because the force of attraction is greater due to the net positive charge on the ion.

    (4) With the second ionization energy, the electron is removed from the third energy level which is the valence (outer) energy level. With the third ionization energy, the next electron is removed from the second energy level, a kernel (inner) energy level. There is a very large difference in energies between these two principal energy levels. In addition, the same effect due to ionic charge as in (3) above also applies here.

28. <u>Overall Strategy</u>: Recall the definition of the four quantum numbers.

n = principal quantum number (energy level)

ℓ = angular quantum number (sublevel within a principal energy level)

range: 0, 1 ......, $n-1$

m (or m_ℓ) = magnetic (orbital within a sublevel)

range: $-\ell, \ldots, 0, \ldots, +\ell$

s (or m_s) = spin (or clockwise or counterclockwise)

range: $+\frac{1}{2}, -\frac{1}{2}$

The relationship between quantum number and spectrographic notation for electron distribution is needed in order to provide thorough answers to many questions on this topic. Recall that electron capacity by energy level can be summarized using the principal quantum number, n. For each principal energy level, n, where n = the number of that principal energy level:

n = number of sublevels

n^2 = total number of orbitals

$2n^2$ = maximum number of electrons

There are seven principal energy levels in ground state atoms with a maximum of four occupied sublevels:

s (one orbital, two electrons)

p (three orbitals, six electrons)

d (five orbitals, ten electrons)

f (seven orbitals, fourteen electrons)

(A) Orbital a.

(1) quantum numbers representing one of the electrons in orbital a: 4, 0, 0, $+\frac{1}{2}$

(2) quantum numbers representing the second electron in orbital a: 4, 0, 0, $-\frac{1}{2}$. The only difference is the sign of the s quantum number representing opposite spin.

(3) maximum number of electrons in the principal energy level containing orbital a: 32, determined by $2n^2$, defined above, where $n = 4$

(B) (1) Three sublevels are allowed in the third principal energy level identified as *s*, *p* and *d*. Note that orbital *d* is part of the 3*d* sublevel.

(2) The specified orbitals, *b, c, d, e,* and *f,* form the 3*d* sublevel. The range of the m_ℓ quantum number for any *d* sublevel is $-l, \to 0, \to +l$. For the 3*d* sublevel, the range is $-2, \to 0, \to +2$.

(C) The orbitals, *g, h, i,* form the 4*p* sublevel. The *l* quantum number that corresponds to the 4*p* sublevel is +1. (The sign for all *l* quantum numbers is positive.)

(D) When a Ge° atom is converted to Ge^{4+}, four electrons are removed from the orbitals *a, g, h.*

Chapter 2
Chemical Bonding

1. Copper wire is a metallic solid where a regular array of Cu^{2+} ions is contained within a diffuse cloud of electrons.

   The correct choice is (B).

2. Iodine crystals form as a molecular solid containing nonpolar I_2 molecules.

   The correct choice is (E).

3. Granular sugar is made of molecules of sucrose, $C_{12}H_{22}O_{11}$. The forces between sucrose molecules are hydrogen bonds – forces between molecules where hydrogen atoms serve as "bridges" to the oxygen atoms of the next molecule.

   The correct choice is (D).

4. Magnesium sulfate is an ionic solid containing the Mg^{2+} and SO_4^{2-} ions.

   The correct choice is (A).

5. Powdered silicon carbide abrasive contains silicon and carbon atoms in an extensive network of covalent bonds.

   The correct choice is (C).

6. The electron pair distribution associated with dsp^3 hybridization is trigonal bipyramidal with two electron pairs at opposite ends of the longitudinal axis. Three additional electron pairs are located equidistant from each other in a plane perpendicular to that axis. Five electon pairs must be accounted for. "Linear" (2 shared, 3 unshared), "T-shaped" (3 shared, 2 unshared), "see-saw" (4 shared, 1 unshared) and trigonal bipyramid (5 shared pairs) account for five electron pairs. Since "octahedral" calls for 6 pairs of electrons, it does not fit the dsp^3 hybridization.

   The correct choice is (D).

7. In the carbon dioxide, CO_2, molecule, the effects of two diametrically opposed polar bonds is canceled out. In the oxygen, O_2, molecule, the 0-0 bond is non-polar since this is a homonuclear molecule. In the hydrogen halides, HBr, HCl, and HI, the bond with the greatest dipole moment (polarity) is HCl because Cl has the greatest attraction for the shared pair of electrons.

   The correct choice is (C).

9

8. NO₂ is an odd-electron molecule. As such, it could never be represented by a "correct" Lewis diagram that illustrates the octet rule. Even the best approximation would have only 7 electrons for the central atom as shown here.

(E) NO₂   :Ö: N ::Ö

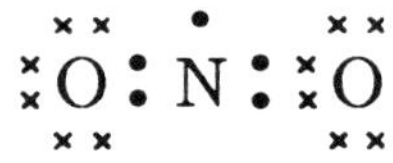

The dot diagrams for the other species illustrate the octet rule as shown below.

(A) NO₃⁻
$$\left[\begin{array}{c} :\overset{..}{O}: \\ :\overset{..}{O}::N:\overset{..}{O}: \end{array} \right]^{-}$$

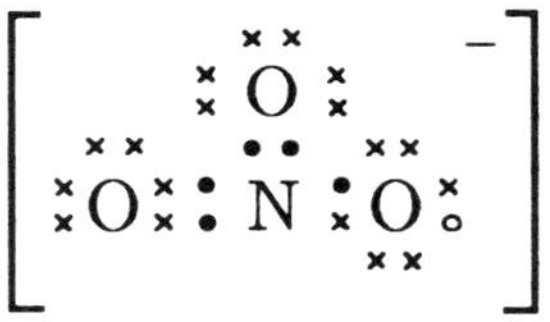

(B) NH₃   H : N : H
                     ·
                     H

(C) NH₄⁺
$$\left[\begin{array}{c} H \\ H:N:H \\ H \end{array} \right]^{+}$$

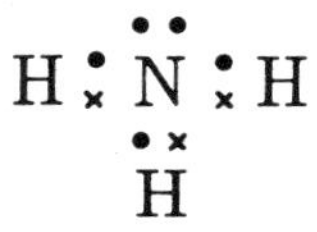

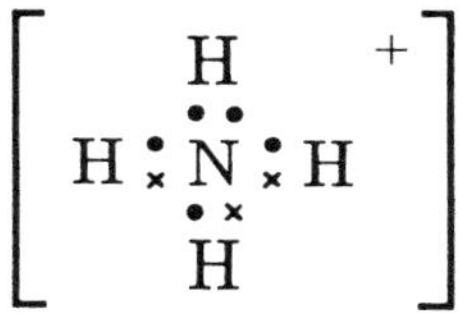

(D) N₂   :N :: N:

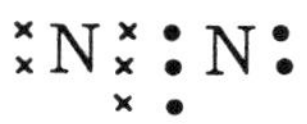

The correct choice is (E).

9. The correct answer must illustrate the rule of 8 and show 24 valence electrons. The correct dot diagram is

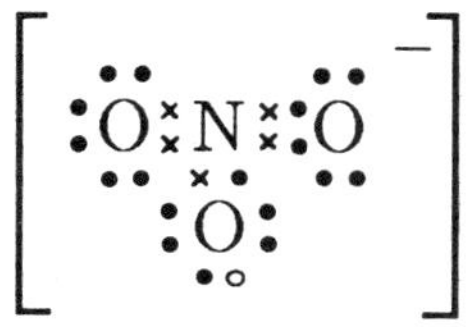

$$\left[\begin{array}{c} :\overset{..}{O}:N:\overset{..}{O}: \\ :\overset{..}{O}: \end{array} \right]^{-}$$

By convention, ions are represented in square brackets with explicit charge indicated.

The correct choice is (D).

Chemical Bonding   Chapter 2   11

Questions 10-12: This Lewis dot diagram helps explain the bonds found in solid potassium hydrogen phosphate. Each phosphorus/oxygen bond is a single covalent bond. The oxygen/hydrogen bond is a single covalent bond. The potassium/hydrogen phosphate bond is an ionic bond between oppositely charged ions, K$^+$ and HPO$_4^{2-}$.

$$[K^+] \begin{bmatrix} :\overset{..}{\underset{..}{O}}: \\ :\overset{..}{\underset{..}{O}}:P:\overset{..}{\underset{..}{O}}:H \\ :\overset{..}{\underset{..}{O}}: \end{bmatrix}^{2-} [K^+]$$

There are no double bonds, resonance bonds or hydrogen bonds in potassium hydrogen phosphate.

10. The correct choice is (C).

11. The correct choice is (A).

12. The correct choice is (C).

---

13. The resonance structures below help explain the electron arrangement in SO$_2$ molecules.

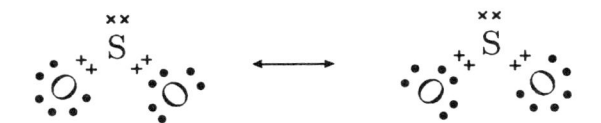

    Note one unshared electron pair, one shared pair at each of two bond sites and one resonance electron pair delocalized over both bond sites. The bond order of each S–O bond is 1.5. Each S–O bond is stronger than a single bond but weaker than a double bond.

    The correct choice is (E).

14. The Lewis dot diagram for HCOOH helps explain the distribution of electron pairs around the central atom, carbon. Note two single bonds and one double bond.

    The correct choice is (A).

15. The greatest ionic character is associated with compounds containing active metals in combination with active nonmetals. Of the elements in the compounds listed, magnesium is the most active metal. (Chlorine, an active nonmetal, is found in all choices.)

    The correct choice is (D).

16. The Lewis dot diagram for IO_3^- helps explain its shape.

    $$\left[\begin{array}{c} \ddot{\underset{\cdot\cdot}{\text{O}}} \overset{\times\times}{\underset{\times\times}{\text{I}}} \ddot{\underset{\circ\circ}{\text{O}}} \\ \ddot{\underset{\cdot\cdot}{\text{O}}} \end{array} \right]^-$$

    Note four electron pairs arranged at the four corners of a tetrahedron as explained by sp^3 hybridization. Three of those four corners are occupied by oxygen atoms, giving the trigonal pyramidal shape.

    The correct choice is (E).

17. The carbon-carbon bond in C_2H_2 is a triple bond. The carbon-carbon bond in C_2H_4 is a double bond. The triple bond has more electrons (three pairs), is stronger and has a shorter bond length.

    The correct choice is (D).

18. Except for mercury, Hg, metals are characterized by moderate to high melting points and high thermal conductivity. Characteristics I and III are not correct. Metals are characterized by high malleability and high electrical conductivity. Characteristics II and IV are correct.

    The correct choice is (D).

19. Zinc chloride is an ionic solid. Its lattice points are occupied by Zn^{2+} cations and Cl^- anions. Zinc is a metallic solid, containing Zn^{2+} cations dispersed in a diffuse electron cloud with enough electrons to match the charge on the cations, producing a net neutral solid. Neither substance contains molecules or isolated atoms.
    The correct choice is (B).

Chemical Bonding   **Chapter 2**   13

20. The shape of both BH_3 and CO_3^{2-} is trigonal planar. $BrCl_3$ is T-shaped; I_3^- is linear. PH_3 is trigonal pyramidal. No member of this list has the see-saw shape.

    The correct choice is (B).

21. In PF_5, the valence shell of phosphorus is expanded to accommodate five electron pairs which allows for the formation of five single bonds (shared electron pairs). The hybridization that accounts for this distribution is dsp^3 which generates the trigonal bipyramidal shape. One F-P-F bond angle is 180° (along the longitudinal axis). However, other F-P-F bond angles are 120° (on the equatorial plane) or 90° (axial F to equatorial F). No resonance structures are needed to account for the shape of this molecule.

    The correct choice is (B).

22. sp hybrids: SCN^-

    sp^2 hybrids: NO_2^-, NO_3^-

    sp^3 hybrids: NH_4^+, NH_2^-

    Only choice (A) identifies ions with the same orbital hybridization.

    The correct choice is (A).

23. All three statements give correct comparisons between single bonds with equal sharing of electrons and those with unequal sharing. Unequal sharing gives bonds at least some ionic character. These bonds are stronger and have greater bond energy. A smaller difference in electronegativity accounts for more nearly equal sharing.

    The correct choice is (E).

24. The number of orbitals associated with sp^3 hybridization is always four. In the case of the H_3O^+ ion, three of the four account for bond formation. One sp^3 hybrid orbital is occupied by an unshared pair of electrons.

    The correct choice is (D).

25. *Sigma*, σ, and *pi*, π, bond specification is shown in the structural formula below.

$$\begin{array}{c} \quad\quad\quad\quad H \quad\quad\quad\quad\quad\quad\quad\quad H \\ \quad\quad\quad\quad |\sigma \quad\quad \pi \quad\quad |\sigma \\ H \overset{\sigma}{-} C \overset{\sigma}{-} C \overset{\sigma}{=} C \overset{\sigma}{-} C \overset{\sigma}{-} Cl \\ \quad\quad\quad\quad |\sigma \quad\quad \pi \quad\quad |\sigma \\ \quad\quad\quad\quad H \quad\quad\quad\quad\quad\quad\quad\quad H \end{array}$$

Note that all single bonds are *sigma* bonds. A multiple bond – double or triple – contains one *sigma* bond and one *pi* bond (double bond) or two *pi* bonds (triple bond). In the case of 1-chloro-2-butyne, there are nine *sigma* and two *pi* bonds.

The correct choice is (D).

Free-Response Questions

26. **Overall Strategy:** The phosphorus atom has five electrons $\cdot \overset{\cdot \cdot}{\underset{\cdot}{P}} \cdot$

The chemical properties of phosphorus may be similar to those of its analog, nitrogen.

$$\cdot \overset{\cdot \cdot}{\underset{\cdot}{N}} \cdot$$

However, phosphorus has the capacity for a third principal energy level with its vacant d sublevel. This allows for expansion of its valence shell octet into a configuration with capacity for five or six electron pairs, some of which may be shared. With four bond sites and four shared pairs of electrons, sp^3 hybridization and tetrahedral geometry is suggested. With five bond sites and five pairs of electrons, sp^3d hybridization and trigonal bipyramidal geometry is expected. Six bond sites with six shared electron pairs corresponds to sp^3d^2 octahedral geometry.

(A) PCl_3

PCl_4^+

PCl_5

PCl_6^-

(B) PCl$_3$ – pyramidal, sp^3 hybridization

PCl$_4^+$ – tetrahedral, sp^3 hybridization

PCl$_5$ – trigonal bipyramidal, sp^3d hybridization

PCl$_6^-$ – octahedral, sp^3d^2 hybridization

(C) The Cl-P-Cl bond angle is larger in PCl$_4^+$. In the case of PCl$_4^+$, each Cl atom is located at one of the four corners of a regular tetrahedron. In the case of PCl$_3$, three corners of the tetrahedron are occupied by a Cl atom. However, an unshared electron pair is located at the fourth corner. This arrangement produces a trigonal pyramid, also known as an irregular tetrahedron. The unshared electron pair is "spread out" forcing the three Cl atoms closer together, producing a smaller Cl-P-Cl bond angle.

(D) In PCl$_5$, there are three different Cl-P-Cl bond angles: 90°, 120° and 180°. The Cl-P-Cl bond involving both axial Cl atoms is 180°. The three Cl-P-Cl bonds that include only equatorial Cl atoms are 120°. The six Cl-P-Cl bonds that include one each of axial and equatorial Cl atoms are 90°. See diagram above.

(E) In PCl$_6^-$, there are two different Cl-P-Cl bond angles: 90° and 180°. The Cl-P-Cl bond involving both axial Cl atoms is 180°. The four Cl-P-Cl bonds that include only equatorial Cl atoms are 90°. The eight Cl-P-Cl bonds that include one each of axial and equatorial Cl atoms are also 90°. See diagram above.

27. <u>Overall Strategy</u>: The major categories of bonding include covalent bonding (shared electrons) and ionic bonding (coulombic attraction between oppositely charged structures). Among the other categories of forces of attraction are van der Waals forces, London dispersion forces, dipole-dipole attractions, hydrogen bonding, induced dipole forces and ion-dipole attraction. Still another bonding force is the metallic bond. Refer to properties associated with these categories of intermolecular forces when responding to the four questions.

(A) The forces of attraction between molecules of iodine are stronger than the corresponding forces between molecules of chlorine. These intermolecular forces forces are sometimes known as van der Waals forces or London forces. For nonpolar, symmetrical molecules such as chlorine and iodine, these forces are greater where the number of electrons in the molecules is greater. Each iodine molecule has 106 electrons; each chlorine molecule has 34 electrons. Thus, the forces of attraction between molecules are stronger in iodine, accounting for its higher normal boiling point. From another perspective, larger molecules are described as more "polarizable". Due to the large electron cloud, induced dipole forces between molecules are greater.

(B) Silver metal, whether melted or solid, illustrates metallic conduction of electricity. In both solid and liquid (melted or fused) silver, the diffuse electron cloud surrounding the regular array of Ag^+ ions provides for the transfer of electrons observed as conduction. Ionic conduction of electricity is observed in molten or dissolved silver nitrate. For ionic conduction to occur, ions must be present and "mobile"; that is, free to move. Both requirements are met in dissolved $AgNO_3$ and melted $AgNO_3$. However, in solid $AgNO_3$, even though ions are present, they are not mobile. Therefore, conduction of electricity is not observed.

(C) Higher boiling point is generally associated with stronger forces between molecules. In H_2O, hydrogen bonding and strong dipole forces between molecules cause its normal boiling point to be higher than that of H_2S. There is no evidence of hydrogen bonding between H_2S molecules.

(D) Arsenic is a metalloid; that is, it has properties of both metals and nonmetals. In the presence of a strong reducing agent such as sodium, arsenic acts like a nonmetal and takes on three electrons as it is reduced to the arsenide ion, As^{3-}. The resulting compound is the ionic solid, sodium arsenide, Na_3As. In the presence of a good oxidizing agent such as chlorine, arsenic acts as a reducing agent and shares its valence electrons with the oxidizing agent to form a molecular compound, in this case, arsenic (III) chloride, $AsCl_3$. Note that most metals, when oxidized, form cations. Arsenic, a metalloid, does not illustrate this property.

18   Chapter 2   Chemical Bonding

28. <u>Overall Strategy:</u> Recognize CO_3^{2-} as a polyatomic ion with three oxygen atoms bonded to the central carbon atom and net charge of 2−. Application of the octet rule and evidence that the three bonds are equivalent suggests three resonance bonds with bond strength, bond energy and bond length somewhere between single and double bond, each equal to about $1\frac{1}{3}$ bond.

(A)

(B) With three equivalent coplanar bonds, the hybridization of atomic orbitals on the carbon atom is most likely to be sp^2. A *sigma* bond is found between the central carbon atom and each of the three oxygen atoms. *Pi* bond electron density is delocalized across all three C-O bond sites. This electron cloud lies above and below the plane of the molecule, as defined by the coplanar arrangement of the nuclei of the four bonded atoms. The *pi* bond does not play a role in determining molecular geometry.

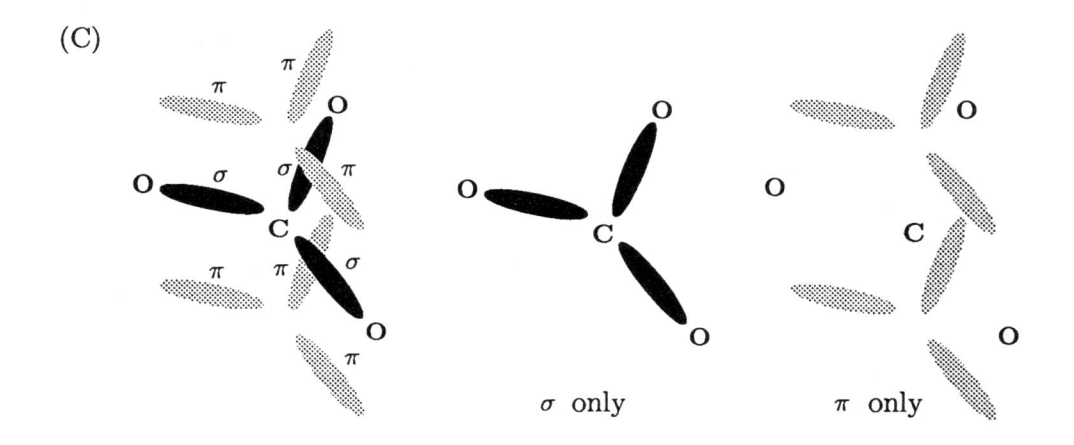

(C)

σ only π only

The diagram shows a σ bond electron cloud coplanar with C and O atoms. The electron cloud for the resonance π bond is above and below the plane of the σ bond electron cloud.

(D) Calcium carbonate is an ionic solid. Ions are found at its lattice points.

cation sites: Ca^{2+} anion sites: CO_3^{2-}

Chapter 3
The Phases of Matter - Solid, Liquid, and Gas

1. During the period from point *b* to point *c*, the system is a melting solid. The length of the line is determined by the heat of fusion of the substance.

   The correct choice is (A).

2. The change in potential energy is greatest between points *d* and *e*. During this time, potential energy increases as energy is added to the system and the liquid is converted to gas (vaporized).

   The correct choice is (D).

3. In region *d-e*, the liquid is becoming a gas (vaporization). In region *b-c*, the solid is becoming a liquid (fusion). Because energy is added at a constant rate and the amount of time required for vaporization is greater, the heat of fusion must be less than the heat of vaporization.

   The correct choice is (D).

4. In the region *c-d*, as time increases, temperature increases. Note also that region *c-d* is preceded by one period of constant temperature (a phase change) and followed by another. In region *c-d*, the system is in the liquid phase. Therefore, the best description of the system is liquid with increasing temperature.

   The correct choice is (D).

5. Rotational energy is related to movement around an axis. Translational energy is related to movement from place to place. In region *a-b*, the solid is being warmed. In the solid, with particles in fixed positions, the amount of translational energy is negligible. Rotational energy is present. Therefore, the ratio of rotational energy to translational energy is greatest.

   The correct choice is (A).

6. The phrase, "a sample", implies that no molecules may be added or removed. In order to increase the distance between molecules in the gas phase, the volume of the system must increase. Only the "increase in temperature at constant pressure" allows for an increase in volume.

   The correct choice is (C).

7. Density of gas is proportional to its molar mass. Therefore, the relationship $MW_1 \times D_2/D_1$ will permit calculation of the molar mass of the unknown gas. MW_1 (32 g·mol^{-1}) and D_1 refer to oxygen. D_2 refers to the unknown gas.

$$32 \text{ g·mol}^{-1} \times \frac{1.65 \text{ g·L}^{-1}}{1.10 \text{ g·L}^{-1}} = 48, \text{ one of the responses.}$$

   Note that since 1.65/1.10 = 1.5, no other response is reasonable. The actual arithmetic is not needed. The other choices represent various incorrect substitutions and solutions.

   The correct choice is (D).

8. Since samples of gas at the same temperature have the same average kinetic energy ($KE_1 = KE_2$), the equation $\frac{1}{2}m_1v_1^2 = \frac{1}{2}m_2v_2^2$ can be used for a quantitative result. If gas_1 is methane, (molar mass = 16) then the equation becomes

$$\frac{1}{2}(16)(12)^2 = \frac{1}{2}m_2(8.0)^2$$

Solving for m_2 (while looking for easy cancellations),

$$\frac{1}{2}m_2 = \frac{1}{2}\left[\frac{(16)(12)(12)}{(8.0)(8.0)}\right] \quad \text{or} \quad m_2 = \frac{16}{8} \times \frac{12 \times 12}{8}$$

the result is 36, one of the choices. The other responses represent various incorrect substitutions and solutions.

The correct choice is (D).

9. Using the ideal gas law, for mixtures of gases:

$$(PV)_{total} = n_{total}RT$$

$$(P_1V_1) + (P_2V_2) + (P_3V_3) = (PV)_{total} = n_{total}RT$$

$$(4 \times 2) + (2 \times 3) + (2 \times 5) = (PV)_{total} = n_{total}RT$$

$$24 = (PV)_{total} = n_{total}RT$$

If $PV = 24$ and $V = 12$, then $P = 2.0$ atm. The other values represent various incorrect substitutions and solutions.

The correct choice is (A).

10. The question asks about a density as grams per (one) liter, thus referring to a volume of 1 liter at nonstandard conditions. Assuming ideal behavior, krypton has a molar mass of 83.8 grams and a molar volume of 22.4 liters at STP. To correct the volume to nonstandard conditions, application of Boyle's and Charles's Law to the molar volume, 22.4 liters at STP, is needed. The increase in temperature causes the volume to increase (a temperature correction factor greater than 1). The decrease in pressure also causes the volume to increase (a pressure correction factor greater than 1). Note that only volume (in the denominator) is directly affected by the temperature and pressure changes. Choice (B) has these algebraic expressions correctly applied.

$$(B) \quad \frac{83.8}{22.4 \times \frac{760}{745} \times \frac{298}{273}}$$

The other choices represent various incorrect substitutions and solutions.

The correct choice is (B).

11. Deviation from ideal behavior is partly due to the existence of forces of attraction between molecules. At low temperature this attraction accounts for lower than predicted volume for some gases. Another cause of deviation that does not apply here is the absolute volume of the gas molecules. This accounts for higher than predicted volume for samples of some gases at very high pressures.

    The correct choice is (B).

12. In order to boil, the forces of attraction between molecules of a liquid must be overcome. In the case of sulfur dioxide, its normal boiling point is −10°C. This relatively high boiling point is due to forces of attraction between SO_2 molecules.

    The correct choice is (B).

13. In the sample of "wet" hydrogen gas, both $H_{2(g)}$ and $H_2O_{(g)}$ occupy the same volume and have the same temperature. At ordinary temperature and pressure, the partial pressure of $H_2O_{(g)}$ (the vapor pressure of water) is much less than the partial pressure of $H_{2(g)}$. The molar mass of $H_2O_{(g)}$ is 18. The molar mass of $H_{2(g)}$ is 2. Choice (A) claims that the gases occupy different volumes. This is incorrect. Since both gases occupy the same enclosed space, both have the same volume.

    The correct choice is (A).

14. Of the properties listed, all must be "measured" as laboratory observations except the vapor pressure of water. Once the temperature is "measured", the vapor pressure of water is determined from a reference table.

    The correct choice is (B).

15. All the properties listed, except molar mass, are related to the polarity of the H_2S molecule. Molar mass is determined by the number of protons and neutrons in the atoms of the molecule. The contribution of electrons to molar mass is negligibly small.

    The correct choice is (A).

16. Since mass and volume are the same for all systems, their densities are the same. Since they are at the same temperature, the molecules with the lowest molar mass have the highest velocity; therefore, neon molecules have the greatest velocity. Since neon molecules have the lowest molar mass, more neon molecules will be found in a 2.50 gram sample. Only statement II is correct.

    The correct choice is (A).

22 Chapter 3 The Phases of Matter

17. For reasons described in 16, the number of neon molecules is the greatest. The piston containing the most molecules at the same temperature and volume must have the greatest pressure.

    The correct choice is (E).

18. At 1 atm and 273 K, 0.10 mole of an ideal gas occupies 2.24 L, the original volume specified for the pistons at some nonstandard pressure. When changing to standard pressure, any sample greater than 0.10 mole will experience an increase in volume. Any sample less than 0.10 mole will experience a decrease in volume. Less than 0.10 mole is present for Ar (39.9 g/mol) and Kr (83.8 g/mol). More than 0.10 mole is present for Ne (20.2 g/mol). The volume of the Ne sample will increase. The volumes of each of the other two will decrease.

    The correct choice is (D).

19. Molecules added to a sample at constant temperature and constant volume will cause a change in pressure, the only property of those listed that will change. Constant temperature assures constant average molecular velocity. Note that the ideal gas law shows that P is directly proportional to n when no change in volume or temperature occurs.

    $$P \text{ (the dependent variable)} = n \text{ (the independent variable)} \times \frac{RT}{V} \text{ (a constant)}$$

    The correct choice is (D).

20. Average kinetic energy of a system is directly proportional to kelvin temperature. To account quantitatively for kinetic energy changes in samples of gas, the temperature change in kelvins must be used. In the case of a temperature increase from 20°C to 40°C, the corresponding kelvin change is from 293 K to 313 K. There is a corresponding increase in kinetic energy in direct proportion to the change in kelvin temperature.

    The correct choice is (B).

21. Since this phase change occurs at constant temperature ("at the normal boiling point"), no change in average kinetic energy occurs. Added energy appears as an increase in potential energy. As forces of attraction are overcome, the molecules move to relatively large distances away from each other. Only statements I and II are correct.

    The correct choice is (C).

22. As shown in the labeled diagram below, any system at −56.6°C with pressure greater than 5.1 atm must be in the solid phase.

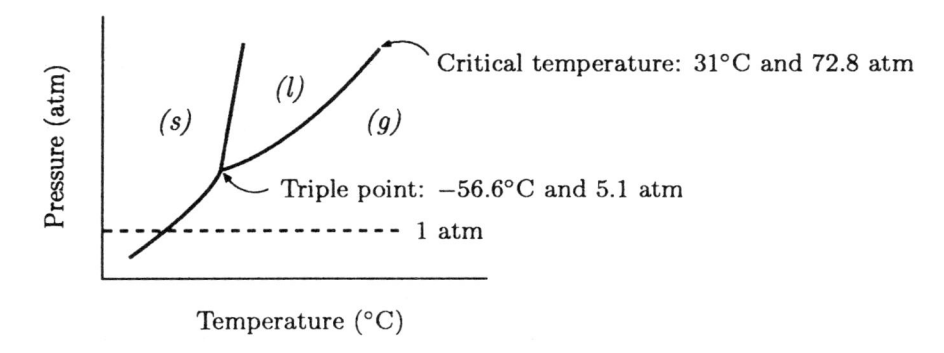

The correct choice is (A).

23. The normal boiling point is the temperature at which the vapor pressure of the liquid is equal to one atmosphere. For carbon dioxide, at one atmosphere, no liquid exists at any temperature. Therefore, no normal boiling point exists for carbon dioxide.

The correct choice is (E).

24. See the constant pressure line traced at 1.0 atm in the diagram for question 22 above. That line intersects with the solid/gas boundary at some temperature less than −56.6°C. The solid/gas phase equilibrium occurs at that temperature. No other phase equilibrium is observed at that pressure.

The correct choice is (B).

25. Since the metal tank is sealed, its volume cannot change. In this temperature range, nitrogen molecules do not undergo any chemical change. The increase in temperature will cause an increase in average molecular velocity, hence, an increase in the pressure of the confined gas.

The correct choice is (C).

24   Chapter 3   The Phases of Matter

Free-Response Questions

26. Overall Strategy: The Ideal Gas Law is a collection of principles known separately as Boyle's Law and Charles's Law. One might also include Dalton's Law and Avogadro's Hypothesis. "Ideal" behavior assumes that each molecule of a gas occupies no actual volume and exerts no forces of attraction (or repulsion) on even its nearest neighbors. In the case of actual substances in the gas phase, some space is occupied and some forces do exist. The heaviest and most polar molecules deviate most from ideal behavior.

   (A) Ideal gases have no forces of attraction between molecules and occupy no actual space, i.e. have no dimension or volume. Real gases have forces between molecules including van der Waals forces and dipole-dipole attractions. Real gas molecules have actual dimensions and do, in fact, occupy some actual space or volume.

   (B) When gases are cooled, their molecular velocities decrease. At some low molecular velocity (low temperature), the colliding molecules no longer have sufficient kinetic energy to overcome attractive forces and rebound. This results in gas molecules actually "sticking" together to form the liquid phase. When gases are compressed, the distance between molecules decreases. This also creates an increase in the effectiveness of attractive forces. The greater effectiveness of these attractive forces results in the molecules bonding together to form the liquid phase.

   (C) At low temperature, molecular velocity is less than predicted by the ideal gas law, again, due to the attractive forces between molecules. That attractive force prevents the gases from expanding to the volume predicted by the ideal gas law. The lower molecular velocity also results in fewer collisions per second between molecules and the wall of the container. Thus, the PV product at low temperature can be smaller than the value predicted.

   (D) At high pressure, where the distance between molecules is very small, the electron clouds of the molecules repel each other. Thus, as pressure is increased, the volume of the gas does not decrease to the value predicted by the ideal gas law due to mutual repulsion of the molecules. The PV product at high pressure can be greater than the predicted value.

27. <u>Overall strategy</u>: In order for a solid to be formed from the liquid or gas phase, forces of attraction between fundamental particles must become effective. Forces become effective when temperature is low (low molecular velocity) and when pressure is high (distance between molecules is small). These forces could be

- weak attractions between molecules such as van der Waals forces, London forces or dipole-dipole attractions that produce molecular solids (part A).
- metallic bonds between cations and a diffuse electron cloud that explain the properties of metallic solids (part B)
- coulombic attractions between cations and anions that form ionic solids (part C)
- electrons shared between atoms as covalent bonds that account for the strong forces in network (covalent) solids; sometimes called atomic solids (part D)

	(1) example	(2) particle	(3) attractive force
A. molecular solid	CO_2	molecule	van der Waals forces
B. metallic solid	Cu	cation	metallic bond
C. ionic solid	NaCl	cation/anion	ionic bond
D. network covalent solid	$C_{diamond}$	atom	covalent bond

(Answers will vary based upon the substances selected to illustrate each category.)

(A) (1) CO_2 (dry ice) or any other molecular solid
 (2) CO_2 molecules; molecules only, no ions or nonbonded atoms
 (3) intermolecular forces such as van der Waals forces, London forces or dipole-dipole attractions due to attractions between nonsymmetrical electron clouds including induced dipole-dipole attractions; such nonsymmetry of the electron cloud is transitory in nonpolar molecules where the magnitude of induced dipole-dipole attractions is related to the size of the electron cloud.

(B) (1) Cu or any other metallic element; alloys also acceptable
 (2) Cu^{2+}, cations, only, at lattice point
 (3) metallic bond; positively charged particles (cations) in a diffuse cloud of negative charge (electrons)

(C) (1) NaCl or any other ionic solid
 (2) Na^+ and Cl^-; anions and cations in a regular array
 (3) coulombic (electrostatic) attraction between ions of opposite charge

(D) $C_{diamond}$, $C_{graphite}$, SiO_2 or any other network (covalent) solid
 (1) C or SiO_2
 (2) C atoms or Si and O atoms; atoms, only; no ions or molecules
 (3) covalent bonds (shared electron pairs) between atoms

28. <u>Overall Strategy:</u> A phase diagram is a graphic representation of the equilibrium relationship between phases of a substance or a solution. It is a plot of pressure/temperature values for a closed system. No air is present; no material can enter or leave the system. Ordinarily, the simplest versions of these plots represent two or three phase systems, identifying the boundaries between those phases.

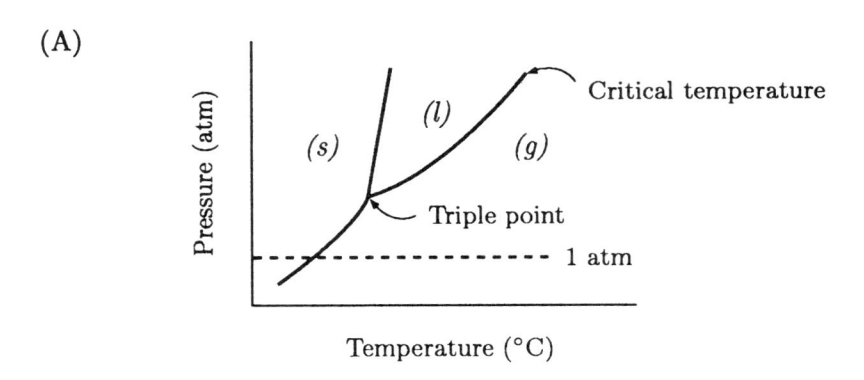

(A)

Pressure (atm) vs. Temperature (°C): regions labeled (s), (l), (g), with Critical temperature, Triple point, and 1 atm indicated.

(B) (1) At one atmosphere of pressure, there is no solid/liquid equilibrium and there is no liquid/gas equilibrium at any temperature.

(2) When the solid/liquid boundary is tilted to the right (has positive slope), the solid is more dense than the liquid. That is, for a sample at a given temperature in the liquid phase, as pressure increases at constant temperature, the phase change to solid will occur at some increased value in pressure.

(C) The temperature of the dry ice/acetone slush is most likely to be closest to the temperature of the liquid/solid phase change at 1 atm of pressure, the normal melting point. At 1 atm, dry ice sublimes to the gas phase and bubbles out of the slush at the temperature of the gas/solid phase change, the sublimation temperature. At laboratory conditions, this mixture is unlikely to get much warmer, because any heat which enters from the surroundings will be absorbed by the sublimation process. Similarly, the mixture is unlikely to get much colder, because the temperature of its container will be very near the room temperature of the laboratory. This provides a continuing source of energy.

Chapter 4
Solutions

1. Determine [Cl⁻] for each sample:

   NH_4Cl: $\dfrac{0.30 \text{ mol solute}}{1 \text{ L solution}} \times \dfrac{1 \text{ mol Cl}^-}{1 \text{ mol solute}} = 0.30$ $[Cl^-] = 0.30$

   $NaCl$: $\dfrac{0.10 \text{ mol solute}}{1 \text{ L solution}} \times \dfrac{1 \text{ mol Cl}^-}{1 \text{ mol solute}} = 0.10$ $[Cl^-] = 0.10$

   KCl: $\dfrac{0.20 \text{ mol solute}}{1 \text{ L solution}} \times \dfrac{1 \text{ mol Cl}^-}{1 \text{ mol solute}} = 0.20$ $[Cl^-] = 0.20$

   $MgCl_2$: $\dfrac{0.20 \text{ mol solute}}{1 \text{ L solution}} \times \dfrac{2 \text{ mol Cl}^-}{1 \text{ mol solute}} = 0.40$ $[Cl^-] = 0.40$

   $FeCl_3$: $\dfrac{0.10 \text{ mol solute}}{1 \text{ L solution}} \times \dfrac{3 \text{ mol Cl}^-}{1 \text{ mol solute}} = 0.30$ $[Cl^-] = 0.30$

   The highest concentration of Cl⁻ ions is found in solution D, 0.20 M $MgCl_2$.

   The correct choice is (D).

2. Determine the highest concentration of all ions; [Cl⁻] is given above. Add the concentration of the cation for each solution.

   NH_4Cl: $[NH_4^+] = 0.30$ $[Cl^-] = 0.30$ concentration of all ions = 0.60 M

   $NaCl$: $[Na^+] = 0.10$ $[Cl^-] = 0.10$ concentration of all ions = 0.20 M

   KCl: $[K^+] = 0.20$ $[Cl^-] = 0.20$ concentration of all ions = 0.40 M

   $MgCl_2$: $[Mg^{2+}] = 0.20$ $[Cl^-] = 0.40$ concentration of all ions = 0.60 M

   $FeCl_3$: $[Fe^{3+}] = 0.10$ $[Cl^-] = 0.30$ concentration of all ions = 0.40 M

   The NaCl solution has the lowest concentration of all ions. Its freezing point is highest, that is, closest to the freezing point of pure water.

   The correct choice is (B).

3. The solution with the highest vapor pressure is the solution that has the lowest concentration of all ions. See solution to question (2) above.

   The correct choice is (B).

28 Chapter 4 Solutions

4. Of the samples listed, the solution with the greatest mass is 500 mL of 0.10 M NaCl, choice (B). At 500 mL of solution, the mass of the system includes nearly 500 g H_2O plus about 2.9 grams (0.05 mol) of solute. The next closest value is 400 mL of 0.030 M NH_4Cl, with nearly 400 g H_2O.

   The correct choice is (B).

5. Estimate mass of solute for each solution:

   (A) NH_4Cl: $0.400 \text{ L} \times \dfrac{0.30 \text{ mol solute}}{1 \text{ L solution}} \times \dfrac{53.5 \text{ g}}{1 \text{ mol solute}} \approx 0.12 \times 54 \approx 6$

   (B) NaCl: $0.500 \text{ L} \times \dfrac{0.10 \text{ mol solute}}{1 \text{ L solution}} \times \dfrac{58.5 \text{ g}}{1 \text{ mol solute}} \approx 0.05 \times 59 \approx 3$

   (C) KCl: $0.200 \text{ L} \times \dfrac{0.20 \text{ mol solute}}{1 \text{ L solution}} \times \dfrac{74.5 \text{ g}}{1 \text{ mol solute}} \approx 0.04 \times 75 \approx 3$

   (D) $MgCl_2$: $0.100 \text{ L} \times \dfrac{0.20 \text{ mol solute}}{1 \text{ L solution}} \times \dfrac{95.3 \text{ g}}{1 \text{ mol solute}} \approx 0.02 \times 95 \approx 2$

   (E) $FeCl_3$: $0.200 \text{ L} \times \dfrac{0.10 \text{ mol solute}}{1 \text{ L solution}} \times \dfrac{162 \text{ g}}{1 \text{ mol solute}} \approx 0.02 \times 160 \approx 3$

   The question appears to call for calculations. However, a satisfactory answer can be obtained by estimating values. Estimation is also a valuable timesaver when precise calculation is not required.

   The correct choice is (A).

6. Cl^- ions come from both sources:

   $$0.250 \text{ L} \times \dfrac{0.20 \text{ mol } CaCl_2}{1 \text{ L solution}} \times \dfrac{2 \text{ mol } Cl^- \text{ ion}}{1 \text{ mol } CaCl_2} = 0.10 \text{ mol } Cl^- \text{ ions}$$

   $$0.250 \text{ L} \times \dfrac{0.40 \text{ mol KCl}}{1 \text{ L solution}} \times \dfrac{1 \text{ mol } Cl^- \text{ ion}}{1 \text{ mol KCl}} = 0.10 \text{ mol } Cl^- \text{ ions}$$

   Mixing together in 0.50 liter of solution

   $$\dfrac{0.20 \text{ mol } Cl^- \text{ ions}}{0.50 \text{ liters of solution}} = 0.40 \text{ M}$$

   Other answers are results when the values provided are used incorrectly.

   The correct choice is (D).

Solutions   Chapter 4   29

7. This system illustrates solubility equilibrium established according to the equation

$$Na_2CO_{3(s)} \rightleftharpoons 2Na^+_{(aq)} + CO_3^{2-}_{(aq)}$$

Statement I is correct.

Molality is defined as moles solute per kilogram solvent; molarity is defined as moles solute per liter of solution. For most aqueous solutions, the value for molality is generally greater than the corresponding value for molarity. This is especially true at high concentrations where the solute may form an appreciable fraction of the volume of the solution. Statement II is not correct.

The dissolving process is represented in the equation above. Note that two moles of the cation dissolve for every one mole of anions. Statement III is correct.

The correct choice is (D).

8. Sucrose is a nonvolatile solute. The vapor pressure of this solution will be less than the vapor pressure of pure water. As the dissolving process occurs, the vapor pressure of the solution decreases until it becomes $\frac{10}{10.5} \times 17.5$ mmHg. This corresponds to a decrease of $\frac{0.5}{10.5} \times 17.5$ mmHg.

The correct choice is (E).

9. Density is defined as mass per unit volume. When molality is known, moles of solute per kilogram of solution can be calculated.

$$\text{molality} = \frac{\text{mol solute}}{\text{kg solvent}}$$

To obtain mol solute per kilogram of **solution**, add mass of solute present to 1.00 kg solvent as shown above.

$$\frac{6.0 \text{ mol sucrose}}{\left(6.0 \text{ mol sucrose} \times \frac{0.342 \text{ kg sucrose}}{1 \text{ mol sucrose}}\right) + 1 \text{ kg solvent}}$$

The denominator gives the mass of the solute + solvent (the solution). In order to calculate density, a connection to volume of solution must be known. Such a connection is molarity, moles of solute per liter of solution. The expression below shows how to use the known information to obtain density.

$$\frac{\text{kg solution}}{\text{mol solute}} \times \frac{\text{mol solute}}{\text{L solution}}$$

The correct choice is (B).

30   Chapter 4   Solutions

10. Mole fraction is defined as the ratio of moles of solute to the sum of the moles of all components in the mixture. Thus, the mole fraction of sulfuric acid dissolved in water is given by

$$\frac{\text{mole H}_2\text{SO}_4}{\text{mole H}_2\text{SO}_4 + \text{mol H}_2\text{O}}$$

For the given solution,

$$\frac{3.0 \text{ mole H}_2\text{SO}_4}{3.0 \text{ mol H}_2\text{SO}_4 + \left(90 \text{ g H}_2\text{O} \times \dfrac{1 \text{ mol H}_2\text{O}}{18 \text{ g H}_2\text{O}}\right)}$$

rearranged to a form simple fraction

$$\frac{3.0 \text{ mole H}_2\text{SO}_4}{3.0 \text{ mol H}_2\text{SO}_4 + 5.0 \text{ mol H}_2\text{O}} = \frac{3}{8}$$

The correct choice is (B).

11. Molarity is defined as moles of solute per liter of solution. The number of moles of solute determined by calculation is generally measured by weighing. However, the quantity of solution is specified as a volume. Of those listed, the device for measuring volume with the greatest precision is the volumetric flask.

The correct choice is (B).

12. Percent methanol by mass calls for mass of methanol in the numerator and mass of solution (solute + solvent) in the denominator.

$$\frac{20 \text{ g methanol}}{20 \text{ g methanol} + 30 \text{ grams water}} = 0.40 = 40\%$$

The correct choice is (C).

Solutions   Chapter 4   31

13. If the final rinsing of a buret in a titration experiment is taken with water rather than the standard solution, the standard solution becomes slightly diluted by residual water in the buret as its initial volume reading is taken. Thus, an apparently slightly larger quantity of the standard solution will have been added to the reaction mixture when the endpoint is reached. This causes the number of moles of base used to be reported too large and therefore the number of moles of acid reacting is also reported too large. The mistake does not affect the volume of solute used for the solid acid. (That volume is not used in any calculation for the assigned result.) Only statement III is correct.

The correct choice is (C).

14. Parts per million refers to mass of solute per million units of mass of solvent. Drinking water with 0.050 ppm arsenic contains 0.050 g arsenic per 10^6 (million) grams of water. One way to respond to this question is to change each answer to the same units as given, i.e., ..?.. g arsenic per 10^6 (million) grams of water.

(A) $\dfrac{0.050 \text{ mg As}}{1 \text{ mL water}} \times \dfrac{1 \text{ g}}{1000 \text{ mg}} \times \dfrac{1 \text{ mL water}}{1 \text{ g water}} \times \dfrac{10^6}{\text{million}} = \dfrac{50 \text{ g As}}{\text{million g water}}$

(B) $\dfrac{0.050 \text{ mg As}}{1 \text{ liter water}} \times \dfrac{1 \text{ g}}{1000 \text{ mg}} \times \dfrac{1 \text{ liter water}}{1000 \text{ g water}} \times \dfrac{10^6}{\text{million}} = \dfrac{0.050 \text{ g As}}{\text{million g water}}$

(C) $\dfrac{0.050 \text{ As}}{10^6 \text{ L water}} \times \dfrac{1 \text{ liter water}}{1000 \text{ g water}} \times \dfrac{10^6}{\text{million}} = \dfrac{0.000050 \text{ g As}}{\text{million g water}}$

(D) $\dfrac{0.050 \text{ mg As}}{10^6 \text{ L water}} \times \dfrac{1 \text{ g}}{1000 \text{ mg}} \times \dfrac{1 \text{ liter water}}{1000 \text{ g water}} \times \dfrac{10^6}{\text{million}} = \dfrac{.000000050 \text{ g As}}{\text{million g water}}$

(E) $\dfrac{0.050 \text{ mg As}}{10^6 \text{ g water}} \times \dfrac{1 \text{ g}}{1000 \text{ mg}} \times \dfrac{10^6}{\text{million}} = \dfrac{50 \text{ g As}}{\text{million g water}}$

The value, 0.050 mg As per liter of water, choice (B), is another way to express 0.050 ppm.

The correct choice is (B).

15. At 35°C, a saturated solution contains between 35 and 40 grams of solute per 100 grams of water. Using estimation arithmetic instead of calculation, $40 \text{ g} \times \dfrac{1 \text{ mol}}{75 \text{ g}} \approx 0.5$. That is approximately 0.5 mol solute/0.1 kg solvent which is 5 m (molal).

The correct choice is (E).

16. At 75°C a saturated solution of KCl contains about 50 g KCl per 100 g water, producing a solution with total mass of 150 g. Thus the percent by mass of KCl is 50/150 or about 1/3, that is, 33%.

    The correct choice is (A).

17. Since no further changes are occurring and the mixture is below the saturation point (45 g KCl per 100 g water), the system must be an unsaturated solution.

    The correct choice is (D).

18. Since a white crystalline solid forms during the cooling process, one can conclude that the solution has become saturated. At the final temperature of 35°C, the 100 grams of solute (H_2O) can dissolve about 35 grams of this solute (KCl), producing 135 grams of solution. Note that choice (C) specifies 100 grams of <u>solution</u> which is not correct.

    The correct choice is (E).

19. The Tyndall effect is the glow observed along the path of a beam of light shining through a colloid. It is caused by the scattering of light as photons strike the dispersed particles of a colloid. This effect is not observed in a solution because the dispersed particles are too small to affect light. Since the particles of a suspension are much larger, that type of dispersion is opaque to visible light.

    The correct choice is (A).

20. The stearate ion, $C_{17}H_{35}COO^-$, is large enough to have a charged part that is attracted to water and an uncharged part that is attracted to nonpolar molecules. Hydrophobic molecules are likely to be nonpolar molecules that form strong intermolecular attractions with each other and thus "repel" water. In the presence of the stearate ion, such repulsion decreases. This accounts for the cleaning action of ordinary soap.

    The correct choice is (B).

21. Adding water to a solution of potassium nitrate will cause the solution to become more dilute in potassium nitrate. In addition, the volume of the solution will increase. At lower concentration, the solution will have higher vapor pressure and higher freezing point. Its mass per unit volume (density) will decrease. Its properties become more like pure water.

    The correct choice is (E).

22. In this solution, the addition of NaCl to water causes density to increase, vapor pressure to decrease, freezing point to decrease, and osmotic pressure to increase. The lower vapor pressure accounts for the increase in the boiling point as the solute is added to the solution.

    The correct choice is (C).

23. In a spontaneous, exothermic dissolving process, ΔG_{soln} is negative (spontaneous process), ΔH_{soln} is negative (exothermic process), and ΔT is positive because the energy given off causes the temperature of the system to increase.

    The correct choice is (C).

24. Increasing the temperature while maintaining contact with excess solute causes more solute to dissolve. Both molality and density of the solution increase. The solution remains saturated because it remains in contact with excess solute.

    The correct choice is (E).

25. Increasing the temperature of any aqueous NaCl solution causes the vapor pressure to increase because the vapor pressure of the solvent increases. The number of ion pairs in solution remains the same because a dilute solution of an ionic solid such as NaCl is fully dissociated. The difference between the boiling point and the freezing point remains the same because the concentration of the solution remains the same.

    The correct choice is (A).

Free-Response Questions

26. <u>Overall Strategy</u>: Salts are ionic solids. The cations and anions become separated from each other due to the attractive forces exerted by the polar water molecules. This process is most correctly called dissociation; however, it is also referred to as ionization. Energy is absorbed by the separation component of this process (lattice energy). Energy is released (hydration energy) as the ions become attracted to and surrounded by the polar water molecules.

   (A) Conductivity (conduction of an electric current) is the result of either the movement of electrons as in a metal wire or the movement of charged particles in solution (ions) as they are attracted to oppositely charged electrodes. Pure water, a molecular solvent, is a nonconductor of electricity. Similarly, solutions of molecular substances such as urea and sugar are also nonconductors. However, when a salt such as KCl dissolves in water, the ionic crystal lattice breaks apart as K^+ and Cl^- ions dissociate. Due to the presence of these mobile ions, the solution is able to conduct electric current.

   (B) When a 1.0 molal aqueous solution of a molecular substance such as sugar or urea is compared to a 1.0 molal aqueous solution of an ionic substance such as sodium chloride or ammonium phosphate, the boiling point of the solution of the ionic solute is higher. Similarly, the freezing point of that solution is lower. The amount of increase in boiling point or decrease in freezing point is not determined by the identity of the solute but only the number of particles that are present in solution. Vapor pressure behaves in a similar way. Boiling point elevation, freezing point depression and decrease in vapor pressure are among several such properties known as colligative properties.

   (C) A solution of any monoprotic strong acid is actually a solution of hydrogen (hydronium), H^+ (H_3O^+), ions. When a strong acid such as HCl or HBr dissolves in water, the acid "ionizes" to form H^+ and the corresponding anion. After dissolving, solutions of both strong acids contain the same cation, H^+ (H_3O^+). When neutralization occurs in an aqueous system, the reaction is actually between the OH^- ion of the base and the H^+ (H_3O^+) ion formed when the acid was first dissolved in water. In both neutralization reactions, it is this cation, not the Cl^- or Br^-, that neutralizes the strong base, OH^-. Because the same changes in bonding occur for each reaction, the heat of reaction (neutralization) is the same.

$$H^+ + Cl^- + K^+ + OH^- \rightarrow K^+ + Cl^- + HOH \qquad \Delta H = -56 \text{ kJ}$$
$$H^+ + Br^- + K^+ + OH^- \rightarrow K^+ + Br^- + HOH \qquad \Delta H = -56 \text{ kJ}$$

$$H^+ + OH^- \rightarrow HOH$$
$$H_3O^+ + OH^- \rightarrow 2HOH$$

(D) Molecules of HCl dissociate in water because the oxygen ends of the polar water molecules attract the hydrogen from the HCl molecules. The hydrogen from the HCl molecule becomes bonded to a molecule of H_2O to form a hydronium ion, H_3O^+. Similarly, the hydrogen end of the water molecules attract the chlorine from the HCl molecules. Each chlorine becomes a hydrated Cl^- ion. Benzene, C_6H_6, is a nonpolar molecule with no special attraction for hydrogen atoms. The covalent bonds between H and Cl atoms in the HCl molecules are stronger than any attractions between HCl and nonpolar C_6H_6 molecules. Thus no change in molecular structure — i.e., no dissociation or ion formation — occurs when HCl dissolves in benzene.

27. <u>Overall Strategy</u>: Dissolving of a solute in a solvent requires separation of solute particles, attraction of solute particles to solvent and separation of solvent particles to provide space for the dissolving solute. As these components of the dissolving process occur, the solute becomes dispersed into the solvent to form the solution, a mixture of molecule-size particles.

- (A) Lattice energy, hydration energy

  - Lattice energy is the energy required to overcome attraction between solute particles in the solid phase and separate the solute into particles small enough to be dispersed in the solvent. Those particles are generally ions or molecules.

  - Hydration energy is the energy released when the solute particles are attracted to the water molecules.

- (B) As an ionic solid dissolves in water, entropy increases. The ionic solid is a highly ordered system. When dissolved in water, the extent of disorder (randomness) increases. Hydrated ions become randomly dispersed throughout the mixture. The entropy change, ΔS, is given by $\Delta S = S_{prod} - S_{react}$. In the dissolving process for an ionic solid, S_{prod} is generally greater than S_{react}; therefore ΔS is positive.

- (C) Providing the lattice energy requires input of energy. Hydration of solute particles releases energy. The balance struck between these changes helps determine the solubility of the ionic solid. When the hydration energy is greater than the lattice energy, (that is, when the algebraic sum of these energy changes is negative), ΔH is negative and solubility tends to be greater. (See also part D below.)

- (D) In order for an ionic solid to be soluble, the value for ΔG for the dissolving process must be negative. In the relationship, $\Delta G = \Delta H - T\Delta S$, ΔS is nearly always positive because the system becomes more disordered as dissolving occurs. The ΔH term is the algebraic sum of the hydration energy (exothermic, negative) and the lattice energy (endothermic, positive). When ΔH is negative and ΔS is positive as above, ΔG is negative at all values of T and the dissolving process occurs at any temperature. However, when ΔH is positive, it is the magnitude of the $T\Delta S$ term that determines whether or not ΔG is negative, that is, whether or not the dissolving process does occur. At higher temperatures, increasing entropy plays a greater role in determining solubility.

- (E) The dissolving process for ammonium nitrate, NH_4NO_3, in water is endothermic.

  - (1) In an endothermic dissolving process, heat is absorbed from the surroundings. The vessel and the system become colder; that is, temperature of the system and its container decreases.

  - (2) If the amount of solute to be dissolved is doubled, the amount of decrease in temperature, ΔT, is expected to be doubled. In the dissolving process, twice as much energy is absorbed from the surroundings in order to overcome the attractive forces between twice as many particles of solute.

Solutions   Chapter 4   37

28. <u>Overall Strategy</u>: Preparation of any solution calls for the determination of measurable amounts in terms of mass or volume of any two of the following

- solute, most often a solid or liquid

- solvent, usually a liquid

- solution, usually a liquid

Measurable amounts could be expressed as mass or volume. The mass and volume of the resulting mixture are determined by the amounts of solute and solvent that are mixed together. Note that masses of solute and solvent must add up to give the mass of the solution. However, the volumes of the solute plus solvent do not necessarily add up to the volume of the solution formed. Thorough mixing of the solute and solvent generally produces a mixture with less volume than the sum of its components. In addition, the volume of a given mass of solid solute to be dissolved is easily affected by the degree of subdivision of that solid.

(A) Measure, precisely to two significant figures, 0.50 mol, that is, 49 grams, of H_2SO_4. A balance may be used for weighing the assigned quantity. Alternatively, to use volumetric equipment such as a graduated cylinder, pipette or buret, the volume that contains the specified mass can be calculated from the specific gravity information supplied with the concentrated sulfuric acid. The assigned quantity of solute is 0.50 mol and the concentration of the solution is to be 1.0 M; therefore, the volume of the solution to be prepared is 0.50 liter. Obtain a heat-resistant (borosilicate) volumetric flask with volume specified as 500 mL. Add enough distilled water so that it is at least half filled. Then carefully add the measured 0.50 mole of liquid H_2SO_4 to the water. (A very noticeable **exothermic reaction** will occur.) Swirl gently to mix. When the mixture has cooled to room temperature, add distilled water to the 500 mL mark on the neck of the flask. (Note: it is **not** correct, and actually unsafe, to add any amount of water to the measured amount of acid.)

(B) Yes. Again, the assigned amount of solute, H_2SO_4, is 0.050 mol (49 grams), obtained either by weighing or taking a measured volume. To use all of this solute, the amount of solvent needed is precisely 500 g (500 mL). The solution must be prepared in a heat-resistant vessel that holds more than 500 mL of solution because the volume of the assigned amount of H_2SO_4 is added to the 500 g (500 mL) of water.

(C) The percent by mass of H_2SO_4 is greater in the 1.0 M solution. The mass of H_2SO_4 used for each solution is the same. For the 1.0 M solution, the mass of water used is some amount less than 500 g (500 mL). The mass of water used for the 1.0 m solution is precisely 500 g. Therefore, the solution with the lesser amount of water has a greater percent by mass of H_2SO_4.

(D) Concentrated H_2SO_4 is very corrosive to the skin. In addition, as it is mixed water, much energy is evolved. To avoid boiling and spattering, sulfuric acid should always be added to water slowly and with constant mixing. Mixing should always be done in heat-resistant glassware and in a sink or other space where dilution of any spills can be carried out safely. As with any laboratory activity, use of safety goggles and protective clothing is necessary.

Chapter 5
Stoichiometry

1. Each of these oxides has the formula MO, where M is an alkaline earth metal. The oxide with the greatest percent by mass oxygen is that oxide with the lightest mass metal, Be.

    The correct choice is (B).

2. The molar mass of $H_2C_2O_4 \cdot 2H_2O$ is 126. The atomic mass of the two carbon atoms is 24. Therefore, the percent by mass carbon is given by the expression

    $$\frac{24}{126} \times 100$$

    The correct choice is (E).

3. Manganese has atomic mass of about 55. Oxygen has atomic mass of about 16. In any formula where the mass of Mn is greater than the mass of oxygen, the percent by mass of manganese is greater than 50%. MnO – formula mass 55 + 16; MnO_2 – formula mass 55 + 32; Mn_2O_3 – formula mass 110 + 48. All three compounds are greater than 50% by mass manganese.

    The correct choice is (E).

4. In this mixture, 0.40 mol CO_3^{2-} and 0.30 mol Cu^{2+} are available. Upon the precipitation of $CuCO_3$, excess CO_3^{2-} remains in solution. $CuCO_3$ is a blue solid. The system is a heterogeneous mixture.

    The correct choice is (A).

5. The number of oxygen atoms in each pair is given below:

    (A) 0.10 mol Al_2O_3 and 0.50 mol BaO: 0.30 + 0.50 mol O atoms

    (B) 0.20 mol Cl_2O and 0.10 mol HClO: 0.20 + 0.10 mol O atoms

    (C) 0.20 mol SnO and 0.20 mol SnO_2:   0.20 + 0.40 mol O atoms

    (D) 0.10 mol Na_2O and 0.10 mol Na_2SO_4:   0.10 + 0.40 mol O atoms

    (E) 0.20 mol $Ca(OH)_2$ and 0.10 mol $H_2C_2O_4$:   0.40 + 0.40 mol O atoms

    The correct choice is (E).

40 Chapter 5   Stoichiometry

6. The mole ratio that applies is

$$\frac{3 \text{ mol KOH}}{1 \text{ mol ScCl}_3}$$

Thus, 0.60 mol KOH will consume 0.20 mol ScCl$_3$, producing 0.20 mol Sc(OH)$_3$ and 0.60 mol KCl. The excess amount of ScCl$_3$ is 0.40 mol.

The correct choice is (B).

7. The properly labeled solution to this problem is

$$15 \text{ g KClO}_3 \times \frac{1 \text{ mol KClO}_3}{122.5 \text{ g KClO}_3} \times \frac{3 \text{ mol O}_2}{2 \text{ mol KClO}_3} \times \frac{32 \text{ g O}_2}{1 \text{ mol O}_2}$$

This matches the numerical values for choice (B). The other choices are various incorrect arrangements of these values.

The correct choice is (B).

8. The properly labeled solution to this problem is

$$25 \text{ g Al} \times \frac{1 \text{ mol Al}}{27 \text{ g Al}} \times \frac{3 \text{ mol Cl}_2}{2 \text{ mol Al}} \times \frac{22.4 \text{ L Cl}_2}{1 \text{ mol Cl}_2}$$

This matches the numerical values for choice (D). The other choices are various incorrect arrangements of these values.

The correct choice is (D).

9. Determine approximately the number of moles of nitrogen atoms in each sample.

(A) 0.20 mol N$_2$O$_{4(g)}$:   0.40 mol N atoms

(B) 0.40 mol N$_{2(g)}$:   0.80 mol N atoms

(C) 40. L NO$_{2(g)}$:   more than 1 mol but less than 2 mol N atoms (22.4 L contains 1 mol N atoms)

(D) 40. g NH$_{3(g)}$:   more than 2 mol but less than 3 mol N atoms (NH$_3$: molar mass −17; 17 g contains 1 mol N atoms)

(E) 80. g N$_2$O$_{4(g)}$:   more than 1 mol but less than 2 mol N atoms (N$_2$O$_4$: molar mass −92; 92 g contains 2 mol N atoms)

The greatest number of nitrogen atoms is found in sample (D).

The correct choice is (D).

10. In this reaction, for every six moles of gas that is consumed, seven moles of product is formed. At constant temperature and volume, this will cause a net increase in total pressure. The mole ratio that applies is

$$\frac{5 \text{ mol } O_2}{1 \text{ mol } C_3H_8}$$

Thus, 0.030 mol C_3H_8 will react with 0.15 mol O_2, producing 0.090 mol CO_2 and 0.12 mol H_2O. The excess amount of O_2 is 0.050 mol.

The correct choice is (D).

11. Based on the law of conservation of mass, the mass of product M is 22 grams. (32 grams of reactants X and Y produce 10 grams of M and ..?.. grams of Z.) That mass of Z is given as 2.0 moles. Therefore, the molar mass of Z is 11.

The correct choice is (A).

12. To solve this problem, the relative number of atoms of each element must be determined. Assuming 100 g of the compound, each percent by mass is divided by the corresponding atomic mass to determine the number of moles of atoms of each element in the 100 g sample.

$$\frac{26.6 \text{ g K}}{39.1 \text{ g/mol K}} \qquad \frac{35.3 \text{ g Cr}}{52.0 \text{ g/mol Cr}} \qquad \frac{38.1 \text{ g O}}{16.0 \text{ g/mol O}}$$

In the case of a three-element compound, those three values give a ratio of atoms. In order to determine the correct empirical formula, those values must be restated as a simple whole-number ratio. However, the decimal fraction values determined from the common fractions above give a reasonable representation of the empirical formula. The values in choice (C) match the values in the properly labeled solution above.

The correct choice is (C).

13. Determine the number of moles of Sr^{2+} in solution

$$0.025 \text{ L} \times \frac{0.10 \text{ mol } Sr^{2+}}{1 \text{ L sol'n}} = 0.0025 \text{ mol } Sr^{2+}$$

One mole Sr^{2+} precipitates one mole CO_3^{2-}; therefore, 0.0025 mol CO_3^{2-} must be added.

$$0.0025 \text{ mol } CO_3^{2-} \times \frac{1 \text{ L sol'n}}{0.20 \text{ mol } CO_3^{2-}} = 0.0125 \text{ L sol'n} \quad \text{(or 12.5 mL)}$$

The correct choice is (B).

14. Without doing calculations, 48 grams of Cu (64 g/mol) can be recognized as 3/4 mol Cu. According to the equation, 2 mol NO_2 is produced for every 1 mol Cu consumed. Therefore, 1.5 mol NO_2 is the amount of $NO_{2(g)}$ expected. At 1 atm and 273 K, that quantity occupies 33.6 L.

$$1.5 \text{ mol} \times \frac{22.4 \text{ L}}{1 \text{ mol}} = 33.6 \text{ L}$$

The correct choice is (C).

15. In this equation, the term **3e⁻** represents 3 moles of electrons, that is, $3 \times 6.02 \times 10^{23}$ electrons. It could also mean $3 \times 96{,}500$ coulombs, but that value is not offered as one of the choices.

    The correct choice is (B).

16. In order to determine the limiting reactant, the appropriate mole ratio is

    $$\frac{7 \text{ mol } O_2}{2 \text{ mol } C_2H_6}$$

    If all 0.40 mol C_2H_6 is consumed, 1.40 mol O_2 is consumed, leaving 0.20 mol O_2 in excess.

    The correct choice is (A).

17. The volume of the reaction mixture is 200 mL. Determine the concentration of Na⁺ as below:

    $$\frac{0.100 \text{ L sol'n} \times \dfrac{0.100 \text{ mol } Na_2CrO_4}{1 \text{ L sol'n}} \times \dfrac{2 \text{ mol } Na^+}{1 \text{ mol } Na_2CrO_4}}{0.200 \text{ L reaction mixture}} = 0.10 \text{ M}$$

    The correct choice is (B).

18. Since the mole ratio is

    $$\frac{2 \text{ mol } Ag^+}{1 \text{ mol } CrO_4^{2-}}$$

    there is excess CrO_4^{2-}. Ag^+ is the limiting reactant. One labeled expression that gives the answer is

    $$0.10 \text{ L solution} \times \frac{0.10 \text{ mol } Ag^+}{1 \text{ L solution}} \times \frac{1 \text{ mol } Ag_2CrO_4}{2 \text{ mol } Ag^+}$$

    The numerical answer is 0.0050 mol Ag_2CrO_4.

    The correct choice is (B).

19. The beaker contains 100 mL of 0.10 M $AgNO_3$. As Na_2CrO_4 is added, the volume of the reaction mixture increases to 200 mL. Because the number of NO_3^- ions remains the same as volume increases, $[NO_3^-]$ decreases. Because Na^+ is being added to the reaction mixture, $[Na^+]$ increases.

    The correct choice is (D).

20. The properly labeled solution to this problem is

$$3 \text{ mol Al} \times \frac{1 \text{ mol Al}_2\text{S}_3}{2 \text{ mol Al}} \times \frac{150 \text{ g Al}_2\text{S}_3}{1 \text{ mol Al}_2\text{S}_3}$$

Completing the arithmetic gives 225 g Al$_2$S$_3$. The other choices result from incorrect arrangements of these values.

The correct choice is (E).

21. The properly labeled solution to this problem is

$$0.40 \text{ mol Zn} \times \frac{1 \text{ mol H}_2}{1 \text{ mol Zn}} \times \frac{22.4 \text{ L H}_2}{1 \text{ mol H}_2}$$

Considering the plausibility of each choice (or completing the arithmetic) gives 9.0 L. The other choices are various incorrect calculations using these values.

The correct choice is (D).

22. Each mass specified must be equal to the atomic mass of the element multiplied by some integer (including 1). Similarly, the difference between any two masses must be equal to the atomic mass of the element multiplied by some integer (including 1). The smallest mass or difference between masses is a reasonable value to propose as the atomic mass. The smallest difference is 14. Every mass and difference in masses is an integral multiple of 14.

The correct choice is (A).

23. In order to determine the limiting reactant, the appropriate mole ratio is

$$\frac{3 \text{ mol Fe}}{4 \text{ mol H}_2\text{O}}$$

There is excess iron. The properly labeled solution to the problem is

$$12 \text{ mol H}_2\text{O} \times \frac{1 \text{ mol Fe}_3\text{O}_4}{4 \text{ mol H}_2\text{O}} = 3 \text{ mol Fe}_3\text{O}_4$$

When all 12 mol H$_2$O is consumed, 9 mol Fe is consumed, leaving 3 mol Fe in excess and 3 mol Fe$_3$O$_4$ produced. These results match the numerical values for choice (D). The other choices result from incorrect arrangemnents of these values.

The correct choice is (D).

24. The chloride ion concentration in 0.20 M $CrCl_3$ is 0.60 M. The 0.500 L of solution provided contains 0.30 mol Cl^-. To increase the Cl^- concentration of that solution to 1.00 M requires the presence of 0.50 mol Cl^- in the solution. Therefore, 0.20 mol KCl must be added.

    The correct choice is (A).

25. In this problem, Fe is the limiting reactant. The properly labeled solution to this problem is

$$6.0 \text{ mol Fe} \times \frac{1 \text{ mol } Fe_3O_4}{3 \text{ mol Fe}} = 2.0 \text{ mol } Fe_3O_4$$

When all 6 mol Fe is consumed, 8 mol H_2O is consumed, leaving 4 mol H_2O in excess and 2 mol Fe_3O_4 produced. However, all gas, including H_2O, escapes. These results match the numerical values for choice (A). The other choices result from incorrect arrangements of these values or overlooking the loss of $H_2O_{(g)}$.

The correct choice is (A).

Stoichiometry Chapter 5 45

Free-Response Questions

26. <u>Overall Strategy</u>: Quantitative relationships apply to this problem. Refer to the list of *Equations and Constants* to find useful information.

   (A) Use ideal gas law as provided in the list of *Equations and Constants* to find moles of gas at specified conditions, then find molar mass.

   $$n = \frac{1.58 \text{ atm} \times 3.00 \text{ L}}{0.0821 \text{ L} \cdot \text{atm} \cdot \text{mol}^{-1} \cdot \text{K}^{-1} \times 800 \text{ K}}$$

   $$n = 7.22 \times 10^{-2} \text{ mol}$$

   Since mass is 3.90 grams and number of moles has been found to be 7.22 x 10-2, molar mass (g/mol) is found as

   $$\frac{3.90 \text{ g}}{7.22 \times 10^{-2} \text{ mol}} = \mathbf{54.0 \text{ g} \cdot \text{mol}^{-1}}$$

   (B) Assume 100 g of compound, thus 76.5 g CO_2 and 23.5 g H_2O

   - find number of mol of each element
   - find simplest whole number ratio of atoms; that is the "empirical formula".

   $$76.5 \text{ g } CO_2 \times \frac{1 \text{ mol } CO_2}{44 \text{ g } CO_2} \times \frac{1 \text{ mol C atoms}}{1 \text{ mol } CO_2} = 1.74 \text{ mol C atoms}$$

   $$23.5 \text{ g } H_2O \times \frac{1 \text{ mol } H_2O}{18 \text{ g } H_2O} \times \frac{2 \text{ mol H atoms}}{1 \text{ mol } H_2O} = 2.61 \text{ mol H atoms}$$

   Thus, $C_{1.74}H_{2.61}$ is the ratio of atoms but not yet the simplest whole number ratio of atoms. Divide this ratio by the smallest subscript to get the simplest whole number ratio of atoms.

   $$C_{\frac{1.74}{1.74}=1} \quad H_{\frac{2.61}{1.74}=1.5}$$

   becomes $C_1H_{1.5}$ or $\mathbf{C_2H_3}$ as the simplest whole number ratio of atoms. That is the **"empirical formula"**.

   (C) The molar mass of the unknown hydrocarbon is **54.0** and its empirical formula is $\mathbf{C_2H_3}$, the molecular formula must be some integral multiple of C_2H_3 for which the formula mass is 27.0. The molar mass of 54 is given by two times 27, the formula mass of the empirical formula. Thus, the molecular formula must be two times the empirical formula or $\mathbf{C_4H_6}$. Its IUPAC name is butyne.

   The equation for the burning of this hydrocarbon includes hydrocarbon and oxygen as the reactants with carbon dioxide and water as the only products.

   $$C_4H_6 + \frac{11}{2}O_2 \rightarrow 4CO_2 + 3H_2O \quad \text{or, when balanced with integers,}$$

   $$\mathbf{2C_4H_6 + 11O_2 \rightarrow 8CO_2 + 6H_2O}$$

46 Chapter 5 Stoichiometry

27. <u>Overall Strategy</u>: Quantitative relationships apply to this problem. Refer to the list of *Equations and Constants* to find useful information. Because a chemical reaction occurs, principles of stoichiometry apply. The energy changes and transfers involved call for the application of principles of Hess's Law and specific heat capacity.

(A) $N_2H_4 + 2H_2O_2 \rightarrow N_2 + 4H_2O$.

(B) Find number of moles of $N_{2(g)}$ produced, then use the ideal gas law to calculate volume at specified conditions.

$$100 \text{ g } H_2O_2 \times \frac{1 \text{ mol } H_2O_2}{34 \text{ g } H_2O_2} \times \frac{1 \text{ mol } N_2}{2 \text{ mol } H_2O_2} = 1.47 \text{ mol } N_2$$

$$V = \frac{1.47 \text{ mol } N_2 \times 0.0821 \text{ L} \cdot \text{atm} \cdot \text{mol}^{-1} \cdot K^{-1} \times 298 \text{ } K}{0.975 \text{ atm}}$$

V = 36.9 L

(C) From the list of *Equations and Constants* provided with the exam, find

$$\Delta H° = \sum \Delta H°_{f \text{ products}} - \sum \Delta H°_{f \text{ reactants}} \quad \text{(often known as Hess's Law)}$$

Use the values for $\Delta H°_f$ provided for all reactants and products to calculate $\Delta H°$.

$$\Delta H° = \left[\Delta H°_{f,N_2} + 4(\Delta H°_{f,H_2O})\right] - \left[\Delta H°_{f,N_2H_4} + 4(\Delta H°_{f,H_2O_2})\right]$$

$$\Delta H° = \left[0 + 4(-241.6)\right] - \left[50.2 + 2(-192.3)\right]$$

$$\Delta H° = [-966.4] - [-334.4] = \mathbf{-632 \text{ kJ}}$$

(D) From part (B), note that the energy given off by 1.47 mol N_2 is used to heat the water. Calculate total energy produced.

$$1.47 \text{ mol } N_2 \times \frac{632 \text{ kJ}}{1 \text{ mol } N_2} = 929 \text{ kJ energy produced}$$

The total energy is 929 kJ. Next calculate temperature change produced by this energy when used to heat 5 kg water.

$$\frac{929 \text{ kJ energy}}{5.00 \text{ kg } H_2O} \times \frac{1000 \text{ J}}{\text{kJ}} \times \frac{1 \text{ g °C}}{4.18 \text{ J}} \times \frac{1 \text{ kg } H_2O}{1000 \text{ g } H_2O} = 44.5°C$$

Then add temperature change to original temperature.

Final temperature is $20.0°C + 44.5°C = \mathbf{64.5°C}$

28. Overall Strategy: Quantitative relationships apply to this problem. Refer to the list of *Equations and Constants* to find useful information. Because a chemical reaction occurs, principles of stoichiometry apply. The ideal gas law is used for quantitative relationships for gases.

(A) $MnO_2 + 4H^+ + 2e^- \rightarrow Mn^{2+} + 2H_2O$

Note that a reduction half-reaction has the electron term as a reactant.

(B) In the list of *Equations and Constants* provided, find the definition of molarity as moles solute/liter of solution. Using density as specified, 1 mL of solution has a mass of 1.189 g, part HCl and part H_2O. Find mass, then moles, of HCl per liter of solution. This gives molarity.

In 1 mL of solution: $1.189 \text{ g sol'n} \times \dfrac{38.0 \text{ g HCl}}{100 \text{ g sol'n}} = 0.4518 \text{ g HCl}$

thus, $\dfrac{0.4518 \text{ g HCl} \times \dfrac{1 \text{ mol HCl}}{36.5 \text{ g HCl}}}{0.00100 \text{ L sol'n}} = \mathbf{12.4 \text{ M}}$

(C) Use the ideal gas law as provided in the list of *Equations and Constants* to find moles of chlorine gas at specified conditions.

$n = \dfrac{0.975 \text{ atm} \cdot 1.50 \text{ L}}{0.0821 \text{ L} \cdot \text{atm} \cdot \text{mol}^{-1} \cdot \text{K}^{-1} \times 298 \text{ K}}$

$n = \mathbf{5.98 \times 10^{-2} \text{ mol } Cl_2}$

(D) Use mol Cl_2 to find mol MnO_2, then mass MnO_2, then percent of MnO_2 in the impure sample.

$5.98 \times 10^{-2} \text{ mol } Cl_2 \times \dfrac{1 \text{ mol } MnO_2}{1 \text{ mol } Cl_2} \times \dfrac{87.0 \text{ g } MnO_2}{1 \text{ mol } MnO_2} = 5.20 \text{ g } MnO_2$

thus, $\dfrac{5.20 \text{ g } MnO_2}{10 \text{ g impure sample}} = \mathbf{52.0\% \ MnO_2}$

Chapter 6
Chemical Kinetics

1. A catalyst increases the rate of a chemical reaction by decreasing the potential energy of the activated complex. When the activated complex has a lower potential requirement (barrier), more reactant molecules at any given temperature can meet that requirement. Hence, more collisions are effective and the reaction proceeds at a greater rate.

    The correct choice is (C).

2. Addition of a catalyst provides a new reaction pathway in which the activated complex has a lower energy of activation. See diagram below.

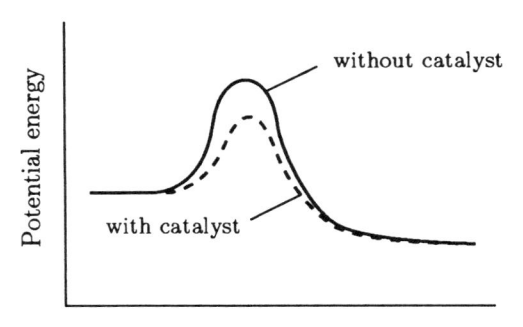

    The correct choice is (E).

3. Referring to the ideal gas law will help determine which changes affect the concentration of $A_{(g)}$. From the equation

    $$PV = nRT \quad \text{rearranged as} \quad \frac{n}{V} = \frac{P}{RT}$$

    the term, $\frac{n}{V}$, is concentration expressed as mol/liter. Thus concentration is directly proportional to P (pressure) and inversely proportional to T (temperature). Whenever V is held constant, addition of molecules (an increase in concentration) causes an increase in pressure, a decrease in temperature, or both. In statements I and III, volume is held constant; therefore the addition of molecules causes an increase in concentration. In statement II, temperature and pressure are held constant; therefore concentration, given as $\frac{n}{V}$, remains the same.

    The correct choice is (D).

4. As this reaction proceeds, molecules of C are produced as molecules of A and B are consumed.

    The correct choice is (D).

48

Chemical Kinetics   Chapter 6   49

5. In this reaction, one mole $XY_{2(g)}$ forms for every two mol Y consumed. Because $XY_{2(g)}$ is a product, its rate of formation has a positive sign. Therefore, the rate of formation of $XY_{2(g)}$ has opposite sign and half the numerical value of the rate of consumption of Y.

$$\frac{\Delta[Y]}{\Delta t} = -5.0 \times 10^{-2} \text{ mol} \cdot \text{L}^{-1} \cdot \text{sec}^{-1}$$

$$\frac{\Delta[XY_2]}{\Delta t} = +2.5 \times 10^{-2} \text{ mol} \cdot \text{L}^{-1} \cdot \text{sec}^{-1}$$

The correct choice is (D).

6. Substituting the values given into the rate law gives

$$\text{Rate} = k[A]^2[B]$$

$$0.048 \text{ mol} \cdot \text{L}^{-1} \cdot \text{sec}^{-1} = k(4.0 \text{ mol} \cdot \text{L}^{-1})^2(1.0 \text{ mol} \cdot \text{L}^{-1})$$

solving for k: $$k = \frac{0.048}{4 \times 4} = 3.0 \times 10^{-3}$$

The correct choice is (E).

7. Referring to the solution above and canceling labels where appropriate

$$0.048 \text{ mol} \cdot \text{L}^{-1} \cdot \text{sec}^{-1} = k(4.0 \text{ mol} \cdot \text{L}^{-1})^2(1.0 \text{ mol} \cdot \text{L}^{-1})$$

solving for k (including units): $k = 3.0 \times 10^{-3} \text{ L}^2 \cdot \text{mol}^{-2} \cdot \text{sec}^{-1}$

The correct choice is (C).

8. When [B] has become $0.4 \text{ mol} \cdot \text{L}^{-1}$, 0.6 mol B has been consumed. According to the mole ratio from the equation, 2 mol A consumed for every 1 mol B consumed. Therefore, 1.2 mol A has been consumed and [A] has become $2.8 \text{ mol} \cdot \text{L}^{-1}$.

The correct choice is (C).

9. As the reaction proceeds, some of the reactant molecules are consumed, decreasing the frequency of their collisions and, therefore, the rate of the reaction. Since temperature is constant, the rate constant is constant, producing no effect on the rate. The concentration of products does not affect the rate of the reaction.

The correct choice is (D).

10. As the reaction proceeds, some of the reactant molecules are consumed, decreasing the frequency of their collisions and, therefore, the rate of the reaction. However, this decrease in concentration does not affect the effectiveness of their collisions.

The correct choice is (C).

11. As temperature increases, more molecules reach the energy of activation requirement; therefore, the rate increases and [A] decreases at a greater rate. At this new, higher temperature, the rate constant has a new, higher value.

    The correct choice is (C).

12. Adding an inert gas has no effect on the reaction rate since it does not affect the concentration of any of the reactants.

    The correct choice is (A).

13. In a reaction mechanism, the coefficients of the reactants can be inferred from the exponents of the corresponding terms in the rate law. Thus, the net coefficients for Br^-, BrO_3^-, and H^+ in the elementary processes (steps) of the reaction mechanism must be 1, 1, and 2, respectively. Only the mechanism

    $$Br^- + H^+ \to Int_1 \quad \text{(given)}$$

    $$Int_1 + BrO_3^- \to Int_2$$

    $$Int_2 + H^+ \to Int_3$$

    meets this requirement.

    The correct choice is (B).

14. The overall order of a reaction is the sum of the exponents in the rate law. Because the rate law is

    $$\text{Rate} = k[Br^-][BrO_3^-][H^+]^2$$

    the overall order is 4.

    The correct choice is (C).

15. Because more H^+ is in the system, more collisions will occur between H^+ and Br^- ions.

    The correct choice is (D).

16. Adding $Br_{2(\ell)}$ to the system adds to its mass. However, a change in the amount of product does not affect the rate of the reaction. Only statement I is correct.

    The correct choice is (A).

17. All three proposed changes will decrease the rate of the reaction. Adding water decreases the concentrations of all reactants. Both addition of OH^- and removal of H^+ have the effect of decreasing $[H^+]$.

    The correct choice is (E).

18. At At constant temperature, only a change in the number of molecules of B or the volume of the reaction vessel can affect the partial pressure of $B_{(g)}$, P_B. Only changes I and II affect P_B. Addition of AB_2, as in change III, increases the total pressure. However, because no reverse reaction is specified or implied, no reverse reaction occurs. P_B is not affected by change III.

    The correct choice is (C).

19. Only mechanism II is consistent with the rate law specified.

    The rate law for mechanism I is Rate = $[H_2]^{\frac{1}{2}}[I_2]$

    The rate law for mechanism III is Rate = $[H_2][I_2]^2$

    The correct choice is (B).

20. The change shown at Time 1 is an abrupt increase in the concentration of X. Addition of X would cause this change. Because no equilibrium is implied or specified, changes in Y and Z do not affect concentration of X.

    The correct choice is (A).

21. Between Time 1 and Time 2, the reaction will proceed as usual, with [X] and [Y] decreasing and [Z] increasing.

    The correct choice is (E).

22. The coefficients of X and Y give the mole ratio by which consumption of X and Y, (ΔX and ΔY), $\frac{\Delta X}{\Delta Y}$ occurs. The coefficients of Y and Z give the mole ratio for the production of Z, $\frac{\Delta Z}{-\Delta Y}$. The coefficients do not express quantities available such a [Y] or [Z]. The coefficients also do not give the simple change in quantity such as ΔZ. Only the ratios of changes can be determined from the coefficients of the balanced equation.

    The correct choice is (D).

23. Increase in temperature causes an overall shift in the curve toward higher X values. Since the area under the curve remains constant because the number of molecules remains the same, the new high point must be at a lower value.

    The correct choice is (D).

24. In an exothermic reaction, the potential energy of the products is less than that of the reactants. In an endothermic reaction, the potential energy of the products is greater than that of the reactants. Differences in amount of activation energy are not related to the exo- or endo- thermic nature of the reaction.

The correct choice is (A).

25. The value for the potential energy of the activated complex is shown as the highest value on the plot of the progress of the reaction. The energy of activation is the difference between the potential energy of the reactants and that of the activated complex. Choice (B) shows higher E_a (left) and lower E_a (right), the order of comparison specified. Choice (E) shows lower E_a, then higher E_a, opposite to the order of comparison specified. Choices (A), (C) and (D) show same E_a but different ΔH. Differences in the exo- or endo- thermic nature of the reaction are unrelated to differences in the energy of activation.

The correct choice is (B).

Free-Response Questions

26. Overall Strategy: Compare information about each of the four trials to determine the experimental rate law. Substitute information from any one of the trials in the experimental rate law as determined to solve for the specific rate constant, including its units. Note that rate laws reflect the stoichiometry of the elementary processes in the reaction mechanism up to and including the "slow" step.

(A) Strategy:

- Compare trials to look for change in one concentration, then find the corresponding change in the initial rate of formation.

- Find another similar variation or look for a way to apply information learned from the first comparison.

In this problem, when [B] doubled with [A] held constant (compare trials II and III), rate doubled. Hence, order in B is 1 (first order). Comparing trials I and II, rate doubles as both [A] and [B] double. Doubling of [B] alone accounts for doubling of the rate. Doubling [A] has no effect, hence order in A is 0.

$$\text{Rate} = k[A]^0[B]^1$$

(B) Strategy: To calculate the rate constant, k, choose any trial and substitute its values, including labels, in the rate law as determined in part (A).

From trial I, 8.0×10^{-4} mol L^{-1} sec^{-1} = k(0.4 mol L^{-1})^0(0.20 mol L^{-1})^1

$$k = \frac{8.0 \times 10^{-4} \text{ mol L}^{-1} \text{ sec}^{-1}}{0.20 \text{ mol L}^{-1}}$$

$$k = 4.0 \times 10^{-3} \text{ sec}^{-1}$$

(C) Strategy: Recognize that as [A] has decreased to 0.400 M, [B] has also changed. Based on the stoichiometry of the reaction,

$$\frac{2 \text{ mol A}}{1 \text{ mol B}}$$

when [A] has decreased by 0.200 M, then [B] has decreased by 0.100 M from 0.600 M to 0.500 M.

Applying the rate law as above,

$$\text{Rate}_C = k[A]^0[B]^1 = 4.0 \times 10^{-3} \text{ sec}^{-1} \times 0.500 \text{ M} = \mathbf{2.0 \times 10^{-3} \text{ M sec}^{-1}}$$

or

$$\mathbf{2.0 \times 10^{-3} \text{ mol L}^{-1} \text{ sec}^{-1}}$$

54 Chapter 6   Chemical Kinetics

(D) <u>Strategy</u>: The mechanism must match the stoichiometry and the rate law.

(1) $A + B \xrightarrow{slow} M$ (2) $A + A \underset{}{\overset{fast}{\rightleftharpoons}} M$ (3) $B \xrightarrow{slow} M$

$A + M \xrightarrow{fast} C$ $B + M \underset{}{\overset{slow}{\rightleftharpoons}} C$ $M + A \xrightarrow{fast} N$

$N + A \xrightarrow{fast} C$

In this problem, all mechanisms match the stoichiometry (2 mol A reacts with 1 mol B). The rate law for mechanism 1 is first order in both A and B. That is not correct. Mechanism 2 is second order in A and first order in B. That is also not correct. In mechanism 3, the first step determines the mechanism because it is the slow step. The mechanism is first order in B and zero order in A. This matches the rate information and the experimental rate law. The order of a reaction with respect to any one reactant is given by the sum of the coefficients for that reactant in the steps of the mechanism up to and including the slow step. The overall order is the sum of the orders of all the reactants.

27. Overall Strategy: Use the given information to determine the experimental rate law. Use the rate law to propose a consistent reaction mechanism. Use the potential energy diagram to represent the specified charcateristics for each compound of the system. Use graphs with quantity/time axes to represent the change in amounts (not concentrations) of each of the three substances in the sytem.

(A) Strategy: A rate law has the form Rate = $k[A]^m[B]^n$ where k is the specific rate constant and A and B represent the reactant species. Each exponent defines the order of the reaction with respect to the species with which it is associated. In a first order reaction, the exponent is 1, in a second order, 2, etc.

Because the reaction is identified as "first order" in each reactant, the rate law for this reaction is

$$\text{Rate} = k[PCl_3][Cl_2]$$

The values of m and n are 1. As such, these exponents are generally omitted from explicit inclusion in the rate law.

The factors that determine the value of k include the identity of the reactants and the temperature at which the reaction takes place. Different substances undergoing a similar reaction may have a totally different value for k. If the reaction takes place at a higher temperature, the value for k increases. The value of k in this example is based on expressing the concentration of each substance in moles per liter. Because these are gases, concentrations may also be expressed as pressures, in which case, a different value and label is determined for k.

The exponents m and n are determined by the number of collisions in the reaction mechanism. The values of the exponents are the coefficients of those reactants in the elementary processes (single step collisions of reactants) in the reaction mechanism up to and including the rate-determining ("slow") step.

(B) Strategy: Note the information above. In its simplest version, the reaction mechanism involves only one simple elementary process, a bimolecular collision (one step).

$$PCl_{3(g)} + Cl_{2(g)} \rightarrow PCl_{5(g)}$$

At a more complex level, a mechanism with more steps could be proposed.

(C) <u>Strategy</u>: In the context of chemical change, the energies are sometimes called enthalpies. The absolute enthalpy of a substance cannot be determined. In chemical changes, only enthalpy changes can be identified. On the graph, the chemical formulas represent the relative potential energies stored in the specified substances. The differences in their y-values represent values for ΔH (enthalpy change) for the corresponding change in structure.

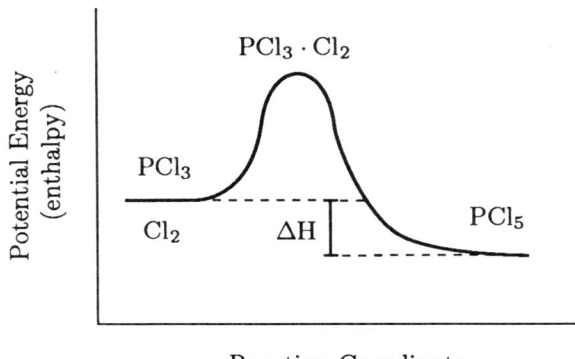

```
                              PCl₃ · Cl₂
                                 ___
                                /   \
Potential Energy               /     \
  (enthalpy)                  /       \
              PCl₃ _____/          \
                                        \
              Cl₂        ΔH  |           _____ PCl₅
                             |_____
```

Reaction Coordinate
(time, progress of the reaction)

(D) <u>Strategy</u>: As the reaction proceeds, the quantities of each substance present changes; product increases and reactants decrease. Note that as one mole of PCl₃ and one mole of Cl₂ react, one mole of PCl₅ is formed.

On the graph, PCl₃ must start at 3.0 moles, as given, and end at approximately 2.4 moles (0.60 mole of PCl₃ is lost). Similarly, Cl₂ must start at 1.0 mole, as given, and end at approximately 0.4 moles (0.60 mole of Cl₂ is lost). The product, PCl₅, must start at 0.0 moles, as given, and end at approximately 0.60 moles.

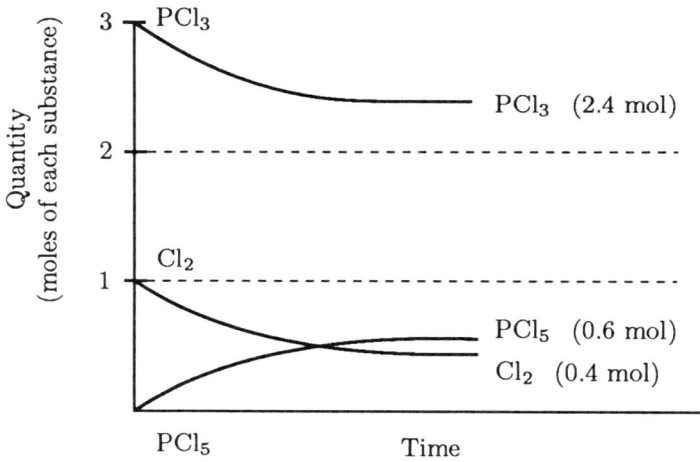

```
                    3 ┬ PCl₃
Quantity              │\
(moles of each        │ _____ PCl₃  (2.4 mol)
 substance)         2 ┼────────────────────────
                      │
                      │
                      │ Cl₂
                    1 ┼─\──────────────────────
                      │  _____ PCl₅  (0.6 mol)
                      │  /                    Cl₂   (0.4 mol)
                      │ /
                      └─────────────────────────
                        PCl₅         Time
```

28. Overall Strategy: When asked to "predict the effect", answers can often be expressed as "increase, decrease or no effect (remains the same)". For that type of question, it is good style to specify the conclusion explicitly first, then provide explanation. For this problem, consider each of the changes proposed. Determine whether or not the change specified causes a corresponding change in the collision frequency, concentration of the reactants, the kinetic energy of the reactants, the nature of the reaction mechanism or other pertinent property. Specify your conclusion, then give a brief explanation. Scoring of this type of question will most likely assign one point for the explicit conclusion and a second point for an adequate explanation.

(A) Strategy: **Initial rate of the reaction increases.** When hydrogen gas is added at constant volume and temperature, the concentration of hydrogen increases. The frequency of collisions between H_2 and I_2 molecules increases and the corresponding rate of reaction increases.

(B) Strategy: **Initial rate of the reaction decreases.** When the volume of the reaction vessel increases at constant temperature, the concentrations of each gas phase reactant decreases. At decreased concentration, the frequency of collisions decreases and the corresponding rate of reaction decreases.

(C) Strategy: **Initial rate of the reaction increases.** When a catalyst is present, a different reaction mechanism is available for reaction. The catalyzed mechanism includes an activated complex that has a lower energy of activation. Because a lower energy of activation is required, more reactant molecules possess the minimum energy (activation energy, E_a) required to form the activated complex. The heat of reaction, ΔH, does not change.

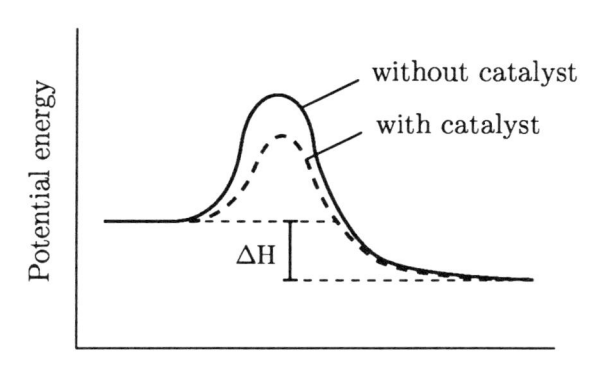

(D) Strategy: **Initial rate of the reaction increases.** At the higher temperature, more reactant molecules possess the minimum energy required to form the activated complex.

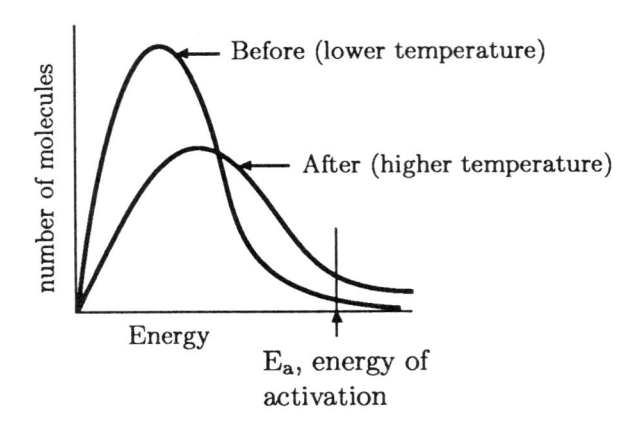

Chapter 7
Chemical Equilibrium

1. $K_p = K_c$ when the number of moles in the gas phase is the same for both products and reactants. For choice (A), that characteristic is present as one mole of gas each for reactant and product. The system described in choice (A) is a heterogeneous system. Note that $S_{(s)}$ is not expressed in either K_c or K_p. The concentration of $S_{(s)}$ is not variable. For each of the other choices, the numbers of moles of gases are as follows:

    (B)   2 mol $(g) \to$ 3 mol (g)

    (C)   4 mol $(g) \to$ 2 mol (g)

    (D)   1 mol $(g) \to$ 2 mol (g) (also a heterogeneous system)

    (E)   2 mol $(g) \to$ 1 mol (g)

    The correct choice is (A).

2. The reaction in question is the reverse of the original reaction. Therefore

$$K_{c,new} = \frac{1}{K_{c,orig}}$$

   The reaction in question also includes twice the amounts of reactants and products. Combining both differences

$$K_{c,new} = \frac{1}{(K_{c,orig})^2} = \frac{1}{(49)^2}$$

   The correct choice is (C).

3. As SO_4^{2-} is added, more collisions occur between Pb^{2+} and SO_4^{2-} ions. In terms of le Chatelier's principle, the reaction shifts to the left to favor formation of reactants (mass of $PbSO_4$ increases) and loss of products ($[Pb^{2+}]$ decreases).

The correct choice is (D).

4.
$$PbCl_{2(s)} \rightleftharpoons Pb^{2+}_{(aq)} + 2Cl^-_{(aq)}$$

The K_{sp} for $PbCl_2$ is given by

$$K_{sp} = [Pb^{2+}][Cl^-]^2 = 1.6 \times 10^{-5}$$

Substituting known values

$$1.6 \times 10^{-5} = 0.010[Cl^-]^2$$

Solving for maximum $[Cl^-]$ that would be permitted with no precipitation

$$[Cl^-]^2 = 1.6 \times 10^{-3}$$

$$[Cl^-]^2 = 16 \times 10^{-4}$$

$$[Cl^-] = 4 \times 10^{-2}$$

Thus, even the largest quantity offered as a response can be added without causing the precipitation.

The correct choice is (E).

Questions 5-9: (To help you analyze this problem, the tabular format from the question book is shown below. Values in bold print are those given in the problem. Values in ordinary type are those resulting from calculations. It is unlikely that this format will appear on the examination. However, its use will help you work through some quantitative principles of chemical equilibrium.)

$$4H_{2(g)} + CS_{2(g)} \rightleftharpoons CH_{4(g)} + 2H_2S_{(g)}$$

	$H_{2(g)}$	$CS_{2(g)}$	$CH_{4(g)}$	$H_2S_{(g)}$
mol available	**2.50**	**1.50**	1.50	**2.0**
mol change	+1.00	+0.25	-0.25	-0.50
mol at equil.	3.50	1.75	1.25	1.50
concentration	0.70	0.35	**0.25**	0.30

To obtain the values above:

First, use mol per liter CH_4 as given to find mol CH_4 at equilibrium.

$$5.0 \text{ L} \times \frac{0.25 \text{ mol } CH_4}{1.0 \text{ liter}} = 1.25 \text{ mol } CH_4 \text{ at equilibrium}$$

Based on the given information, it can be concluded that the system proceeds in the reverse direction to favor production of the reactants, since there is a decrease in $[CH_4]$. Calculate change in number of moles of CH_4.

1.50 mol CH_4 available $-$ 1.25 mol CH_4 at equilibrium $=$ 0.25 mol CH_4 lost

Once the number of mol CH_4 "lost" is determined, then find corresponding number of moles of H_2S lost and number of moles of H_2 and CS_2 produced. Using mole ratios from the balanced equation, the change in moles of the other three components can be calculated.

$$0.25 \text{ mol } CH_4 \text{ lost} \times \frac{2 \text{ mol } H_2S \text{ lost}}{1 \text{ mol } CH_4 \text{ lost}} = 0.50 \text{ mol } H_2S \text{ lost}$$

$$0.25 \text{ mol } CH_4 \text{ lost} \times \frac{1 \text{ mol } CS_2 \text{ produced}}{1 \text{ mol } CH_4 \text{ lost}} = 0.25 \text{ mol } CS_2 \text{ produced}$$

$$0.25 \text{ mol } CH_4 \text{ lost} \times \frac{4 \text{ mol } H_2 \text{ produced}}{1 \text{ mol } CH_4 \text{ lost}} = 1.00 \text{ mol } H_2 \text{ produced}$$

Moles of each component remaining at equilibrium and concentration of each in the 5-liter vessel can be calculated.

5. The balanced equation shows that, in the reverse reaction, two moles of H_2S are lost for every one mole CS_2 produced.

    The correct choice is (C).

62 Chapter 7 Chemical Equilibrium

6. The principles used to complete the table above show that the change in number of moles of H_2S is -0.50.

   The correct choice is (B).

7. The principles used to complete the table above show that the change in number of moles of CS_2 is $+0.25$. Adding that value to the original quantity shows that 1.75 mol CS_2 is present at equilibrium.

   The correct choice is (E).

8. The principles used to complete the table above show that the change in number of moles of H_2 is $+1.00$. Thus 3.50 mol H_2 is present at equilibrium in a 5.0 liter vessel, giving a concentration of 0.70 mol H_2 per liter.

   The correct choice is (B).

9. Since the system proceeded to equilibrium by shifting to form reactants, the value for ΔG at mixing was positive and the value for Q was greater than the value for K_{eq}. Moving toward equilibrium, where $\Delta G = 0$, will move ΔG toward zero from a positive value. Moving toward equilibrium, where Q = K, will decrease the numerator of Q and increase its denominator, producing an overall lower value.

   The correct choice is (C).

Questions 10-13:

$$2SO_{2(g)} + O_{2(g)} \rightleftharpoons 2SO_{3(g)} + \text{heat}$$

Consider an equilibrium system based on the reaction above. This equilibrium mixture is contained in a piston.

10. According to the Le Chatelier's principle, as volume increases, the system will shift to produce more molecules to fill this larger volume. A shift favoring formation of reactants would provide more molecules. The number of molecules of SO_2 will increase as SO_3 molecules are decomposed to SO_2 and O_2. For every two SO_3 molecules lost, two molecules of SO_2 and one molecule of O_2 are formed for a net increase in total number of molecules. Because temperature remains constant, K_p does not change.

    The correct choice is (C).

11. A decrease in the force on the piston causes an increase in the volume of the system and is accompanied by a decrease in the total pressure of the system. The phrase, "this system" implies that no substances are added. As volume increases, the changes occur as described in number 10 above occur.

    The correct choice is (C).

12. According to the Le Chatelier's principle, an increase in temperature can be regarded as an addition of heat. This addition of heat will shift the equilibrium to favor greater formation of reactants. The number of molecules of SO_2 as well as the total number of molecules will increase. K_p is given by

$$K_p = \frac{(P_{SO_3})^2}{(P_{SO_2})^2 \times P_{O_2}}$$

Thus, the new K_p, with a smaller numerator and a larger denominator, will decrease compared to the original K_p.

The correct choice is (E).

13. According to the Le Chatelier's principle, addition of reactants will shift the system to favor formation of more products due to greater frequency of collisions. Since not all of the added O_2 will be consumed and for every existing SO_2 molecule consumed, a molecule of SO_3 will be produced, there will be a net increase in the total number of molecules. Since temperature is constant, there will be no change in K_p.

The correct choice is (B).

14. $$HgO_{(s)} + 4I^-{}_{(aq)} + H_2O \rightleftharpoons HgI_4{}^{2-}{}_{(aq)} + 2OH^-{}_{(aq)} \qquad \Delta H < 0$$

Addition of HNO_3 will decrease [OH^-], thus shifting the equilibrium to favor the formation of more $HgI_4{}^{2-}{}_{(aq)}$. Adding $KI_{(s)}$, a soluble salt and source of $I^-{}_{(aq)}$, will also shift the equilibrium to favor formation of products. Increasing the mass of $HgO_{(s)}$ will not affect the equilibrium since there is already excess $HgO_{(s)}$ in this heterogeneous equilibrium system. Furthermore, as in any heterogeneous equilibrium, the concentration of the solid phase cannot be changed. Its concentration is not a variable term in the mass action expression (Q) or the equilibrium constant (K_{eq}) for this system.

The correct choice is (C).

15. $$CaSO_{4(s)} \rightleftharpoons Ca^{2+}{}_{(aq)} + SO_4{}^{2-}{}_{(aq)}$$

For $CaSO_4$

$$K_{sp} = [Ca^{2+}][SO_4{}^{2-}]$$

Since the molar solubility for $CaSO_4 = 1.2 \times 10^{-3}$

$$[Ca^{2+}] = [SO_4{}^{2-}] = 1.2 \times 10^{-3}$$

$$K_{sp} = [1.2 \times 10^{-3}][1.2 \times 10^{-3}] = [1.2 \times 10^{-3}]^2$$

The correct choice is (B).

Questions 16-19:

$$N_{2(g)} + 3H_{2(g)} \rightleftharpoons 2NH_{3(g)} + 92 \text{ kJ}$$

The questions below apply to an equilibrium system based on the reversible reaction given above.

16. Since volume is unchanged and the phrase "such [a] system" implies no change in the total mass of substances in the system, density (mass per unit volume) remains unchanged. The increase in temperature specified (addition of heat) causes pressure and average kinetic energy to increase. Addition of heat also causes the equilibrium to shift to favor formation of reactants, including $N_{2(g)}$.

    The correct choice is (A).

17. The addition of heat favors the reaction with the highest energy of activation; that is, the endothermic reaction, in this case the reverse reaction. Since the system shifts to favor formation of reactants, the value for K_p decreases.

    The correct choice is (D).

18. Equilibrium exists when there is no further change in the macroscopic properties of the system. Of the five observations offered, only constant pressure of hydrogen qualifies as evidence for existence of equilibrium. Density and mass of the system are always constant. The odor of ammonia can be detected even at non-equilibrium conditions. Decreasing pressure is evidence that equilibrium has NOT yet been achieved.

    The correct choice is (D).

19. All three changes will occur since the system is shifted to favor formation of $NH_{3(g)}$, an exothermic reaction.

    The correct choice is (E).

---

20. An increase in temperature causes the rate of any chemical reaction to increase. Note also when comparing the rates of opposing reactions as in this problem, the rate of the endothermic reaction is subject to a greater effect due to temperature change than is the rate of the exothermic reaction. However, this question does not address such a comparison of rates.

    The correct choice is (E).

Questions 21-25:

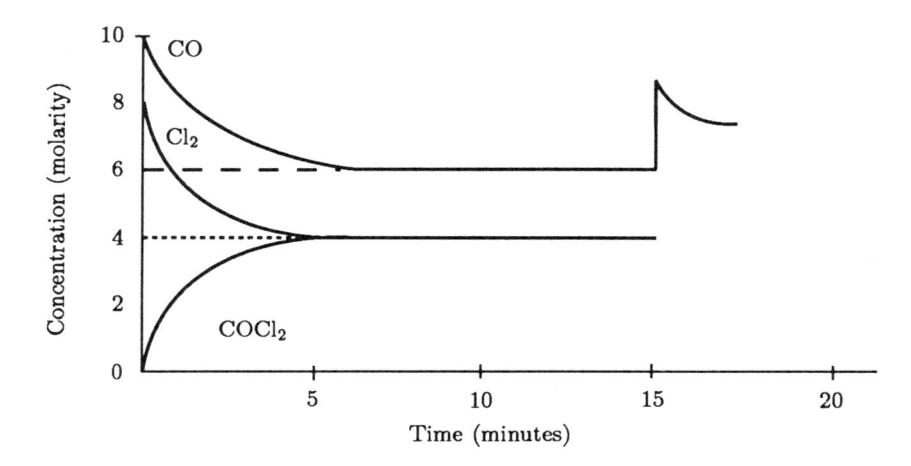

21. Read the concentration of each species from the graph provided and substitute those values in the equilibrium expression. Note that equilibrium is achieved at about time 5 minutes and lasts until time 15 minutes.

    Set up the equilibrium expression as

    $$\frac{[COCl_2]}{[CO][Cl_2]} = \frac{4}{6 \times 4}$$

    The correct choice is (C).

22. Note that $[COCl_2]$ does not appear on the graph at time 20 minutes. Its value can be determined by using the principle that 1 mol $[COCl_2]$ is produced for every mole of CO consumed. From time 15 to time 20, [CO] decreases by about 1 M. Therefore, $[COCl_2]$ increases by about 1 M. Thus the value of $[COCl_2]$ becomes approximately 5 M.

    The correct choice is (D).

23. The abrupt increase in [CO] at time 15 minutes can be explained by the addition of CO. The subsequent loss in [CO] and increase in $[Cl_2]$ is caused by the forward reaction which proceeds at a greater rate than the reverse reaction until equilibrium is reestablished at time 20 minutes.

    The correct choice is (C).

24. At equilibrium, the rates of the opposing reactions are always equal. This principle helps to account for the constant properties of any system observed at equilibrium.

    The correct choice is (E).

25. Between times 15 and 20 minutes, [CO] decreases. The rate of the forward reaction, consuming Cl_2, is greater than the rate of the reverse reaction which produces Cl_2. When [CO] decreases, $[Cl_2]$ also decreases and $[COCl_2]$ increases.

    The correct choice is (C).

Free-Response Questions

26. <u>Overall Strategy</u>: Note first that the value for K_p, being substantially greater than 1, favors the formation of products. Note also that the stoichiometry of this system specifies that one mole of $PCl_{5(g)}$ decomposes to form one mole each of $PCl_{3(g)}$ and $Cl_{2(g)}$.

    (A) At equilibrium, $[PCl_3] = [Cl_2]$. For every mole of PCl_3 formed, one mole of Cl_2 is also formed.

    (B) At equilibrium, $[PCl_5] < [PCl_3]$. Because $K_p > 1$, the reaction must proceed to favor formation of the products. Thus, $[PCl_5]$ decreases from its original value (equal to $[PCl_3]$) as $[PCl_3]$ increases.

    (C) At equilibrium, **RATE_{forward} = RATE_{reverse}**. When these rates are equal, there is no further net change in concentration (or pressure) of any components of the system. Thus, equal rates accounts for the establishment of equilibrium.

    (D) (1) **The number of moles of PCl_5 decreases.** When the volume of the system at equilibrium is increased, the rates of the opposing reactions are no longer equal. In order to reestablish the equilibrium, the system will shift to favor formation of more molecules of gas. According to le Chatelier's principle, the stress of increased volume is relieved when more molecules are produced to fill that volume. In a larger volume, the frequency of collisions between PCl_3 and Cl_2 molecules decreases, reducing the number of PCl_5 molecules formed by the reverse reaction. The total number of molecules increases as the number of molecules of $PCl_{5(g)}$ decreases and more molecules of $PCl_{3(g)}$ and $Cl_{2(g)}$ are formed.

    (2) **The value of K_p remains the same.** Because the temperature remains the same, the value for K_p, which is the ratio, $\frac{\text{products}}{\text{reactants}}$, remains the same.

Chemical Equilibrium   Chapter 7

27. **Overall Strategy:** This problem illustrates solubility equilibrium. The dissolving/dissociation equation and the K_{sp} expression for each dissolving process are needed. Where two equilibria are involved as in the case where Cl^- and CrO_4^{2-} ions are in contact with Ag^+ in water solution, the concentration of the ion common to both equilibria has the same value.

 (A) $AgCl_{(s)} \rightleftharpoons Ag^+_{(aq)} + Cl^-_{(aq)}$ $K_{sp} = [Ag^+][Cl^-]$

        $K_{sp} = (1.3 \times 10^{-5})(1.3 \times 10^{-5}) = 1.7 \times 10^{-10}$

 (B) $Ag_2CrO_{4(s)} \rightleftharpoons 2Ag^+_{(aq)} + CrO_4^{2-}_{(aq)}$ $K_{sp} = [Ag^+]^2[CrO_4^{2-}]$

        Note that two moles of Ag^+ are formed for every mole of $Ag_2CrO_{4(s)}$ that dissolves.

        $K_{sp} = (2 \times 1.3 \times 10^{-4})^2(1.3 \times 10^{-4}) = 8.8 \times 10^{-12}$

 (C)   Calculate $[Ag^+]$ present at saturation when a solution is 0.050 M in both CrO_4^{2-} and Cl^-.

        Use K_{sp} values determined above.

        $K_{sp} = 1.7 \times 10^{-10} = [Ag^+][Cl^-] = [Ag^+] \times 0.050$

        $[Ag^+] = 3.4 \times 10^{-9}$

        $K_{sp} = 8.8 \times 10^{-12} = [Ag^+]^2[CrO_4^{2-}] = [Ag^+]^2 \times 0.050$

        $[Ag^+] = 1.3 \times 10^{-5}$

        Since the AgCl precipitates at a lower concentration of Ag^+, the AgCl precipitates first. The concentration of Ag^+ when AgCl first begins to appear is 3.4×10^{-9} M.

 (D)   Recognize that AgCl is least soluble. Therefore as Ag^+ is added, it reacts with the available Cl^- first until $[Cl^-]$ is driven to a very low value. Then any additional Ag^+ reacts with CrO_4^{2-}. Essentially all of the Cl^- must precipitate before the $Ag_2CrO_{4(s)}$ begins to form. Thus, 0.050 mol $AgCl_{(s)}$ has been formed when $Ag_2CrO_{4(s)}$ begins to precipitate.

28. **Overall strategy:** This problem illustrates a homogeneous gas phase equilibrium. The equilibrium expression, K_c, for this system is needed. When K_c (rather than K_p) is specified for the equilibrium expression, its value is determined using concentrations in moles/liter. Note that the quantity present at equilibrium is given for only one species. The equilibrium quantities for the other species must be calculated using principles of stoichiometry. Concentrations for all species must also be calculated. In the last part of this problem, a shift in equilibrium is caused by adding more of one of the reactants.

(A) $K_c = \dfrac{[HI]^2}{[H_2][I_2]}$

(B) This table is provided to help summarize the changes and final concentrations.

	H_2	I_2	HI
mol orig	2.0	3.0	—
chg mol due to rxn	−0.95	−0.95	+1.90
mol at equil	1.05	2.05	1.90
[ ] at equil	$\dfrac{1.05}{3}$ = 0.350	$\dfrac{2.05}{3}$ = 0.683	$\dfrac{1.90}{3}$ = 0.633

$$K_c = \dfrac{[HI]^2}{[H_2][I_2]} = \dfrac{(0.633)^2}{(0.350)(0.683)} = 1.68$$

(C) The number of moles of $I_{2(g)}$ is calculated above. Use the ideal gas law as found on the list of *Equations and Constants* to determine the partial pressure of $I_{2(g)}$.

$$P = \dfrac{nRT}{V}$$

$$P = \dfrac{2.05 \text{ mol} \times 0.0821 \text{ L} \cdot \text{atm} \cdot \text{mol}^{-1} \cdot \text{K}^{-1} \times 700 \text{ K}}{3.0 \text{ L}} = 39.3 \text{ atm}$$

(or choose 0.683 mol and 1.0 liter to substitute for n and V)

Chemical Equilibrium   **Chapter 7**   69

(D) The new mixture now has 3.0 mol each of H_2 and I_2. Use K_c, previously calculated to determine $[I_2]$. Then use ideal gas law to determine partial pressure from moles per liter.

	H_2	I_2	HI
mol orig	**3.0**	**3.0**	—
chg mol due to rxn	$-X$	$-X$	$+2X$
mol at equil	$3.0 - X$	$3.0 - X$	$2X$
[ ] at equil	$\dfrac{3.0 - X}{3}$	$\dfrac{3.0 - X}{3}$	$\dfrac{2X}{3}$

$$K_c = \frac{[HI]^2}{[H_2][I_2]} = 1.68$$

$$1.68 = \frac{\left(\dfrac{(2X)}{(3)}\right)^2}{\dfrac{3.0-X}{3} \times \dfrac{3.0-X}{3}} \quad \text{(note: volumns cancel)}$$

$$1.68 = \frac{(2X)^2}{(3.0-X)^2}$$

$$\sqrt{1.68} = \sqrt{\frac{(2X)^2}{(3.0-X)^2}}$$

$$1.30 = \frac{(2X)}{(3.0-X)} \quad \text{(by taking square root of both sides)}$$

$X = 1.18 \quad 2X = 2.36$ mol HI at equilibrium

Use the ideal gas law to determine partial pressure of $HI_{(g)}$.

$$P = \frac{nRT}{V}$$

$$P = \frac{2.36 \text{ mol} \times 0.0821 \text{ L} \cdot \text{atm} \cdot \text{mol}^{-1} \cdot \text{K}^{-1} \times 700 \text{ K}}{3.0 \text{ L}} = 45.2 \text{ atm}$$

Chapter 8
Thermodynamics

1. The change in enthalpy, ΔH, is negative for any exothermic reaction.

   The correct choice is (C).

2. The change in Gibbs free energy, ΔG, is negative for any spontaneous change.

   The correct choice is (B).

3. The energy of activation, E_a, is the energy stored in the activated complex. When a catalyst is added to a system, a new activated complex (and perhaps an entire reaction mechanism) becomes available. If the reaction is catalyzed, this new activated complex must have a lower E_a than the former activated complex.

   The correct choice is (E).

4. Entropy, often described as randomness or disorder in a system, is subject to change in any chemical reaction. The value for ΔS can be positive or negative.

   The correct choice is (D).

5. The equilibrium constant is determined by the concentration of reactants and products at equilibrium in a closed system according to the formula

   $$\frac{[\text{products}]}{[\text{reactants}]}$$

   The correct choice is (A).

6. The relationship that applies is

   $$\Delta S° = S°_{\text{prod}} - S°_{\text{react}}$$

   $$\Delta S° = 2S°_{NH_3} - (S°_{N_2} + 3S°_{NH_3})$$

   $$\Delta S° = (2 \times 193) - \left(192 + (3 \times 131)\right)$$

   using arithmetic by estimation

   $$\Delta S° = \text{about } 400 - \text{about } 200 - \text{about } 400$$

   $$\Delta S° = -\text{about } 200 \text{ J} \cdot \text{K}^{-1}$$

   The correct choice is (E).

7. The relationship that applies is

$$\Delta G = \Delta H - T\Delta S$$

Substituting and noting that ΔS from question 1 is -0.200 kJ·K^{-1}

$$\Delta G = -92 \text{ kJ} - (200 \text{ K} \times -0.200 \text{ kJ·K}^{-1})$$

using arithmetic by estimation

$$\Delta G = \text{about } -100 + 40$$

$$\Delta G = \text{about } -60$$

The correct choice is (B).

8. The relationship that applies is

$$\Delta G = \Delta H - T\Delta S$$

Since ΔH is negative and ΔS negative, at low values of T the value of ΔG is negative and the reaction is spontaneous. Again, since ΔH is negative and ΔS negative, as temperature increases, the $-T\Delta S$ term is positive and becomes larger. At some value of T, the value of ΔG becomes positive (increases to values greater than zero) and the reaction becomes non-spontaneous.

The correct choice is (E).

9. For any phase change at the melting point, $\Delta G = 0$. Therefore

$$\Delta G = \Delta H - T\Delta S = 0$$

$$\Delta H = T\Delta S$$

$$\Delta S = \frac{\Delta H}{T}$$

The relationship that applies is

$$\Delta S_{fus} = \frac{\Delta H_{fus}}{T_{mp}}$$

The correct choice is (A).

10. This change includes the heat needed to melt the ice, ΔH_{fus}, and the heat needed to warm the water, C_p, over a temperature increase of 25C°. Note that ΔH and C_p must be expressed in the same units.

$$6010 \frac{\text{joules}}{\text{mol}} + \left(75 \frac{\text{J}}{\text{mol·C°}} \times 25\text{C°}\right)$$

The correct choice is (C).

11. The quantities of reactants available are

$$0.100 \text{ L HCl sol'n} \times \frac{3.0 \text{ mol H}^+}{1 \text{ L HCl sol'n}} = 0.30 \text{ mol H}^+$$

$$0.100 \text{ L KOH sol'n} \times \frac{1.0 \text{ mol OH}^-}{1 \text{ L KOH sol'n}} = 0.10 \text{ mol OH}^-$$

In this reaction, since 0.30 mol H$^+$ and 0.10 mol OH$^-$ are available, the amount of H$^+$ neutralized is 0.10. The amount of heat released is

$$0.10 \text{ mol H}^+ \times \frac{60 \text{ kJ}}{1 \text{ mol H}^+} = 6.0 \text{ kJ}$$

The correct choice is (D).

12. In general, any reaction that results in an increase in the number of moles of gas illustrates an increase in entropy. Only reaction (D)

$$3\text{Fe}_{(s)} + 2\text{O}_{2(g)} \rightarrow \text{Fe}_3\text{O}_{4(s)}$$

shows a decrease in the number of moles of gas.

The correct choice is (D).

13. The first law of thermodynamics relationship applies to this reaction

$$\Delta H = \Delta E + P\Delta V$$

The term PΔV is equivalent to ΔnRT, where Δn refers to the change in the number of moles of gas. Thus, where Δn is zero, $\Delta H = \Delta E$. The only such reaction of those given is (B).

$$\text{H}_{2(g)} + \text{Cl}_{2(g)} \rightarrow 2\text{HCl}_{(g)}$$

The correct choice is (B).

14. In the standard formation reaction, a compound is formed from its elements provided in the standard state at 298 K and 1 atm of pressure as in reaction (C). Reaction (A) is the "burning" of BaS. Reaction (B) is the precipitation of BaSO$_4$ from aqueous solution. Reaction (D) is a nonsense reaction. Reaction (E) is the neutralization of Ba(OH)$_2$ by H$_2$SO$_4$.

The correct choice is (C).

15. At 298 K, ice melts; thus the change is spontaneous and $\Delta G < 0$. Solid ice is converted to liquid water, an increase in entropy with $\Delta S > 0$. Energy, the heat of fusion, is taken on as the phase change proceeds with $\Delta H > 0$.

The correct choice is (E).

16. The relationship that applies is Hess's Law expressed as

$$\Delta H° = \sum \Delta H°_{f,\ products} - \sum \Delta H°_{f,\ reactants}$$

$$\Delta H° = \left(\left(\Delta H°_{f,\ CO_2}\right) + \left(2 \times \Delta H°_{f,\ H_2O}\right)\right) - \left(\left(\Delta H°_{f,\ CH_4}\right) + \left(2 \times \Delta H°_{f,\ O_2}\right)\right)$$

substituting known values and noting that $\Delta H°_{f,\ O_2} = 0$

$$-889 = \left((-393) + (2 \times (-286))\right) - \left(\Delta H°_{f,\ CH_4} + (0)\right)$$

Rearranging

$$\Delta H°_{f,\ CH_4} = 889 + \left((-393) + (2 \times (-286))\right)$$

or

$$\Delta H°_{f,\ CH_4} = 889 - 393 - (2 \times 286)$$

The correct choice is (E).

17. In this system, some and perhaps all, of the ice melts. This is an increase in potential energy with a corresponding decrease in the average kinetic energy (temperature) of the system, once the system reaches a new equilibrium. Since the system is totally insulated, there is no decrease in total energy. The conversion from solid to liquid is associated with an increase in entropy.

The correct choice is (D).

74   Chapter 8   Thermodynamics

18. The relationship states that any change in internal energy ΔE is seen as heat, q, plus work, w. Sign conventions in chemistry are taken from the standpoint of the system. Thus, heat, q, added the system is given a positive sign. Heat lost by the system (added to the surroundings) is given a negative sign. Similarly, work, w, done on the system is given a positive sign and work done on the surroundings a negative sign. (Note: When ΔE is given as q − w, a different sign convention is used for w.)

The correct choice is (D).

19. The first law of thermodynamics relationship applies to this reaction.

$$\Delta H = \Delta E + P\Delta V$$

The term $P\Delta V$ is equivalent to ΔnRT, where Δn refers to the change in the number of moles of gas. For this reaction Δn is +2. Thus, the equation becomes

$$\Delta H = \Delta E + \Delta nRT$$

$$\Delta H = \Delta E + 2RT$$

The correct choice is (C).

20. Since reaction proceeds spontaneously from the initial standard state conditions, the value for ΔG must be negative. In the standard state, the value for Q, the mass action expression, is unity (1). Again, since the reaction proceeds, it must favor the formation of products. Thus, the value of Q increases to a value greater than 1, eventually reaching equilibrium concentrations where the mass action expression becomes equal to the numerical value of the equilibrium constant, K_{eq}. No information is given about enthalpy change, ΔH.

The correct choice is (C).

Thermodynamics   Chapter 8   75

21. The relationship that applies is Hess's Law expressed as

$$\Delta H° = \sum \Delta H°_{f, \text{ products}} - \sum \Delta H°_{f, \text{ reactants}}$$

$$\Delta H° = \left(\left(3 \times \Delta H°_{f, CO_2}\right) + \left(4 \times \Delta H°_{f, H_2O}\right)\right) - \left(\left(\Delta H°_{f, C_3H_8}\right) + \left(5 \times \Delta H°_{f, O_2}\right)\right)$$

substituting known values and noting that, for CO_2 and H_2O, $\Delta H°_{comb} = \Delta H°_f$ and that $\Delta H°_{f, O_2} = 0$

$$\Delta H°_{comb} = \left(\left(3 \times (-394)\right) + \left(4 \times (-286)\right)\right) - \left(-104 + \left(5 \times (0)\right)\right)$$

Rearranging and simplifying

$$\Delta H°_{comb} = \left(\left(-3 \times (394)\right) + \left(-4 \times (286)\right)\right) - \left(-104\right)$$

The correct choice is (E).

22. The relationship that applies is

$$\Delta G = \Delta H - T\Delta S$$

Since the reaction is not spontaneous at any temperature, ΔG **is always positive**, never negative. If ΔH were negative (favoring spontaneity), ΔG would become negative at some low temperature, no matter what the sign or (reasonable) magnitude of ΔS. Therefore, ΔH **must be positive**. If ΔS were positive (favoring spontaneity), ΔG would become negative at some high temperature even if ΔH were positive. Therefore, ΔS **must be negative**.

The correct choice is (B).

23. The relationship that applies is

$$\Delta G = \Delta H - T\Delta S$$

When the reaction has negative values for both ΔH and ΔS, spontaneity depends upon absolute temperature. Since ΔH is negative, this is an exothermic reaction. (Description II applies). At low temperatures, the effect of negative ΔH predominates and the reaction is spontaneous with negative ΔG. As temperature increases, the role of ΔS in determining spontaneity increases. As the temperature increases, the negative value of ΔG increases (becomes more positive), approaching zero. (Description III applies). Eventually at some higher temperature, ΔG becomes positive and the reaction is no longer spontaneous. (Description I is not true.)

The correct choice is (D).

76 Chapter 8   Thermodynamics

24. The relationship that applies to this question is

$$\Delta G° = -RT \ln K_{eq} = -2.303 \, RT \log K_{eq}$$

The temperature is given as 298 K. The units "kilojoules" identifies $0.00831 \, kJ \cdot mol^{-1} \cdot K^{-1}$ as the proper value for R. Substituting known values

$$\Delta G° = -0.00831 \times 298 \times \ln 10^{-5} = -2.303 \times 0.00831 \times 298 \times \log 10^{-5}$$

Simplifying

$$\Delta G° = -2.303 \times 0.00831 \times 298 \times \log 10^{-5}$$

Then estimating the arithmetic

$$\Delta G° = - \text{ about } 2 \times \text{ about } 0.008 \times \text{ about } 300 \times (-5)$$

$$\Delta G° = - \text{ about } 2 \times \text{ about } 2.4 \times (-5)$$

$$\Delta G° = + \text{ about } 10 \times \text{ about } 2.4$$

$$\Delta G° = \text{ about } 24$$

(precise to 3 significant figures $\Delta G° = 28.5$)

The correct choice is (B).

25. The statement provided shows

$$\Delta S_{universe} > 0$$

Simply stated, this says that the entropy of the universe increases for any spontaneous process.

The correct choice is (A).

Thermodynamics   Chapter 8

Free-Response Questions

26. <u>Overall Strategy</u>: This system should be recognized as illustrating an ordinary dissolving process in which an ionic solid mixes with the polar solvent water and is dissociated into hydrated anions and cations. Since the highly ordered ionic solid is changed into the more random dispersion of hydrated ions, entropy increases. The temperature decrease indicates that energy is absorbed by the system from the surroundings, causing a decrease in the temperature of the surroundings, in this case the solution and the beaker.

   (A) **Entropy increases** due to increased randomness as the ionic crystal lattice breaks down and the particles dissolve as hydrated ions. **Enthalpy increases** as evidenced by the decrease in temperature of the water. Energy is taken on as bonds are broken between NH_4^+ cations and Cl^- anions. The energy given off as bonds form (hydration) is less than the energy required to separate the ions. **Free energy decreases** until it is a minimum. For solute/solvent systems, free energy is at a minimum when the solution is saturated. The problem states that the salt dissolves; therefore, the solution does not become saturated and free energy decreases during this process.

   (B) **ΔG has a negative sign. Both ΔH and ΔS have positive signs.** See above. According to the definition of $\Delta G (= \Delta H - T\Delta S)$, when both ΔH and ΔS are positive, the sign and value for ΔG are dependent upon the temperature in kelvins. Because the dissolving process is observed to occur, the value for ΔG must be negative; the increased entropy effect favoring spontaneity is great enough to override the opposing effect of increasing enthalpy, a positive value for ΔH.

   (C) **The magnitude of the temperature change increases. The apparent heat of solution increases.** That is, more energy would be taken from the water causing its temperature to decrease to a lower value. The plastic foam of the cup has little energy to give up. Its specific heat capacity is very low. In comparison, the specific heat capacity of glass is substantially higher.

   (D) If the temperature were to increase, **the sign of ΔG would remain the same (still negative) and the magnitude of ΔG would increase.** (ΔG would become "more negative".) In the equation for ΔG, $\Delta G = \Delta H - T\Delta S$, as temperature increases, the contribution of the entropy change term, $T\Delta S$, to the value for ΔG increases. Since entropy change is positive (system becomes more disordered), when this same process occurs at a higher temperature, the magnitude of ΔG increases. Note that ΔH is assumed to be constant over the temperature range in question.

78   Chapter 8   Thermodynamics

27. Overall Strategy: Quantitative relationships apply to this problem. Refer to the list of *Equations and Constants* to find useful information. Note that the system is at equilibrium. No further change in concentrations occur.

(A) From the list of *Equations and Constants* provided with the exam, find

$$\Delta H° = \sum \Delta H°_{f,products} - \sum \Delta H°_{f,reactants} \quad \text{(often known as Hess's Law)}$$

Note that values for $\Delta H°_f$ are provided for all reactants and products. Note also that, because bromine is a gas (rather than a liquid, its standard state) for the reaction in question, $\Delta H°_f$ for $BrCl_{(g)}$ is not the $\Delta H°$ for this reaction.

$$\Delta H° = \left[2(\Delta S°_{f,BrCl_{(g)}})\right] - \left[\Delta H°_{f,Br_{2(g)}} + \Delta H°_{f,Cl_{2(g)}}\right]$$

$$\Delta H° = \left[2(14.7)\right]kJ - \left[30.7 + (0)\right]kJ = \mathbf{-1.30\ kJ}$$

(B) From the list of *Equations and Constants* provided with the exam, find

$$\Delta S° = \sum S°_{products} - \sum S°_{reactants}$$

Note that values for $S°$ are provided for all reactants and products.

$$\Delta S° = \left[2(S°_{BrCl_{(g)}})\right] - \left[S°_{Br_{2(g)}} + S°_{Cl_{2(g)}}\right]$$

$$\Delta S° = \left[2(239.7)\right]J\ K^{-1} - \left[152.2 + 222.8\right]J\ K^{-1} = \mathbf{+104.4\ J\ K^{-1}}$$

(C) From the list of *Equations and Constants* provided with the exam, find

$$\Delta G°_f = \Delta H°_f - T\Delta S°_f \quad \text{(providing the definition of Gibbs free energy change)}$$

The values of $\Delta G°_f$ and $\Delta H°_f$ are provided for $BrCl_{(g)}$. Using these values, $\Delta S°_f$ can be calculated by substituting known values in the equation above.

$$\Delta G°_f = \Delta H°_f - T\Delta S°_f$$

$$-0.88\ kJ = 14.7\ kJ - (298\ K \times \Delta S°_f)$$

$$\Delta S°_f = \frac{-0.88\ kJ - 14.7\ kJ}{-298\ K} = 0.0523\ kJ\ K^{-1} = \mathbf{52.3\ J\ K^{-1}}$$

(D) From the list of *Equations and Constants* provided with the exam, find

$\Delta G° = -R\, T\, \ln K_p$ (providing the quantitative relationship between standard free energy change and the equilibrium constant)

Since $\Delta G°$ is not known for this reaction, it can be calculated using the equation below found in the list of *Equations and Constants*

$\Delta G° = \sum \Delta G°_{f,\text{products}} - \sum \Delta G°_{f,\text{reactants}}$ (analogous to Hess's Law)

Note that values for $\Delta G°_f$ are provided for all reactants and products. Note also that, because bromine is a gas (rather than a liquid, its standard state) for the reaction in question, $\Delta G°_f$ for $BrCl_{(g)}$ is not $\Delta G°$ for this reaction.

$\Delta G° = \left[2(\Delta G°_{f,BrCl_{(g)}})\right] - \left[\Delta G°_{f,Br_{2(g)}} + \Delta G°_{f,Cl_{2(g)}}\right]$

$\Delta G° = [2(-0.88)]\text{ kJ} - [3.14 + 0]\text{ kJ} = -4.90\text{ kJ}$

Once $\Delta G°$ has been determined, it can be used with the other known values in the first equation above.

$\Delta G° = -8.31\text{ J mol}^{-1}\text{ K}^{-1} \times T \times \ln K$

$-4.90\text{ kJ} \times \dfrac{1000\text{ J}}{1\text{ kJ}} = -8.31\text{ J mol}^{-1}\text{ K}^{-1} \times 298\text{ K} \times \ln K_p$

$\ln K = \dfrac{-4900}{-8.31 \times 298}$

$K_p = \mathbf{7.23}$

28. Overall Strategy: Quantitative relationships apply to this problem. Refer to the list of *Equations and Constants* to find useful information. Because a chemical reaction occurs, principles of stoichiometry apply. The energy changes and transfers involved call for the application of principles of Hess's Law and heat capacity.

(A) $6C_{(s)} + 6H_{2(g)} + 3O_{2(g)} \rightarrow C_6H_{12}O_{6(s)}$

Note that symbols for phase have been included as instructed.

(B) From the list of *Equations and Constants* provided with the exam, note that

$$\Delta S° = \sum S°_{products} - \sum S°_{reactants}$$

Substitute known values for S° as provided, then calculate the unknown value, $\Delta S°_{f, C_6H_{12}O_6}$.

$$\Delta S°_f = \left[(S°_{C_6H_{12}O_6})\right] - \left[6(S°_C) + 6(S°_{H_2}) + 3(S°_{O_2})\right]$$

$$\Delta S°_f = \left[(212.1)\right] - \left[6(5.69) + 6(130.58) + 3(205.0)\right]$$

$$\Delta S°_f = \left[(212.1)\right] - \left[1,432.62\right] = -1,220.5 \text{ J mol}^{-1} \text{ K}^{-1}$$

(C) From the list of *Equations and Constants* provided with the exam, find

$$\Delta G°_f = \Delta H°_f - T\Delta S°_f \quad \text{(providing the definition of Gibbs free energy change)}$$

The value for $\Delta H°_f$ is given. The value of $\Delta S°_f$ was calculated in part B. Substitute these values and the temperature, 298 K, in the equation above, then calculate $\Delta G°_f$.

$$\Delta G°_f = -1,273.02 - \left(298 \text{ K} \times (-1,220.5 \text{ J K}^{-1})\right) \times \frac{1 \text{ kJ}}{1000 \text{ J}}$$

$$\Delta G°_f = -909.3 \text{ kJ mol}^{-1}$$

(D) Write the chemical equation for the burning of glucose. Then use Hess's Law as provided in the list of *Equations and Constants* to calculate the unknown ΔH°_{comb} for that combustion reaction.

$$C_6H_{12}O_{6(s)} + 6O_{2(s)} \rightarrow 6O_{2(g)} + 6H_2O_{(l)}$$

$$\Delta H^\circ_{comb} = \left[6(\Delta H^\circ_{f,CO_2}) + 6(\Delta H^\circ_{f,H_2O})\right] - \left[\Delta H^\circ_{f,C_6H_{12}O_6} + 6(\Delta H^\circ_{f,O_2})\right]$$

$$\Delta H^\circ_{comb} = \left[6(-393.5) + 6(-285.83)\right] - \left[-1,273.02 + 6(0)\right]$$

$$\Delta H^\circ_{comb} = \left[(-2,361) + (-1,715.0)\right] - \left[-1,273.02\right]$$

$$\Delta H^\circ_{comb} = -2,803 \text{ kJ mol}^{-1}$$

Chapter 9
Acid-Base Systems

1. To meet the specified criteria, the species must have a vacancy for an electron pair to be shared and no proton to be donated. These conditions are found only in AlCl$_3$ which can accept a share in a pair of electrons from Cl$^-$, for example, to form AlCl$_4^-$. Both HC$_2$H$_3$O$_2$ (acetic acid) and NaHCO$_3$ (sodium hydrogen carbonate) are Bronsted Lowry acids but do not act as Lewis acids.

    The correct choice is (A).

2. An amphiprotic species can both accept and donate a proton. Of the species provided as choices, only HCO$_3^-$ in NaHCO$_3$ exhibits such a property.

    The correct choice is (E).

3. In order to be nonconducting, a solution must contain no ions. Of the five solutes listed, only CH$_3$OH dissolves readily but does not produce ions. All other species produce hydrated ions in water solution.

    The correct choice is (B).

4. Some salts undergo hydrolysis in water solution. Such a salt is K$_2$C$_2$O$_4$. The C$_2$O$_4^{2-}$ ion reacts with water to form a basic solution according to the equation below:

$$C_2O_4^{2-} + H_2O \rightleftharpoons HC_2O_4^- + OH^-$$

   The correct choice is (D).

5. An ester is formed when an alcohol reacts with an organic acid. Sulfuric acid is generally used as a dehydrating agent in an esterification reaction. Choice B is methanol, an alcohol.

    The correct choice is (B).

6. A Lewis acid accepts a share in a pair of electrons. Such a substance is called "electrophilic". AlCl$_3$ and BF$_3$ are good examples of Lewis acids.

    The correct choice is (A).

Acid-Base Systems   Chapter 9   83

7. In liquid ammonia, only NH_3 molecules are present. They behave much like water with one NH_3 molecule donating a proton to another NH_3 molecule as in equation (C).

   The correct choice is (C).

8. Compound III, H_3AsO_4 undergoes three stages of ionization like the polyprotic acid, H_3PO_4, forming in successive stages $H_2AsO_4^-$, $HAsO_4^{2-}$ and AsO_4^{3-}. The anion, $H_2PO_4^-$, from compound II undergoes two stages of ionization forming first HPO_4^{2-}, and then PO_4^{3-}. The compound NaH_2PO_4 is a polyprotic acid, more specifically a diprotic acid. Compound I, $Ca(NO_3)_2$, is not an acid.

   The correct choice is (C).

9. In a conjugate acid/base pair, the base contains one less proton (hydrogen nucleus) than the acid. In the case of HF, HSO_4^- and $H_2PO_4^-$, their respective conjugate bases are F^-, SO_4^{2-} and HPO_4^{2-}. List (B) contains only these conjugate bases.

   The correct choice is (B).

10. When potassium oxide, K_2O, is added to water, each oxide ion accepts a proton from water, immediately forming two OH^- ions. In water solution, OH^- ion is a strong base.

    $$O^{2-} + H_2O \rightarrow 2OH^-_{(aq)}$$

    The correct choice is (E).

11. The ion, $H_2PO_4^-$, illustrates amphoteric behavior in that it can either accept or donate a proton. In equations I, II and V, $H_2PO_4^-$ acts as a proton donor. In equations III and IV, $H_2PO_4^-$ acts as a proton acceptor. Only response (E) contains one equation illustrating each type of reaction.

    The correct choice is (E).

12. When potassium hydride, KH, is added to water, each hydride ion accepts a proton from water, immediately forming OH⁻ ion and H₂ gas. In water solution, OH⁻ ion is a strong base.

$$KH + H_2O \rightarrow H_{2(g)} + OH^-_{(aq)} + K^+_{(aq)}$$

The correct choice is (E).

13. An acid anhydride is a chemical compound that is an oxide of a nonmetal that dissolves in water to form an acid, generally a ternary Arrhenius acid such as HNO_3 or H_3PO_4. SO_2 (option I) dissolves to form H_2SO_3. SO_3 (option II) dissolves to form H_2SO_4. SO_4^{2-} (option III) dissolves in water as the anion of a salt. It is not part of an oxide. It is not an acid anhydride.

The correct choice is (C).

14. When 0.10 mol NaOH is added to 100 mL of 1.0 M HCl, neutralization occurs with no excess acid or base remaining. Water is formed. The other product is NaCl which does not hydrolyze. The resulting solution is neutral with pH = 7.

The correct choice is (C).

15. Amphoteric behavior is the capacity to act as either acid or base, that is, to both donate or accept a proton. In (A), HS⁻ is amphoteric. In (C), all are amphoteric. In (D), $H_2PO_4^-$ and NH_2^- are amphoteric. In (E), $Al(OH)_3$ and $Zn(OH)_2$ are amphoteric. In (B), no species could both donate and accept a proton.

The correct choice is (B).

16. When potassium carbonate, K_2CO_3, dissolves, the dissolved species are dissociated K⁺ and CO_3^{2-} ions. Thus, answer (E) is not true. All other answers are correct descriptions of the solution. CO_3^{2-} undergoes hydrolysis to produce a basic solution (choices A and D). No colored ions are present (choice B). As this compound dissolves, the increase in concentration of ions accounts for increased conductivity (choice C).

The correct choice is (E).

17. Using the example, hydrolysis occurs as

$$CO_3^{2-} + H_2O \rightleftharpoons HCO_3^- + OH^-$$

Since the solution is alkaline, addition of water will decrease $[CO_3^{2-}]$ and $[OH^-]$ causing $[H_3O^+]$ to increase. Addition of water provides a dilution effect which is greater than its effect as proton donor. Water molecules are already present in substantial excess. Note that $K_w = [H_3O^+][OH^-]$. (Removal of H_2O would cause $[OH^-]$ to increase). Addition of more solute would cause $[OH^-]$ to increase. Addition of precipitate or phenolphathalein will have no effect on pH. Addition of $NaOH_{(aq)}$ will cause $[OH^-]$ to increase and $[H_3O^+]$ to decrease.

The correct choice is (A).

18. When H_3PO_4, an acid molecule, is neutralized to form PO_4^{3-} in water solution, three protons are donated by each H_3PO_4 molecule to the base (proton acceptor). No transfer of electrons or change in oxidation number occurs.

The correct choice is (B).

19. In this reaction, Na^+ and SO_4^{2-} do not undergo any chemical change. Both are present as ions at the beginning and end of the reaction. Any HSO_4^- present acts as a proton donor, as does H_3O^+ (or H^+); OH^- is the proton acceptor.

The correct choice is (C).

20. In the original solution of H_2SO_4, most SO_4^{2-} is present as the protonated form HSO_4^-. As OH^- is added, protons are donated to OH^- by H_3O^+ and HSO_4^-. This accounts for an increase in $[SO_4^{2-}]$. At the beginning of the reaction all of the Na^+ is present as ions in $NaOH_{(aq)}$ and not part of the reaction mixture. As $NaOH_{(aq)}$ is added from the buret, $[Na^+]$ in the reaction mixture increases; Na^+ does not participate in any chemical reaction.

The correct choice is (A).

21. One properly labeled solution to this problem is

$$\frac{0.0264 \text{ L NaOH sol'n}}{0.0250 \text{ L H}_2\text{SO}_4 \text{ sol'n}} \times \frac{0.125 \text{ mol NaOH}}{1 \text{ L NaOH sol'n}} \times \frac{1 \text{ mol H}_2\text{SO}_4}{2 \text{ mol NaOH}}$$

The correct choice is (C).

86　Chapter 9　Acid-Base Systems

22. The mistake described in the question would have no effect on any value in the data table. This mistake does not change the quantity of H_2SO_4. Similarly, this mistake would also have no effect on the results for the reported molarity of the original unknown H_2SO_4 solution. However, that value is not reported in the data table and is not related to the question.

    The correct choice is (E).

23. This mistake causes the actual concentration of $NaOH_{(aq)}$ to be decreased. However, since this mistake is unknown to the technician, it will not appear in the data table. Again, since the concentration is lower, a greater volume of this solution will be needed to reach neutralization. Since a greater volume was required, the final volume, $NaOH_{(aq)}$ will be reported larger. This would also cause the reported molarity of H_2SO_4 to be reported larger but that value is not part of the data table.

    The correct choice is (A).

24. Hydrolysis of $C_2O_4^{2-}$ occurs according to the equation

    $$C_2O_4^{2-}{}_{(aq)} + H_2O \rightleftharpoons HC_2O_4^{-}{}_{(aq)} + OH^{-}{}_{(aq)}$$

    The mass action expression that matches this equation is

    $$\frac{[HC_2O_4^-][OH^-]}{[C_2O_4^{2-}]}$$

    The correct choice is (C).

25. When diluted with an equal quantity of water, 0.0040 M HBr becomes 0.0020 M HBr (2.0×10^{-3} M). Like HCl, HBr is nearly 100% ionized. Using the definition of pH

    $$pH = -\log[H^+] = -\log(2.0 \times 10^{-3}) = 3 - \log 2 \approx 2.7$$

    Actual calculation is not necessary, since the student should recognize that log 2 is less than 0.5 and that, of the choices given, only 2.7 is possible.

    The correct choice is (B).

Acid-Base Systems Chapter 9 87

Free-Response Questions

26. (A) Strategy: Use definition of molarity to first find moles then find mass of the solute.

$$0.750 \text{ L} \times \frac{0.200 \text{ mol}}{1 \text{ L sol'n}} \times \frac{136 \text{ g KHSO}_4}{1 \text{ mol KHSO}_4} = \textbf{20.4 g KHSO}_4$$

(B) (1) Strategy: Note that 1 mol KHSO$_4$ is needed to neutralize exactly 1 mol KOH

$$\frac{0.0234 \text{ L KHSO}_4 \text{ sol'n}}{0.0250 \text{ L KOH sol'n}} \times \frac{0.200 \text{ mol KHSO}_4}{1 \text{ L sol'n}} \times \frac{1 \text{ mol KOH}}{1 \text{ mol KHSO}_4} = \textbf{0.187 M}$$

(2) Strategy: There are three components to total final volume of the reaction mixture

25.0 mL original KOH solution containing 0.00468 mol K$^+$

25.0 mL additional water

23.4 mL KHSO$_4$ solution added for neutralization containing an additional 0.00468 mol K$^+$ for a total of 73.4 mL of reaction mixture containing 0.00936 mol K$^+$ at the equivalence point (neutralization)

$$\frac{0.00936 \text{ mol K}^+}{0.0734 \text{ L}} = \textbf{0.128 M}$$

(C) (1) Strategy: (See suggestions in the solution to part (B) (2) above). The volume of KHSO$_{4(aq)}$ **is the same for both experiments.** The additional water does not affect the number of moles of KOH that must be neutralized. Therefore the volume of KHSO$_{4(aq)}$ needed to reach the equivalence point remains the same.

(2) Strategy: (See suggestions in the solution to part (B) (2) above). The value for [K$^+$] is **smaller** in the second experiment. The same number of moles of K$^+$ is present but that amount is dissolved in a greater volume of solution; hence [K$^+$] is smaller.

27. Overall Strategy: The reaction between Ba(OH)$_{2(aq)}$ and H$_2$SO$_{4(aq)}$ produces H$_2$O and BaSO$_{4(s)}$ as products. When Ba(OH)$_{2(aq)}$ is titrated against H$_2$SO$_{4(aq)}$, at least two "kinds" of endpoints can be observed. One endpoint is based upon the first evidence of excess OH$^-_{(aq)}$ using phenolphthalein as the indicator. Another endpoint is based upon evidence that the conductivity of the reaction mixture has reached a minimum. A glowing lamp or an ammeter provides such evidence. When an additional quantity of is Ba(OH)$_{2(aq)}$ added past the endpoint, the lamp begins to glow again.

(A) Strategy: Both reactants are ionic solutions and conduct electricity. One product, BaSO$_{4(s)}$, is a nearly insoluble solid. The other product, water is a molecular liquid. Very few ions are present at the point of exact neutralization. Both products are poor conductors of electricity. Net ionic equation:

$$Ba^{2+}{}_{(aq)} + 2OH^-{}_{(aq)} + 2H^+{}_{(aq)} + SO_4^{2-}{}_{(aq)} \rightarrow BaSO_{4(s)} + 2H_2O$$

(B) Strategy: The light goes out because the number of ions present is too small to allow enough current to pass to illuminate the lamp. However, the number of ions present does allow a small but detectable current to flow. As Ba(OH)$_2$ solution is added, SO$_4^{2-}$ ions are removed by precipitation as BaSO$_4$; OH$^-$ ions react with H$^+$ ions to form water. The decreasing concentration of ions in solution accounts for the extinguishing of the lamp. The amount of current that passes is too small to allow for lighting of the lamp but can be detected by the ammeter.

(C) Strategy: Illumination of the lamp requires a conducting solution. When the Ba(OH)$_2$ solution added is in excess, there is no H$_2$SO$_4$ available to react. The light goes back on because ions are once again present as excess Ba^{2+} and OH$^-$ ions, resulting in conductance.

(D) Strategy: The unknown concentration is to be expressed in moles of Ba(OH)$_2$ per liter of solution. Use the molarity of the known solution and its volume to find moles of H$_2$SO$_4$, then moles of Ba(OH)$_2$ that are present in the observed volume of Ba(OH)$_2$ solution. Then calculate the molarity of the Ba(OH)$_2$ solution.

$$\frac{0.0250 \text{ L H}_2\text{SO}_4 \text{ sol'n}}{0.0278 \text{ L Ba(OH)}_2 \text{ sol'n}} \times \frac{0.0500 \text{ mol H}_2\text{SO}_4}{1 \text{ L H}_2\text{SO}_4 \text{ sol'n}} \times \frac{1 \text{ mol Ba(OH)}_2}{1 \text{ mol H}_2\text{SO}_4} = \frac{0.0450 \text{ mol Ba(OH)}_2}{1 \text{ L Ba(OH)}_2 \text{ sol'n}}$$

(E) Strategy: Recognize that concentration of the Ba(OH)$_2$ solution decreases as the volume required to neutralize the fixed quantity of H$_2$SO$_4$ solution increases.

If one chose the color change of the indicator as the endpoint, the value of the concentration of the Ba(OH)$_2$ solution would decrease. According to the information given, a larger volume of the Ba(OH)$_2$ solution is needed to reach this endpoint. The number of moles of acid and base reacting remains the same. Therefore, moles of base per liter of solution decreases.

Similarly, if one chose the reappearance of the glowing lamp as the endpoint, the value of the concentration of the Ba(OH)$_2$ solution would decrease even further. A larger quantity of that solution is needed to reach this endpoint. The number of moles of acid and base reacting remains the same. Therefore, moles of base per liter of solution decreases.

28. (A) Strategy: A buffer solution is a solution to which substantial quantities of acid or base can be added with little change in pH. A buffer solution is also defined as a solution that resists change in pH when acid or base is added. The solution in this problem is a buffer because it contains a weak acid, CH_3COOH, and its conjugate base, CH_3COO^-. Acid added to this solution donates protons to the base, CH_3COO^-. Base added to this solution accepts protons from the acid, CH_3COOH. Thus, substantial changes in pH are not observed until the quantities of acid and base (proton donor and acceptor) available in the buffer have been consumed.

The pH of the solution is given by the equation:

$$pH = pK_a + \log\bigl[[CH_3COO^-]/[CH_3COOH]\bigr]$$

This is known as the Henderson Hasselbalch equation and is found in the list of *Equations and Constants* provided with part of the examination. As long as the ratio, $[CH_3COO^-]/[CH_3COOH]$, has a value near 1, its logarithm is close to zero and the pH of the solution remains nearly equal to pK_a, i.e., nearly constant.

(B) Strategy: In structural formulas, it is common to use a dash , —, for a shared pair of electrons and a pair of dots, : , for unshared electrons. (Other similar representations are permitted.)

$$H-\underset{\underset{H}{|}}{\overset{\overset{H}{|}}{C}}-C\overset{\overset{\cdot\cdot}{O}}{\underset{OH}{\diagdown}}\left[H-\underset{\underset{H}{|}}{\overset{\overset{H}{|}}{O}}\!:\right]^{+}$$

(C) Strategy: $[CH_3COOH]$ increases and $[CH_3COO^-]$ decreases. Note that proton transfer causes changes in the concentrations of all species involved. In this problem, HSO_4^- is the stronger acid; CH_3COO^- is the stronger base. As proton transfer occurs, $[HSO_4^-]$ and $[CH_3COO^-]$, the reactants, decrease while $[CH_3COOH]$ and $[SO_4^{2-}]$, the products, increase. Each HSO_4^- donates a proton to CH_3COO^-; thus, 0.15 mole of protons is transferred from $[HSO_4^-]$ to CH_3COO^- to form 0.15 mole of "new" CH_3COOH. The capacity of the buffer has not been exceeded. There is still some CH_3COO^- remaining (0.10 mole) to accept more protons from any added acid. The amount of acid, CH_3COOH, present has increased to 0.40.

(D) Strategy: [CH$_3$COOH] decreases and [CH$_3$COO$^-$] increases. This is approximately the opposite of the changes that occur in part (C). Some of the OH$^-$ added accepts protons from CH$_3$COOH. Of the 0.40 mol OH$^-$ added, 0.25 mol OH$^-$ accepts protons from CH$_3$COOH forming CH$_3$COO$^-$ ions and H$_2$O molecules. Nearly all 0.25 mol CH$_3$COOH is consumed as 0.25 mole CH$_3$COO$^-$ is formed. The number of moles of protons transferred is nearly 0.25. Due to the presence of the excess 0.15 mole OH$^-$, [OH$^-$] becomes 0.15 M. The capacity of the buffer has been exceeded. The pH of the solution increases to about 13.

29. <u>Overall Strategy</u>: In order to write the best net reaction with the correct formulas for reactants and products, describe the kind of chemical change that occurs in the laboratory situations. Try to associate each reaction with some familiar category of reactions. Reference to the Periodic Table may help determine symbols and formulas for some reactants and products.

  (A) An excess quantity of a dilute solution of hydrochloric acid is added to a solution of sodium sulfite.

  $$SO_3^{2-} + H^+ \rightarrow H_2O + SO_2$$

  Proton transfer; gas formed; H_2SO_3 may not be allowed; no evidence for its existence; HSO_3^- not allowed, excess H^+ specified

  (B) Excess potassium hydroxide solution is added to a solution of zinc chloride.

  $$OH^- + Zn^{2+} \rightarrow Zn(OH)_4^{2-}$$

  possible alternates: reactant $Zn(H_2O)_4^{2+}$; product ZnO_2^{2-}

  Proton transfer; amphoteric hydroxide; "excess" implies that full proton transfer occurs; $Zn(OH)_2$ not allowed as product because "excess" specified.

  (C) Solid sodium acetate is added to concentrated sulfuric acid.

  $$NaCH_3COO + H_2SO_4 \rightarrow CH_3COOH + Na^+ + HSO_4^-$$

  possible alternate reactant: H^+

  Proton transfer; molecular, nonionized product formed

  (D) Boron trifluoride gas is mixed with ammonia gas in a closed container.

  $$BF_3 + NH_3 \rightarrow BF_3NH_3$$

  Lewis acid-base reaction; molecule forms by sharing pair of electrons

  (E) Ammonia gas is mixed with hydrogen chloride gas in a closed container.

  $$NH_3 + HCl \rightarrow NH_4Cl$$

  Proton transfer; no solvent, hence, product not dissociated into its ions

  (F) Some crystals of solid ammonium chloride are added to a warm solution of sodium hydroxide.

  $$NH_4Cl + OH^- \rightarrow NH_3 + H_2O + Cl^-$$

  Proton transfer; nonionized product formed; molecular NH_4OH not shown; best represented as $NH_3 + H_2O$

(G) A solution of 0.1 M sodium dihydrogen phosphate is added to an equal volume of 0.1 M sodium hydroxide.

$H_2PO_4^- + OH^- \rightarrow H_2O + HPO_4^{2-}$

Proton transfer; limiting reactant is OH^-; PO_4^{3-} as a product is not an acceptable answer

(H) A lump of calcium carbonate is placed in a solution of dilute nitric acid.

$CaCO_3 + H^+ \rightarrow H_2O + CO_2 + Ca^{2+}$

Proton transfer; nonionized product formed; molecular H_2CO_3 not shown; best represented as $CO_2 + H_2O$

Chapter 10
Electrochemistry

1. The oxidation number for each element is given below:

    (A) C^{+3} O^{-2}
    (B) Cr^{+6} O^{-2}
    (C) Mn^{+7} O^{-2}
    (D) N^{-3} H^{+1}
    (E) Sn^{+2}

    The element with the highest oxidation number is found in MnO_4^- where the oxidation number of Mn is +7.

    The correct choice is (C).

2. The oxidation number for each element is given in question 1 above. The species with the most negative (lowest) oxidation number is NH_2^- where the oxidation number of N is −3.

    The correct choice is (D).

3. Refer to the list of oxidation numbers given in question 1. Of the metals given, Cr, Mn and Sn, only Cr as $Cr_2O_7^{2-}$ is reduced in acid solution to the +3 oxidation state as $Cr^{3+}_{(aq)}$.

    The correct choice is (B).

4. Of the choices given, only Sn^{2+} can be oxidized to the +4 state as a cation.

    The correct choice is (E).

5. Of the choices given, $C_2O_4^{2-}$ can be oxidized to form a gas. That gas is CO_2 where the oxidation state of carbon is +4, oxidized from +3 in $C_2O_4^{2-}$. CO_2 is nearly insoluble and odorless. When the gas NH_3 is formed from NH_2^-, no oxidation occurs. In addition, NH_3 is very soluble and has a distinct odor.

    The correct choice is (A).

6. The equation that applies to this question is

    $$\Delta G° = -n\mathcal{F}E°$$

    Note that 1.10 volts is equivalent to 1.10 joules/coulomb. One properly labeled solution to this problem is given by

    $$\Delta G° = -2 \text{ mol e}^- \times \frac{96,500 \text{ coul}}{1 \text{ mol e}^-} \times \frac{1.10 \text{ joule}}{1 \text{ coul}} \times \frac{1 \text{ kJ}}{1,000 \text{ joule}}$$

    The correct choice is (C).

7. The equation that applies to this question is

$$E = E° - \frac{0.0592}{n} \log K_{eq}$$

At equilibrium, E = 0; with substitution and rearranging

$$E° = \frac{0.0592}{2} \log K_{eq}$$

$$1.10 = \frac{0.0592}{2} \log K_{eq}$$

$$\log K_{eq} = \frac{2 \times 1.10}{0.0592}$$

Completing the arithmetic by estimation

$$\log K_{eq} = \frac{2 \times 1.10}{0.0592} = \text{about } \frac{2.20}{0.06} = \text{about } \frac{2.40}{0.06} = \text{about } 40$$

Thus, the exponent for 10 in the equilibrium constant is closest to 40 of the choices given.

(precise to 3 significant figures, $\log K_{eq} = 37.2$)

The correct choice is (E).

8. The equation that applies to this question is

$$E = E° - \frac{0.0592}{2} \log \frac{[Zn^{2+}]}{[Cu^{2+}]}$$

substituting the appropriate values

$$E = 1.10 - \frac{0.0592}{2} \log \frac{0.01}{1.0}$$

$$E = 1.10 - \frac{0.0592}{2} \times (-2)$$

$$E = 1.10 + 0.0592 \text{ volts}$$

The correct choice is (A).

9. Referring to the equation above, addition of Cu^{2+}, the oxidizing agent, will increase the value of E. The value of E° is a constant, since, in a standard cell, all concentrations are maintained at 1.0 molar. As this (or any redox) reaction proceeds, the value of E decreases since both oxidizing agent and reducing agent are consumed as more products form.

The correct choice is (D).

Chapter 10 Electrochemistry

Questions 10 and 11: The oxidation numbers and electronic equations for oxidation and reduction are given below.

$$\overset{+1\,+5\,-2}{HNO_3} + \overset{0}{P} + \overset{+1\,-2}{H_2O} \to \overset{+1\,+5\,-2}{H_3PO_4} + \overset{+2\,-2}{NO}$$

oxidation: $\quad 3(P^0 \to P^{+5} + 5e^-)$

reduction: $5(N^{+5} + 3e^- \to N^{+2})$

The balanced equation for this reaction is

$$5HNO_3 + 3P + 2H_2O \to 3H_3PO_4 + 5NO$$

10. The sum of the coefficients in the balanced equation is $5 + 3 + 2 + 3 + 5 = 18$.

    The correct choice is (E).

11. The oxidizing agent is HNO_3, the reactant that contains the element whose oxidation number decreases because it takes on electrons.

    The correct choice is (E).

12. The negative $I^-_{(aq)}$ ions are attracted to the anode where electrons are removed from the $I^-_{(aq)}$ ions to form $I_{2(aq)}$ molecules. (Some may argue that the species formed is really $I_2 \cdot I^-$ or $I_3^-{}_{(aq)}$.)

    The correct choice is (B).

13. In this system, $K^+_{(aq)}$ ions undergo no chemical change. As positive ions, they are attracted to the negative electrode, the cathode of an electrolytic cell. They are called spectator ions.

    The correct choice is (A).

14. At the cathode, reduction of H_2O occurs. At the anode, oxidation of I^- occurs.

    oxidation: $\quad 2I^- \to I_{2(aq)} + 2e^-$

    reduction: $\quad 2H_2O + 2e^- \to H_{2(g)} + 2OH^-_{(aq)}$

    Where hydrogen gas is produced, the solution becomes basic due to the production of OH^- ions. Thus, the pH increases.

    The correct choice is (C).

15. Note that 1 mole of electrons (one faraday) is equal to 96,500 coulombs and that a current of 2.5 amps tranfers electrons at the rate of 2.5 coulombs per second. One properly labeled solution to this problem is given by

$$0.10 \text{ mol } I_2 \times \frac{2 \text{ mole } e^-}{1 \text{ mol } I_2} \times \frac{96,500 \text{ coul}}{1 \text{ mol } e^-} \times \frac{1 \text{ sec}}{2.5 \text{ coul}} \times \frac{1 \text{ min}}{60 \text{ sec}} \times \frac{1 \text{ hr}}{60 \text{ min}}$$

The correct choice is (D).

16. The oxidation number of S changes from -2 in H_2S to 0 in S, an uncombined element. The oxidation number of S in H_2SO_4 does not change.

The correct choice is (C).

17. In this standard elctrochemical cell, the lead chamber must have a lead metal electrode. The Fe^{2+}/Fe^{3+} chamber must contain an unreactive metal (not iron) as the electrode. Platinum is a suitable electrode. The cations must be obtained from soluble iron-containing salts, such as $Fe(NO_3)_3$ (description III). Of the descriptions provided, iron metal as in description I, is not permitted in a standard Fe^{2+}/Fe^{3+} half-cell. The source of Fe^{2+} cannot be $Fe(OH)_2$ since that substance is not soluble (description II).

The correct choice is (B).

18. As this reaction proceeds, the mass of the unreactive metal electrode (#2) remains the same. The mass of electrode #1 (lead) decreases since this metal is the reactant (reducing agent) for this cell.

The correct choice is (B).

19. The standard potential for the cell is calculated by adding the voltages for the two half-reactions.

$$\text{oxidation:} \quad Pb^0{}_{(s)} \to Pb^{2+}{}_{(aq)} + 2e^- \qquad E° = +0.13 \text{ volts}$$

$$\text{reduction:} \quad 2\left(Fe^{3+}{}_{(aq)} + e^- \to Fe^{2+}{}_{(aq)}\right) \qquad E° = +0.77 \text{ volts}$$

$$\text{overall:} \quad Pb^0 + 2Fe^{3+}{}_{(aq)} \to Pb^{2+}{}_{(aq)} + 2Fe^{2+}{}_{(aq)} \qquad E° = +0.90 \text{ volts}$$

The correct choice is (B).

98 Chapter 10 Electrochemistry

20. The equation that applies to this question is

$$E = E° - \frac{0.0592}{2} \log \frac{[Pb^{2+}][Fe^{2+}]^2}{[Fe^{3+}]^2}$$

substituting the appropriate values

$$E = 1.10 - \frac{0.0592}{2} \log \frac{(0.010)^2}{(1.0)^2}$$

$$E = 1.10 - \frac{0.0592}{2} \times (-4)$$

$$E = 1.10 + (2 \times 0.0592) \text{ volts}$$

The correct choice is (E).

21. For metals, chemical activity refers to the ability to behave as a reducing agent. According to the information given, X is the best reducing agent; that is, it is the most likely to give off electrons to become a positive ion. Put another way, compared to Y and Z, X has the least ability to hold electrons and is most easily converted to its cation. Atoms of Y can reduce cations of Z but not X. In general, atoms of metals cannot be reduced. Thus, only II is a correct description.

The correct choice is (B).

22. In this standard half cell, solid AgCl is in contact with $Cl^-_{(aq)}$ where $[Cl^-] = 1.0$M. Some AgCl dissolves according to the reaction

$$AgCl(s) \rightleftharpoons Ag^+_{(aq)} + Cl^-_{(aq)}$$

AgCl is a nearly insoluble salt with a low value for K_{sp}. (Its K_{sp} is actually 1.6×10^{-10} but that value is not used in this problem.) With $[Cl^-]$ at 1.0 M, $[Ag^+]$ in the saturated solution is driven to a very low value.

The correct choice is (E).

23. When $E° > 0$, the reaction is spontaneous. The corresponding value for $\Delta G°$ must be negative (< 0) and the value for $K_{eq} > 1$ because formation of products is favored. Note that the value for K_{eq} is never < 0 (negative).

The correct choice is (B).

24. For the cation, NH_4^+, the oxidation numbers are $+1$ for hydrogen and -3 for nitrogen. For the NO_3^- anion, the oxidation numbers are $+5$ for nitrogen and -2 for oxygen. Note that the rules for oxidation numbers generally assign $+1$ to hydrogen and -2 to oxygen except in such cases as hydrides (-1 for hydrogen) and peroxides (-1 for oxygen).

The correct choice is (D).

25. As with ordinary reactions, atoms in half-reactions may become rearranged into different molecules. Thus, conservation of molecules is not a principle that applies to any equation. However, again as with ordinary reactions, conservation of charge and atoms always applies.

The correct choice is (B).

Free-Response Questions

26. **(A)** Strategy: As with any electrochemical device, oxidation occurs at the anode. When two standard half-cells are properly connected, a path exists for ion migration as well as an external circuit to allow movement of electrons. Electrons flow from the anode toward the cathode through the external circuit.

Find the appropriate half-reactions in the list of *Equations and Constants* provided with the examination. The half-reaction with the larger (more positive) reduction potential is the reduction half-reaction. This is the half-reaction that occurs at the cathode.

$$Fe^{3+} + e^- \rightarrow Fe^{2+} \qquad E° = 0.77$$
$$Sn^{2+} + 2e^- \rightarrow Sn° \qquad E° = -0.14$$

In this case Fe^{3+} is a better oxidizing agent than Sn^{2+}; therefore, reduction occurs in the Fe^{2+}/Fe^{3+} half-cell. To determine the overall reaction, write the reverse of the reduction half-reaction that has the lower reduction potential and change the algebraic sign of the E° value. This becomes the oxidation half-reaction. Choose multipliers for the half-reactions so that the number of electrons lost is equal to the number of electrons gained. Add the half-reactions to get the overall reaction. Add the E° values for the half-reactions to get the E° value for the overall reaction. Note that multipliers are not used with the E° values.

reduction: $\quad 2\left(Fe^{3+} + e^- \rightarrow Fe^{2+}\right) \qquad E° = 0.77$ volts

oxidation: $\qquad\qquad Sn° \rightarrow Sn^{2+} + 2e^- \qquad E° = 0.14$ volts

overall: $\quad \mathbf{2Fe^{3+} + Sn° \rightarrow 2Fe^{2+} + Sn^{2+}} \qquad \mathbf{E° = 0.91}$ **volts**

(B) Strategy: The solution in half-cell B is 1.0 M in each of the cations, Fe^{2+} and Fe^{3+}. The electrode must be an inert substance. A metal that could be used as electrode B is platinum, Pt. Other unreactive substances such as nichrome or graphite are acceptable substitutes. The electrode in half-cell A is tin metal, Sn.

(C) Strategy: Choose a solution for the salt bridge that contains ions that do not react with any of the the ions or the electrodes in the half-cells. Sodium nitrate, $NaNO_3$, is a good choice for such a solution. Neither Na^+ nor NO_3^- reacts with other species present. Other salts with similar properties are also suitable.

(D) Strategy: In any electrochemical cell, electrons, as the product of the oxidation half-reaction, are forced into the external circuit at the anode. The electrons flow from the anode through the external circuit toward the cathode, in this case from electrode A toward electrode B.

(E) Strategy: Refer to the Nernst equation found in the list of *Equations and Constants* provided with the examination to predict the effects of concentration changes on the cell voltage.

$$E_{cell} = E° - \frac{RT}{nF}\ln Q \quad \text{where Q is the reaction quotient (mass action expression)}$$

$$= E° - \frac{0.0592}{2}\log\frac{[Sn^{2+}][Fe^{2+}]^2}{[Fe^{3+}]^2}$$

The same predictions result when le Chatelier's Principle is applied to each situation. Each dilution provides a possible stress on the system. The system shifts to relieve that stress.

(1) No change. Because both ions are diluted equally, there is no net effect on the reduction half-reaction.

(2) Increases. Dilution of the product occurs. Using le Chatelier's principle or the Nernst equation, the voltage (reaction tendency) for the oxidation of Sn increases.

(3) Increases. There is an increase in the voltage of the oxidation half-reaction and no change in the reduction half-reaction. Thus, there is a net increase in the voltage of the overall reaction.

(F) Strategy: Because the cell has operated long enough for $[Sn^{2+}]$ to change by 0.25 M, the concentrations of the other dissolved species have changed, too. Use principles of stoichiometry to calculate the changes. Then use the Nernst equation to find the voltage at the new non-standard conditions. It is expected that the voltage will have decreased from the original standard voltage because some of the reactants have been consumed. Because Sn^{2+} is a product, the change of +0.25 M makes its new concentration 1.25 M. In the reaction, two mol Fe^{3+} is changed to two mol Fe^{2+} for every one mol Sn^{2+} produced. Therefore, the change in $[Fe^{3+}]$ is −0.50 M as $[Fe^{2+}]$ changes by +0.50 M. The new $[Fe^{3+}]$ is 0.50 M and the new $[Fe^{2+}]$ is 1.50 M.

$$E_{cell} = E° - \frac{RT}{nF}\ln Q = E° - \frac{0.0592}{n}\log Q$$

$$= E° - \frac{0.0592}{2}\log\frac{[Sn^{2+}][Fe^{2+}]^2}{[Fe^{3+}]^2} = 0.91v - \frac{0.0592}{2}\log\frac{(1.25)(1.50)^2}{(0.50)^2}$$

$$= 0.91 \text{ volts} - 0.0311 \text{ volts} = \textbf{0.88 volts}$$

27. (A) Strategy: By definition, oxidation occurs at the anode in any electrochemical device. In electroplating cells, metal atoms are oxidized to ions at the anode and the corresponding metal ions are reduced to atoms at the cathode. The object to be plated is connected to the system as a cathode.

oxidation half-reaction: $Cr \to Cr^{3+} + 3e^-$; **occurs at the anode**

(B) From the list of *Equations and Constants* provided with the examination, note that current (amperes) is given as q/t or coulombs sec^{-1}. Note also that one F (faraday) or one mole of electrons contains 96,500 coulombs. Use these relationships to calculate:

- quantity of charge
- moles of Cr
- and finally mass of Cr metal

$$60.0 \text{ min} \times \frac{60 \text{ sec}}{1 \text{ min}} \times \frac{30.0 \text{ coul}}{1 \text{ sec}} \times \frac{1 \text{ F}}{96,500 \text{ coul}} \times \frac{1 \text{ mol Cr}}{3 \text{ F}} \times \frac{52.0 \text{ g Cr}}{1 \text{ mol Cr}} = 19.4 \text{ g Cr}$$

(C) Strategy: The cation, Cr^{3+}, is consumed by the reduction half-reaction as an equal quantity of Cr^{3+} is produced by the oxidation half-reaction. No change in $[Cr^{3+}]$ is observed. For every Cr^{3+} ion reduced from water solution, another $Cr°$ atom is oxidized into solution as a Cr^{3+} ion.

(D) Strategy: Recognize that the reduction half-reaction is

$$2H^+ + 2e^- \to H_2$$

thus, the number of faradays per mole of product is 2

- find moles of H_2 as in part B
- use ideal gas law as provided in list of *Equations and Constants* to find the volume of $H_{2(g)}$

$$60.0 \text{ min} \times \frac{60 \text{ sec}}{1 \text{ min}} \times \frac{30.0 \text{ coul}}{1 \text{ sec}} \times \frac{1 \text{ F}}{96,500 \text{ coul}} \times \frac{1 \text{ mol } H_{2(g)}}{2 \text{ F}} = 0.560 \text{ mol } H_{2(g)}$$

$$V = \frac{0.560 \text{ mol } H_2 \times 0.0821 \text{ L} \cdot \text{atm} \cdot \text{mol}^{-1} \text{ K}^{-1} \times 298 \text{ K}}{0.970 \text{ atm}}$$

V = 14.1 L

28. (A) Strategy: Refer to the Periodic Table of the Elements to verify that chlorine is a stronger reducing agent than iodine. In the experiment, add chlorine water, $Cl_{2(g)} \cdot H_2O$, to the solution of KI. The solution turns yellow or brown. Shake the solution with a small volume of a nonpolar organic solvent such as cyclohexane or mineral oil. The solvent layer remains separate from the water solution layer and turns violet in the presence of iodine, I_2.

(B) Strategy: Recall that the standard reduction potential is based upon determining the voltage generated when the half-cell in question is connected to a standard hydrogen, $H_{2(g)}/H^+_{(aq)}$ half-cell. The reduction potential of the hydrogen half-cell is defined as 0.00 volts. Thus, whenever any standard half-cell is connected to a hydrogen half-cell, the reading on the voltmeter gives the standard reduction potential of the half-reaction being tested. A simple experiment includes the two half cells connected through an external circuit. A path for ion migration is provided using a porous barrier or a salt bridge. A voltmeter is placed in the external circuit. According to the list of *Equations and Constants* provided with the examination, its E° value is −0.76 volts. Therefore, the experimental reading on the voltmeter is expected to be 0.76 volts.

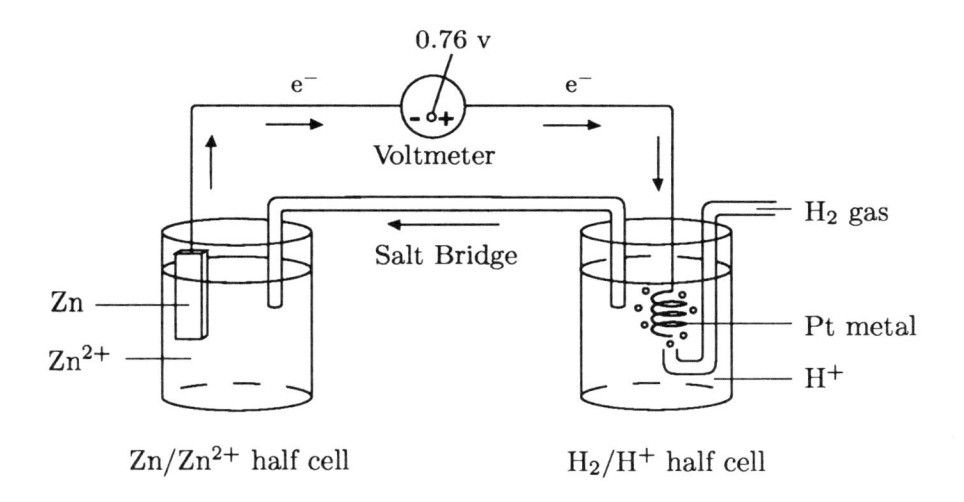

```
                    0.76 v
        e⁻            ⊖ ⊕            e⁻
                   Voltmeter
                       ←
                   Salt Bridge                   ═══ H₂ gas
    Zn ─┤
                                                 ─── Pt metal
    Zn²⁺ ─┤                                      ─── H⁺

    Zn/Zn²⁺ half cell              H₂/H⁺ half cell
```

(C) Overall Strategy: Each metal must be tested by immersion in water solutions of each of the other two cations to determine whether or not the cation will be reduced. If the cation is reduced and the metal reacts (dissolves), that metal is said to be more active, i.e., a better reducing agent, than the metal of the cation tested. For example, when zinc metal is immersed in a solution of Pb^{2+}, the zinc dissolves as Zn^{2+} while the Pb^{2+} ions are reduced to Pb metal. Zinc is more active than metal.

(1) Strategy: Immerse each metal in solutions of the other two cations., for example, metal X in solutions of $Y^{2+}_{(aq)}$ and $Z^{2+}_{(aq)}$. If the metal dissolves, it is described as "more active" than the metal of the cation present in the original solution.

(2) <u>Strategy</u>: Of the three metals tested, the "best" reducing agent will dissolve in solutions of both other cations. The "poorest" reducing agent will not dissolve in either of the other two solutions of cations. Metal Y will dissolve in both $X^{2+}_{(aq)}$ and $Z^{2+}_{(aq)}$. Metal X will not dissolve in $Y^{2+}_{(aq)}$ but will dissolve in $Z^{2+}_{(aq)}$. Metal Z will not dissolve in either $X^{2+}_{(aq)}$ and $Y^{2+}_{(aq)}$.

Chapter 11
Organic Chemistry

1. This hydrocarbon has the molecular formula C_6H_{14}. It matches the general formula C_nH_{2n+2}. It is an alkane, an isomer of hexane.

   The correct choice is (A).

2. This hydrocarbon has the molecular formula C_3H_8. It matches the general formula C_nH_{2n+2}. It is propane, the three-carbon alkane.

   The correct choice is (A).

3. This hydrocarbon has the formula C_4H_8. It matches the general formula C_nH_{2n}. It is 1-butene, a four-carbon alkene.

   The correct choice is (B).

4. This hydrocarbon has the molecular formula C_6H_6. It matches the general formula C_nH_{2n-6}. It is benzene with the ring structure characteristic of the aromatic hydrocarbons.

   The correct choice is (E).

5. This hydrocarbon has the molecular formula C_7H_8. It matches the general formula C_nH_{2n-6}. It is toluene, a six-carbon ring with a methyl group substituted for one hydrogen atom on the benzene ring structure characteristic of the aromatic carbons.

   The correct choice is (E).

6. This hydrocarbon has the molecular formula C_3H_4. It matches the general formula C_nH_{2n-2}. It is propyne, the three-carbon alkyne.

   The correct choice is (C).

7. Of the compounds given, only HCOOH, formic acid, dissolves in water to form enough ions to conduct an electric current. It is a weak electrolyte.

   The correct choice is (C).

8. In the fermentation process, carbohydrates such as sucrose are converted to alcohol and carbon dioxide.

   The correct choice is (D).

9. *Sigma*, σ, and *pi*, π, bond specification is shown in the structural formula for ethyne below.

Note that all single bonds are *sigma* bonds. A multiple bond – double or triple – contains one *sigma* bond and one *pi* bond (double bond) or two *pi* bonds (triple bond). In the case of ethyne, there are three *sigma* and two *pi* bonds.

The correct choice is (C).

10. Butane, C_4H_{10}, is a hydrocarbon. When butane is burned "completely", the products are carbon dioxide and water.

$$2C_4H_{10(g)} + 13O_{2(g)} \rightarrow 8CO_{2(g)} + 10H_2O_{(g)}$$

The correct choice is (D).

11. The structural formula for 1-butene is given below. Note that there are two carbon-carbon single bonds.

$$-C \equiv C - C - C -$$

The correct choice is (B).

12. Structural formulas for all the isomers of butanol are given below. Note that one isomer is 2-methyl-2-propanol.

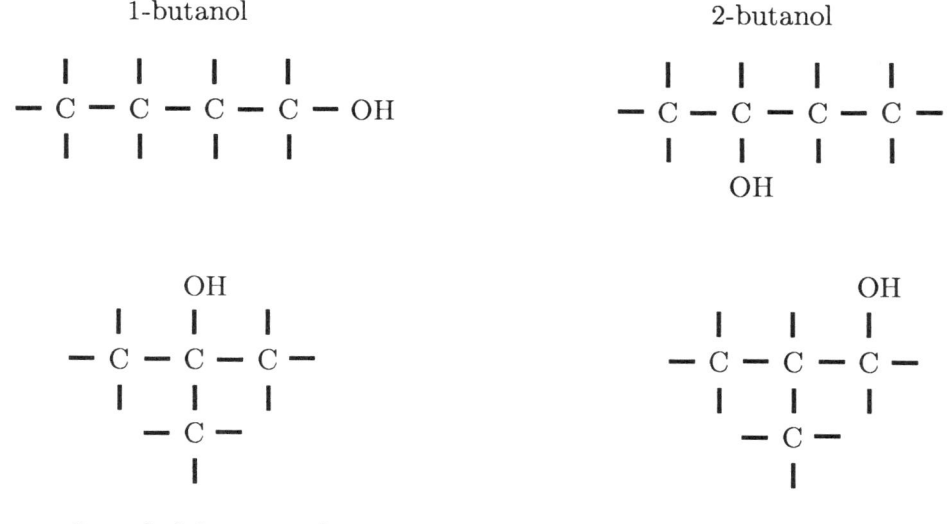

1-butanol

$$-C-C-C-C-OH$$

2-butanol

$$-C-C-C-C-$$
$$OH$$

2-methyl-2-propanol

2-methyl-1-propanol

The correct choice is (C).

13. A good way to think about oxidation in the context of organic chemical reactions is to consider oxidation as the equivalent of dehydrogenation. Thus, the compound with carbon bonded to the fewest hydrogen atoms (or the most oxygen atoms) illustrates the greatest extent of oxidation. To show this relationship, the general formulas for these categories of compounds are given below.

$$\text{acid} \quad R-C\underset{OH}{\overset{O}{\Big\backslash\!\!\!/}}$$

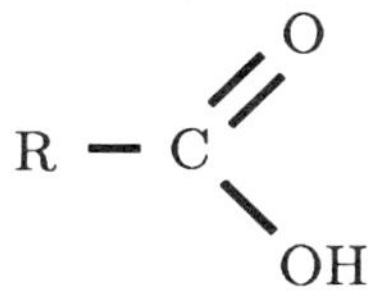

$$\text{ketone} \quad R-\underset{}{\overset{O}{\underset{\|}{C}}}-R' \qquad \text{aldehyde} \quad R-C\underset{H}{\overset{O}{\Big\backslash\!\!\!/}}$$

$$\text{alcohol} \quad R-\underset{|}{\overset{|}{C}}-OH \qquad \text{hydrocarbon} \quad R-\underset{|}{\overset{|}{C}}-$$

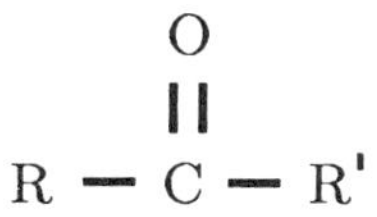

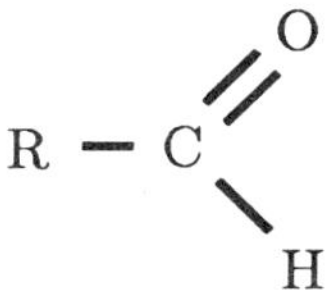

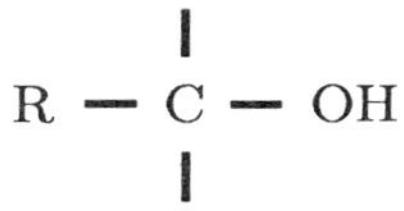

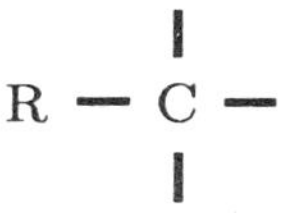

The correct choice is (A).

14. Structural formulas for all three isomers of $C_2H_2Cl_2$ are given below.

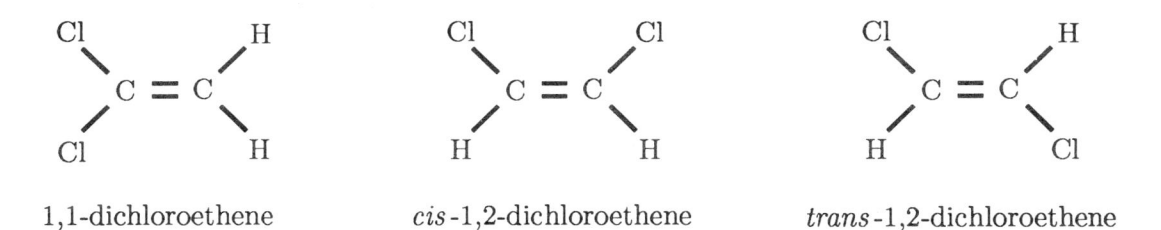

$$\underset{Cl}{\overset{Cl}{\diagdown}}C=C\underset{H}{\overset{H}{\diagup}} \qquad \underset{H}{\overset{Cl}{\diagdown}}C=C\underset{H}{\overset{Cl}{\diagup}} \qquad \underset{H}{\overset{Cl}{\diagdown}}C=C\underset{Cl}{\overset{H}{\diagup}}$$

1,1-dichloroethene   *cis*-1,2-dichloroethene   *trans*-1,2-dichloroethene

The correct choice is (C).

15. Use a structural formula to represent the bonds.

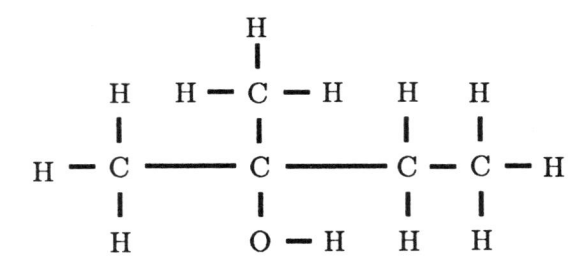

```
                    H
                    |
          H   H — C — H    H   H
          |       |        |   |
      H — C ————— C ————— C — C — H
          |       |        |   |
          H       O — H    H   H
```

Note four **C-C** bonds, eleven **C-H** bonds and one each of **C-O** and **O-H** bonds.

The correct choice is (D).

16. Ethene, C_2H_4, and methane, CH_4, have the same number of hydrogen atoms per molecule. The other characteristics are different for each substance.

The correct choice is (D).

17. Use simplfied structural formulas (C atoms only) to represent the specified molecule and all the answer choices as well, if necessary. Isomers have the same number of atoms (same molecular formula) but different arrangements (different structural formulas) of those atoms.

```
                            |
                          — C —
                   |   |   |   |   |
  2-methypentane  — C — C — C — C — C —
                   |   |   |   |   |
```

(A)
```
        |   |   |   |   |
      — C — C — C — C — C —      pentane
        |   |   |   |   |
```

(B)
```
        |   |   |   |
      — C — C — C — C —          2-methybutane
        |   |   |   |
          — C —
            |
```

(C)

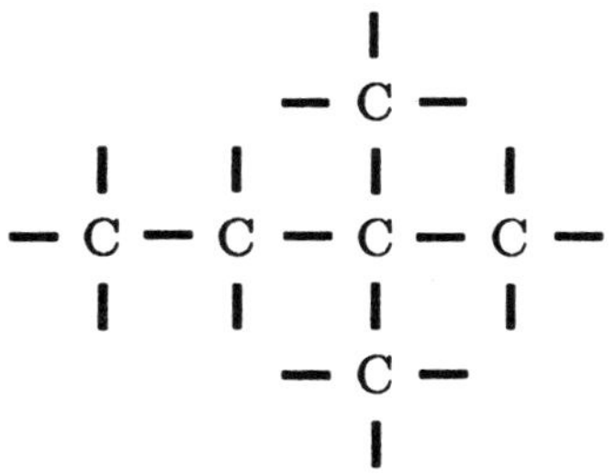

```
        |
      — C —
  |   |   |   |
— C — C — C — C —    2,2-dimethylbutane
  |   |   |   |
      — C —
        |
```

(D)

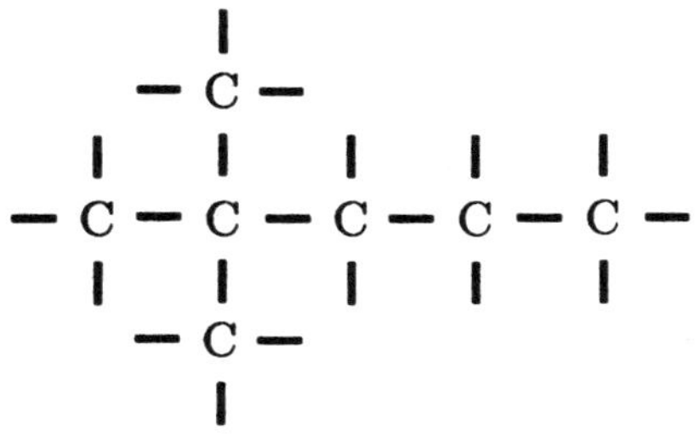

```
        |
      — C —
  |   |   |   |   |
— C — C — C — C — C —    2,2-dimethylpentane
  |   |   |   |   |
      — C —
        |
```

(E)

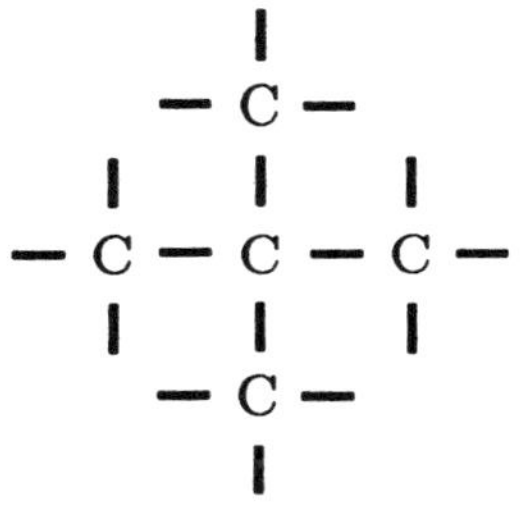

```
        |
      — C —
  |   |   |
— C — C — C —    2,2-dimethylpropane
  |   |   |
      — C —
        |
```

Compared to the given compound, 2-methylpentane, only choice (C) has the same molecular formula and a different structural formula.

The correct choice is (C).

18. In the presence of ethanol in acid solution, $K_2Cr_2O_7$ acts as an oxidizing agent, with chromium becoming reduced from +6 to +3. The redox half-reactions are shown below.

oxidation: $\quad C_2H_5OH \rightarrow CH_3CHO + 2H^+ + 2e^-$

reduction: $\quad 6e^- + 14H^+ + Cr_2O_7{}^{2-} \rightarrow 2Cr^{3+} + 7H_2O$

The correct choice is (C).

19. Since ethanol has a lower normal boiling point than water, a mixture containing water and ethanol can be separated into these components by distillation. Ethanol has a higher normal boiling point than water because it has higher vapor pressure. However, separation cannot become complete because water and ethanol form a low-boiling point mixture at about 95% ethanol.

    The correct choice is (B).

20. Use a structural formula to represent the 2-butyne molecule.

    $$-\overset{|}{\underset{|}{C}} - C \equiv C - \overset{|}{\underset{|}{C}} -$$

    Note one **C-C** triple bond and two **C-C** single bonds for a total of five shared electron pairs.

    The correct choice is (D).

21. An unsaturated hydrocarbon contains at least one double or triple bond between adjacent carbon atoms. C_3H_8 is an alkane; all of its carbon-carbon bonds are single bonds. C_3H_6 is an alkene with one carbon-carbon double bond. It is an unsaturated hydrocarbon. Because the other compounds contain oxygen as well as carbon and hydrogen, they are not hydrocarbons.

    The correct choice is (A).

22. Methanol is a soluble alcohol. Its water solution contains no ions, only molecules of H_2O and CH_3OH. A solution of acetic acid contains H^+ ions and CH_3COO^- ions as well as H_2O and CH_3COOH molecules.

    The correct choice is (E).

23. The structural formula for propyne is

    $$- C \equiv C - \overset{|}{\underset{|}{C}} -$$

    The TOTAL NUMBER of shared electron pairs between adjacent carbon atoms in a molecule of propyne is four, as one single bond and one triple bond.

    The correct choice is (D).

24. The structural formulas that match the general formulas given are

C_nH_{2n+2} — C — C — C — C —   alkane

C_nH_{2n} — C = C — C — C —   alkene

C_nH_{2n-2} — C ≡ C — C — C —   alkyne

C_nH_{2n-4} (no illustration)

C_nH_{2n-6} [benzene ring structure]   benzene (aromatic)

The molecule with one carbon-carbon double bond is an alkene.

The correct choice is (B).

25. Look for pairs of structural formulas with the same molecular formulas as in choices B, C, D and E. Choice A represents two compounds with different molecular formulas, C_3H_7Cl and C_3H_7Br. No special name is given to the relationship between these two alkyl halides.

The correct choice is (A).

Free-Response Questions

26. (A) **Strategy:** Use structural formulas to describe the differences in this bonding. Consider resonance present in the bonding of aromatics such as benzene but not present in aliphatics such as cyclohexane.

Benzene is a planar molecule with one resonance bond between neighboring carbon atoms, producing six bonds with bond order of about 1.5 with *sigma* and *pi* bond distribution of electrons. Cyclohexane exists as a puckered ring with a single covalent bond between neighboring carbon atoms, producing six *sigma* bonds between carbon atoms.

(B) **Strategy:** Use structural formulas to describe the differences in this bonding. Consider the differences in bonding between oxygen atoms and any adjacent atoms.

In diethyl ether, one single covalent bond exists between the oxygen atom and each of two carbon atoms. In 1-butanol, the oxygen atom shares one electron pair with a carbon atom and another electron pair shared with a hydrogen atom.

(C) <u>Strategy</u>: Use structural formulas to describe the differences in this bonding. The molecules illustrate structural isomerism.

Both molecules are planar. The difference in orientation of the chlorine atoms is known as geometrical isomerism, a subset of stereoisomerism. The terms, *cis* and *trans*, are taken from the Latin for *next to* (or near) and *across*, respectively.

$$\underset{cis}{\begin{array}{c}H\\ \diagdown\\ Cl\end{array}C=C\begin{array}{c}H\\ \diagup\\ Cl\end{array}} \qquad\qquad \underset{trans}{\begin{array}{c}H\\ \diagdown\\ Cl\end{array}C=C\begin{array}{c}Cl\\ \diagup\\ H\end{array}}$$

(D) <u>Strategy</u>: Use labeled sketches to describe the differences in this bonding. Consider the bonding that accounts for the solid phase in each substance.

In a polymer, the solid results from the formation of very large molecules based upon covalent bonds between monomers. In a molecular solid, the force of attraction between molecules is due to hydrogen bonding or van der Waals forces. In a molecular solid, no covalent bonds exist between molecules.

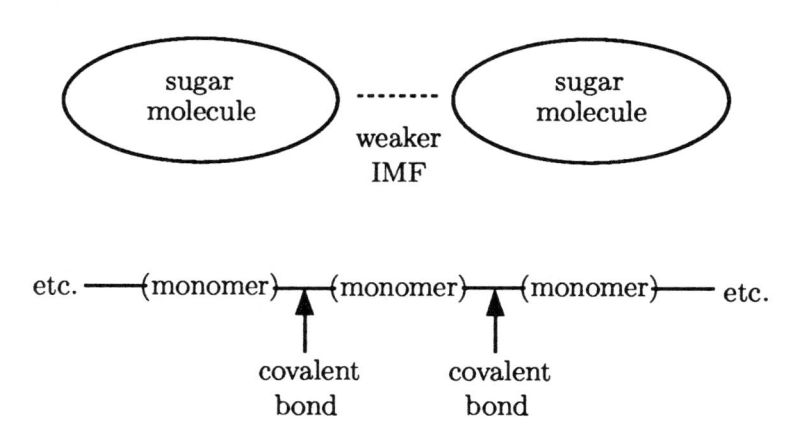

(sugar molecule) - - - - - - - (sugar molecule)
weaker IMF

etc. —(monomer)—(monomer)—(monomer)— etc.
↑ covalent bond   ↑ covalent bond

114 Chapter 11 Organic Chemistry

27. Overall Strategy: For each formula, identify a category of compounds which helps explain its properties and structure.

$$C_2H_6 \quad - \quad \text{alkane}$$
$$C_2H_2Br_2 \quad - \quad \text{substituted alkene}$$
$$C_2H_5OH \text{ and } C_4H_9OH \quad - \quad \text{primary alcohols}$$
$$CH_3COOH \quad - \quad \text{organic acid}$$
$$CHClBrI \quad - \quad \text{multi-substituted alkane}$$

When writing structural formulas, it is customary to omit the symbol H on alkyl chains and use only the dash to represent a hydrogen atom covalently bonded to a carbon atom. For example,

$$-\overset{|}{\underset{|}{C}} - \overset{|}{\underset{\underset{|}{-C-}}{C}} - \overset{|}{\underset{|}{C}} - \qquad \text{2-methylpropane}$$

(A) Strategy: $C_2H_2Br_2$ illustrates *cis-trans* isomerism. Carbon-carbon double bonds are characteristic of alkenes.

$$\underset{Br}{\overset{H}{>}}C=C\underset{Br}{\overset{H}{<}} \qquad\qquad \underset{Br}{\overset{H}{>}}C=C\underset{H}{\overset{Br}{<}}$$

cis-1,2-dibromoethene *trans*-1,2-dibromoethene

These two isomers illustrate geometrical isomerism. A third isomer, 1,1-dibromoethene, also exists.

$$\underset{H}{\overset{H}{>}}C=C\underset{Br}{\overset{Br}{<}}$$

1,1-dibromoethene

The difference between the first two isomers and the third isomer illustrates structural isomerism.

Organic Chemistry   Chapter 11   115

(B) <u>Strategy</u>: Esters are formed as the product of a reaction between an organic acid and an alcohol. The acid is CH₃COOH, acetic acid. The alcohol could be C₂H₅OH, ethanol, or C₄H₉OH, propanol. The ester would then be **CH₃COOC₂H₅** or **CH₃COOC₄H₉**.

$$-\overset{|}{\underset{|}{C}} - C\overset{\displaystyle\nearrow O}{\underset{\displaystyle\searrow O - \overset{|}{\underset{|}{C}} - \overset{|}{\underset{|}{C}} -}{}}$$

ethyl ethanoate
or
ethyl acetate

or

$$-\overset{|}{\underset{|}{C}} - C\overset{\displaystyle\nearrow O}{\underset{\displaystyle\searrow O - \overset{|}{\underset{|}{C}} - \overset{|}{\underset{|}{C}} - \overset{|}{\underset{|}{C}} - \overset{|}{\underset{|}{C}} -}{}}$$

butyl ethanoate
or
butyl acetate

(C) <u>Strategy</u>: Of the substances listed, organic acids are the best proton donors in the presence of OH⁻$_{(aq)}$. The organic acid, **CH₃COOH**, acetic acid, is the strongest proton donor.

$$-\overset{|}{\underset{|}{C}} - C\overset{\displaystyle\nearrow O}{\underset{\displaystyle\searrow OH}{}}$$

(D) <u>Strategy</u>: Optical isomerism exists where there are four different substituents around a tetrahedral carbon atom. These are designated as d- (*dextro*) and l- (*levo*) (right and left) isomers.

```
        H                           H
        |                           |
Cl  —   C                           C   —  Cl
      ╱   ◣                       ◤   ╲
    Br     I                     I      Br
```

(Review this relationship with three-dimensional models, if posssible.)

(E) Strategy: There are three classes of alcohols based on the bonding partners of the carbon atom to which the characteristic —OH group is bonded:

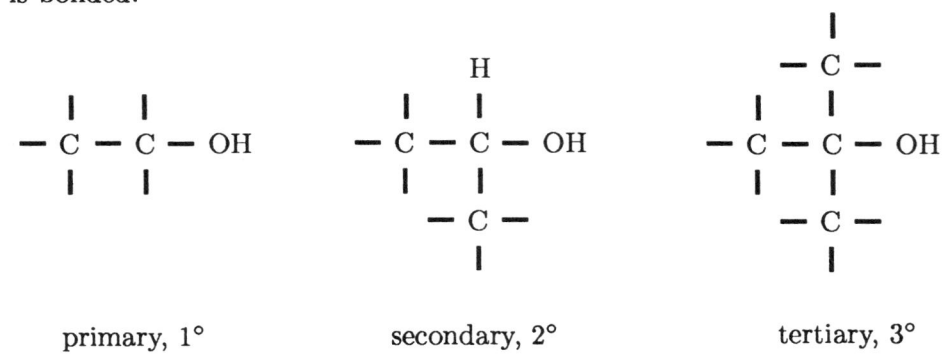

$$-\overset{|}{\underset{|}{C}}-\overset{|}{\underset{|}{C}}-OH \qquad -\overset{|}{\underset{\underset{|}{-\overset{|}{C}-}}{C}}-\overset{H}{\underset{|}{C}}-OH \qquad -\overset{\underset{|}{-\overset{|}{C}-}}{\underset{\underset{|}{-\overset{|}{C}-}}{C}}-\overset{|}{\underset{|}{C}}-OH$$

primary, 1°   secondary, 2°   tertiary, 3°

The four carbon alcohol, C_4H_9OH, exists as four isomers.

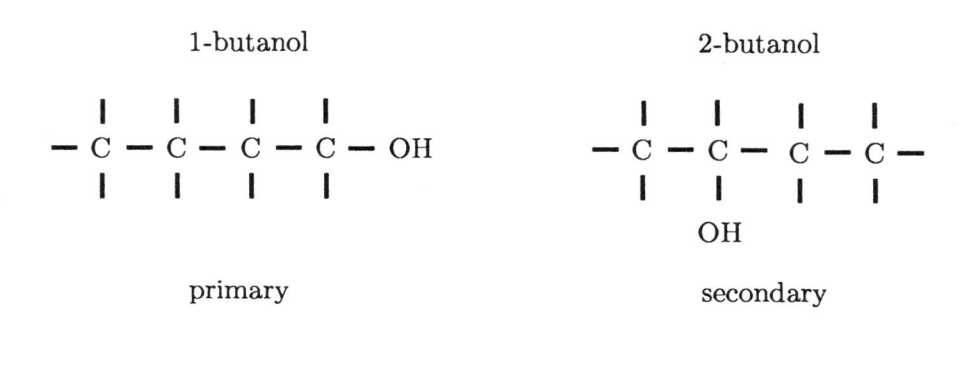

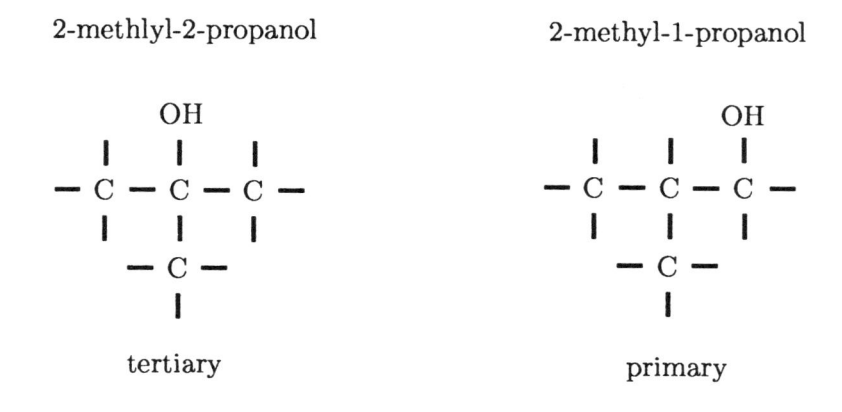

1-butanol

$$-\overset{|}{\underset{|}{C}}-\overset{|}{\underset{|}{C}}-\overset{|}{\underset{|}{C}}-\overset{|}{\underset{|}{C}}-OH$$

primary

2-butanol

$$-\overset{|}{\underset{|}{C}}-\overset{|}{\underset{|}{C}}-\overset{|}{\underset{OH}{C}}-\overset{|}{\underset{|}{C}}-$$

secondary

2-methlyl-2-propanol

$$-\overset{|}{\underset{\underset{|}{-\overset{|}{C}-}}{C}}-\overset{OH}{\underset{|}{C}}-\overset{|}{\underset{|}{C}}-$$

tertiary

2-methyl-1-propanol

$$-\overset{|}{\underset{\underset{|}{-\overset{|}{C}-}}{C}}-\overset{OH}{\underset{|}{C}}-\overset{|}{\underset{|}{C}}-$$

primary

28. Overall Strategy: Review the list of reactions presented on page 150. For each of the four parts A-D choose the best reaction category.

(A) Strategy: Reaction category: <u>Esterification</u>
An alcohol reacts with an acid to form an ester.

$$-\overset{|}{\underset{|}{C}}-\overset{|}{\underset{|}{C}}-\overset{|}{\underset{|}{C}}-\overset{|}{\underset{|}{C}}-OH \;+\; -\overset{|}{\underset{|}{C}}-C\overset{\nearrow O}{\underset{\searrow OH}{}} \;\rightarrow\; -\overset{|}{\underset{|}{C}}-C\overset{\nearrow O}{\underset{\searrow O-\overset{|}{\underset{|}{C}}-\overset{|}{\underset{|}{C}}-\overset{|}{\underset{|}{C}}-\overset{|}{\underset{|}{C}}-}{}}$$

butyl acetate
(butyl ethanoate)

(B) Strategy: Reaction category: <u>Addition</u>
A halogen reacts with an unsaturated hydrocarbon by adding halogen atoms at the double bond location.

1,2-dibromo-*cyclo*-hexane

(C) Strategy: Reaction category: <u>Oxidation</u>
Primary alcohols can be oxidized by oxidizing agents such as $K_2Cr_2O_7$ or $KMnO_4$ to form aldehydes or acids. In the context of organic reactions, it is sometimes helpful to think of oxidation as dehydrogenation.

$$-\overset{|}{\underset{|}{C}}-\overset{|}{\underset{|}{C}}-C\overset{\nearrow O}{\underset{\searrow H}{}} \quad \text{propanal}$$

(D) Strategy: Reaction category: <u>Polymerization</u>
In the presence of a catalyst, ethene (ethylene) molecules can be converted to the ethylene monomer. These monomers bond to form polymers, in this case, polyethylene.

ethene (ethylene)   monomer   polyethylene

Chapter 12
Descriptive Chemistry

Questions 1-5: For each of the mixtures given, a description of the results is given. Where a chemical change occurs, the equation is also given.

1. $$CaCl_{2(aq)} + NaCl_{(aq)} \rightarrow \text{no reaction occurs}$$

    Two colorless solutions are mixed; a colorless mixture with no precipitate and no evolution of gas results.

    The correct choice is (D).

2. $$AgNO_{3(aq)} + KCl_{(aq)} \rightarrow AgCl_{(s)} + KNO_{3(aq)}$$

    $AgCl_{(s)}$ is a white precipitate. The aqueous phase of the mixture is colorless.

    The correct choice is (B).

3. $$K_2CrO_{4(aq)} + (\text{excess})Ba(NO_3)_{2(aq)} \rightarrow BaCrO_{4(s)} + 2KNO_{3(aq)}$$

    $BaCrO_{4(s)}$ is a yellow precipitate. The aqueous phase of the mixture is colorless because excess $Ba^{2+}{}_{(aq)}$ causes all of the $CrO_4{}^{2-}{}_{(aq)}$ to precipitate.

    The correct choice is (A).

4. $$(\text{dilute})HCl_{(aq)} + KHCO_{3(aq)} \rightarrow KCl_{(aq)} + H_2O + CO_{2(g)}$$

    The gas, CO_2, is evolved. The aqueous phase of the mixture is colorless.

    The correct choice is (E).

5. $$CrCl_{3(s)} + (\text{dilute})HNO_{3(aq)} \rightarrow \text{no chemical change}$$

    The $CrCl_{3(s)}$ dissolves to form a dark blue solution with no gas or precipitate formation.

    The correct choice is (C).

---

6. Look first for a component that is insoluble in water. Note that all salts specified are soluble in water. Then look for possible ionic combinations that would produce a precipitate in water. In choice (C), Ca^{2+} would precipitate with $CO_3{}^{2-}$ as $CaCO_3$. However, that substance is soluble in HCl.

    The correct choice is (C).

7. When CO_2 is first bubbled into limewater, a precipitate of $CaCO_3$ forms. Further bubbling of CO_2 causes the precipitate to redissolve. The reactions are represented in the two equations below:

$$CO_{2(g)} + H_2O + Ca^{2+}{}_{(aq)} + 2OH^-{}_{(aq)} \rightarrow CaCO_{3(g)} + 2H_2O$$

$$CaCO_{3(s)} + CO_{2(g)} + H_2O \rightarrow Ca^{2+}{}_{(aq)} + 2HCO_3^-{}_{(aq)}$$

For each of the other choices:

(B) A light blue precipitate is associated with copper-related systems in basic solution.

(C) Two immiscible liquids are often seen when an organic solvent is shaken with water. The layers separate after shaking.

(D) Many chemical reactions are associated with the evolution of energy. Common examples include the dissolving of acids or bases and most acid-base neutralization reactions.

(E) Some chemical reactions are associated with the absorption of energy. Common examples include the dissolving of some salts, especially ammonium salts.

The correct choice is (A).

Questions 8-12:

8. When $NaOH_{(aq)}$ is added to $Cr_2O_7^{2-}$, CrO_4^{2-} is formed. Note that no oxidation-reduction occurs. The oxidation number of chromium remains as +6.

The correct choice is (B).

9. NH_4^+ donates a proton to OH^- according to the equation

$$NH_4^+ + OH^- \rightarrow NH_3 + H_2O$$

Warming drives the $NH_{3(g)}$ out of solution.

The correct choice is (D).

120 Chapter 12   Descriptive Chemistry

10. Al(OH)₃ is amphoteric as shown below. The white precipitate that first forms, re-dissolves in excess OH⁻.

$$Al^{3+} + 3OH^- \rightarrow Al(OH)_{3(s)}$$

$$Al(OH)_{3(s)} + 3OH^- \rightarrow Al(OH)_6^{3-} \quad \text{(or } AlO_2^- + 3H_2O)$$

alternate version: $Al(OH)_{3(s)} + OH^- \rightarrow Al(OH)_4^-$

Al(OH)₃(s) is both proton donor and proton acceptor.

The correct choice is (A).

11. Mg(OH)₂ is a persistent white precipitate in basic solution.

$$Mg^{2+} + 2OH^- \rightarrow Mg(OH)_{2(s)}$$

The correct choice is (C).

12. Ni(OH)₂ is a persistent green precipitate in basic solution.

$$Ni^{2+} + 2OH^- \rightarrow Ni(OH)_{2(s)}$$

The correct choice is (E).

---

13. Consider the five responses provided. CaCO₃, NaHCO₃ and Zn(OH)₂ dissolve in excess acid. BaSO₄ is insoluble in all three reagents: water, excess dilute hydrochloric acid and excess ammonia solution. Of the substances listed, only AgCl is insoluble in water, soluble in excess NH₃ $\left(\text{as } Ag(NH_3)_2^+\right)$, and insoluble in dilute HCl.

The correct choice is (A).

14. Solutions containing cations of the transition elements are colored due to the presence of partially filled d sublevel orbitals. However, in the case of Sc³⁺, the d sublevel is empty; therefore, solutions containing Sc³⁺ are not colored.

The correct choice is (A).

Questions 15-19:

15. One of the oxides of sulfur, SO_3, is a gas that dissolves in water to form H_2SO_4, a strong acid.

    The correct choice is (B).

16. Na_2O dissolves in water to form $NaOH$, a strong base.

    The correct choice is (A).

17. The oxide of silicon is SiO_2, a network solid commonly found as sand or quartz. It is insoluble in water.

    The correct choice is (D).

18. ZnO is a white solid that dissolves in excess acid as Zn^{2+} or in excess base as ZnO_2^{2-} or $Zn(OH)_4^{2-}$.

    The correct choice is (E).

19. The oxide of phosphorus, P_4O_{10}, is a white solid that dissolves in water to form H_3PO_4, a weak acid.

    The correct choice is (C).

---

20. Chlorine water, $Cl_{2(aq)}$, oxidizes both halides, Br^- and I^-, to Br_2 and I_2, respectively. Both molecular substances dissolve in the oil layer.

    The correct choice is (E).

21. In the halogen group, the number of kernel (inner) electrons increases as atomic number increases. This increasing number of electrons also accounts for the corresponding increase in the normal boiling point due to increasing strength of (van der Waals) forces of attraction between molecules.

    The correct choice is (B).

22. All of the elements listed are metals except Ge, germanium. Because it is a semiconductor, germanium is classified as a metalloid (semi-metal).

The correct choice is (A).

23. When dilute hydrochloric acid is added to sodium hydrogen sulfite, the gas, sulfur dioxide, is produced. This gas has a sharp choking odor.

$$HCl_{(aq)} + NaHSO_{3(s)} \rightarrow NaCl_{(aq)} + H_2O + SO_{2(g)}$$

The dark brown gas of choice (A) could be nitrogen (IV) oxide, NO_2. The gas that turns limewater cloudy is carbon dioxide, CO_2. The gas that re-ignites a glowing splint is oxygen, O_2. The gas that has the odor of rotten eggs is hydrogen sulfide, H_2S.

The correct choice is (D).

24. The formulas for the two oxides of tin are SnO and SnO_2. Only choice (B) gives both formulas. Note that the electron configuration of Sn is [Kr core]$4d^{10}5s^25p^2$. This helps to account for oxidation states of +2 and +4.

The correct choice is (B).

25. Only ethanol provides the conditions for hydrogen bond formation, where, within the ethanol molecule, one hydrogen atom is bonded to an oxygen atom. The capacity to form hydrogen bonds between molecules increases solubility in water. Ethanol is soluble in water in all proportions. Some authorities describe water and ethanol as "infinitely miscible".

The correct choice is (A).

Free-Response Questions

26. <u>Overall strategy:</u> Recognize that NaOH is specified as solid pellets or as the solute in water solution. Sodium hydroxide can dissolve in water at a concentration high enough to produce a corrosive solution. Hydrated ions are present. The cation, Na^+, is generally unreactive in water solution. The anion, OH^-, most often acts as a proton acceptor. It also forms precipitates with most Group 2 and transition element cations. Hydroxide ion also acts as a Lewis base in a complexation environment.

(A) The white precipitate that forms after the first few drops is $Al(OH)_{3(s)}$. When excess NaOH is present, the hydrated $Al(OH)_3$ donates protons to the OH^- in solution, producing $Al(H_2O)_2(OH)_4^-$ or other similar soluble species such as $Al(H_2O)(OH)_5^{2-}$ and $Al(OH)_6^{3-}$. Sometimes these species are simply represented as AlO_2^- or $Al(OH)_4^-$.

(B) Energy is given off as bonds form between H_2O molecules and the Na^+ and OH^- ions in solution. This energy loss is seen as a temperature increase in the solution that is formed. This energy is called heat (or energy) of hydration.

(C) The OH^- ions in NaOH are proton acceptors. The quantity of NaOH used could accept 0.020 mol of protons. The HCl solution provides only 0.010 mol of protons. The excess NaOH makes the solution basic with the correspondingly high pH value. The quantity of H_3PO_4 used can still provide more than 0.020 mol protons. The solution of H_3PO_4 is not "neutralized" by the amount of NaOH used. Thus, the H_3PO_4 solution remains acidic.

(D) During the period of exposure, some of the solvent water evaporates, accounting for the loss of volume. During that time, some carbon dioxide from the atmosphere dissolves in the solution according to the equation

$$CO_2 + H_2O \rightarrow HCO_3^- + H^+$$

The dissolved carbon dioxide acts as an acid, reacting with H_2O producing H^+ ions (protons) that neutralize some of the NaOH, thus causing a decrease in pH.

27. Overall strategy: Differences in physical and chemical properties must be used to identify each of the four substances. Sugar is a molecular solid; the others are ionic. Molecular substances such as sugar are nonconductors of electricity in water solution. Solutions of ionic solids such as the other three unidentified samples conduct electricity. The carbonate dissolves in water to form a basic solution. That solution reacts with acid to liberate a gas. The other unidentified substances form neutral solutions and do not react with acid. The sulfate reacts with $BaCl_{2(aq)}$ to form a precipitate. (Similarly, the chloride reacts with Ag^+ ions to form a precipitate. However, that reagent, $AgNO_{3(aq)}$, is not supplied.) Using these differences in properties permits confirmation of identity. When the identities of three of the four are known, the identity of the fourth can be concluded by logical elimination.

Confirming carbonate: The unknown substances are dissolved in separate samples of distilled water. Use of pH paper would be sufficient to identify the sodium carbonate. Of the substances listed, only the solution of Na_2CO_3 would be basic. The others would be neutral.

Confirming sugar: Use of the conductivity apparatus would be sufficient to identify the sugar solution. Its solution is a nonconductor because no ions are present in the sugar solution. All of the other solutions contain mobilized ions in solution. Their solutions conduct electricity.

Confirming sulfate: Use of the barium chloride and hydrochloric acid solutions can distinguish between the remaining two substances. When barium chloride solution is added to solutions of the remaining substances, a white precipitate forms in the solution of sodium sulfate. No change is observed in the solution of sodium chloride. Upon addition of hydrochloric acid, the precipitate from sodium sulfate does not dissolve, confirming the presence of sulfate ions. However, this latter test is not required to identify these four substances. If the carbonate were treated with $BaCl_{2(aq)}$, a precipitate would also form. However, upon addition of $HCl_{(aq)}$, gas bubbles would form and the precipitate of $BaCO_3$ would dissolve.

Confirming chloride: The remaining substance is sodium chloride. It dissolves in water to form a solution that conducts electricity. It does not react with HCl or $BaCl_{2(aq)}$. Its solution is neutral.

Note that ammonia is not used.

28. <u>Overall strategy</u>: The directions specify several broad categories of chemical principles. Acid/base theory includes definitions such as proton donors and acceptors or electron pair donors and acceptors. Those theories also include a characteristic reaction such as neutralization or proton transfer. The oxidation-reduction process is based on changes in oxidation number explained as transfer of electrons. Principles of bonding and intermolecular forces account for the formation of molecules and the attractions between atoms, molecules and ions. These forces include covalent bonds, ionic bonds, metallic bonds and weaker forces of attraction sometimes known collectively as van der Waals forces.

(A) Cyclohexane, a nonpolar liquid, and water are immiscible; that is, they are mutually insoluble. Molecules of cyclohexane and water are not strongly attracted to each other. Hence, two layers form. [The upper layer is the water solution layer. Its density is lower.]

(B) The solution of bromine in cyclohexane is brown. During the shaking process, bromine molecules oxidize iodide ions in the water layer to form iodine molecules that become dissolved in cyclohexane. Cyclohexane is a good solvent for both kinds of halogen molecules since the solvent and both solute molecules are nonpolar. The solution of iodine molecules in cyclohexane has a violet color. Both the NaI and NaBr are colorless in water solution.

(C) Cu^{2+} ions will oxidize Zn atoms to form Zn^{2+} ions. Thus, the zinc dissolves in the water solution. Zn^{2+} ions cannot oxidize copper atoms. Zinc is a more "active" metal than copper. Zinc is a better reducing agent than copper. Zinc loses its valence electrons more readily than copper.

(D) Magnesium metal reduces the H^+ ions to form H_2 molecules. These molecules leave the solution in the form of bubbles of hydrogen gas.

126 Chapter 12   Descriptive Chemistry

29. <u>Overall strategy</u>: For each reaction, choose that reaction category from the list of ten categories that is most closely related to the reactants and conditions specified. Referring to such a category helps narrow the range of probable products. This list is found on page 150.

   (A) Chlorine gas is bubbled through a solution of potassium iodide.

   $Cl_2 + I^- \rightarrow Cl^- + I_2$

   Redox single replacement; more active halogen oxidizes halide ion.

   (B) A solution of sodium carbonate is electrolyzed using inert electrodes.

   $H_2O \rightarrow H_2 + O_2$

   Decomposition; electrolysis of water; Na^+ and CO_3^{2-} ions provide conductivity but do not react.

   (C) Chromium is heated in excess oxygen.

   $Cr + O_2 \rightarrow Cr_2O_3$

   Synthesis; elements combine to form compound.

   (D) A solution of tin (II) chloride is added to a solution of iron (III) nitrate.

   $Sn^{2+} + Fe^{3+} \rightarrow Sn^{4+} + Fe^{2+}$

   Sn^{2+} is a **commonly used reducing agent**. Its oxidation product is Sn^{4+}.

   (E) Sodium chromate crystals are added to a solution of silver nitrate.

   $Na_2CrO_4 + Ag^+ \rightarrow Ag_2CrO_4 + Na^+$

   Double replacement; solid reactant hence not dissociated; precipitate forms.

   (F) A solution of manganese (II) chloride is added to excess solution of sodium hydroxide.

   $Mn^{2+} + OH^- \rightarrow Mn(OH)_2$

   Double replacement; precipitate forms.

   (G) A solution of barium chloride is added to a solution of phosphoric acid.

   $Ba^{2+} + H_3PO_4 \rightarrow Ba_3(PO_4)_2 + H^+$

   Double replacement; H_3PO_4 is a weak acid, hence not ionized; precipitate forms.

   (H) A few crystals of potassium thiocyanate are added to a solution of iron (III) nitrate.

   $KSCN + Fe^{3+} \rightarrow FeSCN^{2+} + K^+$

   Complexation; (also Lewis acid/base reaction); solid reactant hence not dissociated

Sample Examination I

Section I - Multiple-Choice

1. Of the period 4 elements given, Co is the only transition element. As such it has a partially filled $3d$ sublevel. Its electron configuration is [Ar^0 core] $4s^2 3d^7$. The d-sublevel has a capacity of 10 electrons. With only 7 electrons, its d-sublevel is only partially filled.

   The correct choice is (B).

2. Of the period 4 elements given, only Br forms an anion; that is, only Br gains electrons to form its most common ion. Ions formed by the other elements are cations, formed by losing electrons. By gaining one electron, Br acquires a completed $4p$ sublevel to form Br$^-$ ion. As such, it has the greatest ionic radius.

   The correct choice is (A).

3. A low boiling point is associated with weak forces between particles, the same weak forces associated with the liquid or gas phase, rather than the solid phase. Of the period 4 elements given, only Br is a liquid at ordinary conditions. All other elements are solids. Thus, Br, as molecular Br$_2$, has the lowest boiling point.

   The correct choice is (A).

4. The oxide of K is K$_2$O. K$_2$O is a basic anhydride which dissolves in water to form KOH. KOH, in turn, is 100% dissociated in water solution to form the strong base, OH$^-$.

   The correct choice is (D).

5. The element from this list that has four valence electrons is Ge. The electron configuration of Ge is [Ar^0 core] $4s^2 3d^{10} 4p^2$. Thus, Ge has four electrons in the fourth energy level, its valence shell.

   The correct choice is (C).

6. The original condition provided 100 mL Na$_2$CrO$_{4(aq)}$ in a beaker. This is a yellow solution. The Ag$_2$CrO$_{4(s)}$ formed after the addition of AgNO$_3$ is a red precipitate.

   The correct choice is (B).

7. In this double relacement reaction, the two possible products are NaNO$_3$ and Ag$_2$CrO$_4$. Of these two, only Ag$_2$CrO$_4$ is insoluble.

   The correct choice is (D).

128 Sample Examination I

8. The volume of the liquid phase is 200 mL. The quantity of Na$^+$ present is 0.020 mol. Thus, [Na$^+$] = 0.020 mol/0.200 L or 0.10 M.

   The correct choice is (D).

9. Since all of the Ag$^+$ available precipitates due to excess CrO$_4$$^{2-}$, the number of moles of Ag$^+$ in the precipitate is 0.010.

   The correct choice is (A).

10. In the original mixture, 0.010 mol CrO$_4$$^{2-}$ was available. There was enough Ag$^+$ to react with 0.0050 mol CrO$_4$$^{2-}$. Thus, the final concentration of CrO$_4$$^{2-}$ is 0.0050 mol/0.200 L or 0.025 M.

    The correct choice is (B).

11. As with many NH$_4$$^+$ salts, the dissolving of NH$_4$NO$_3$ is endothermic; that is, energy is absorbed and the system becomes colder (choice (D)). In each of the other cases, energy is given off as KOH forms K$^+$ and OH$^-$, H$_2$SO$_4$ forms H$^+$ and HSO$_4$$^-$, metallic Na is oxidized to Na$^+$ and anhydrous CuSO$_4$ takes on water of hydration.

    The correct choice is (D).

12. When a Cl^0 atom takes on an electron, it becomes a Cl$^-$ ion. The radius increases as this electron is added. However, since the mass of an electron is negligibly small, there is no change in its mass. Thus, the Cl^0 atom contains one less electron than the Cl$^-$ ion. Only statement III gives a correct comparison.

    The correct choice is (B).

13. The structural formula for *trans*-1,2-dichloroethene, C$_2$H$_2$Cl$_2$, is

$$\begin{array}{c}\text{Cl} \\ \\ \text{H}\end{array}\!\!\!\!\!\diagdown\!\!\!\diagup\!\!\!\! \text{C}=\text{C}\!\!\!\!\diagup\!\!\!\diagdown\!\!\!\!\begin{array}{c}\text{H}\\ \\ \text{Cl}\end{array}$$

Four single bonds and one double bond account for the six shared pairs of electrons.

The correct choice is (D).

14. Ionization energy is one of several atomic properties that illustrate the Periodic Law. Within a period, as atomic number (Z) increases, ionization energy increases. Within a group, as Z increases, ionization energy decreases. Thus, when Br, Cl and F, as elements in the same group are listed in order of DECREASING Z they are also listed in order of INCREASING ionization energy.

The correct choice is (D).

15. The electron configuration of the Ni atom is [Ar^0 core] $4s^2 3d^8$. Each of the five orbitals in the $3d$ sublevel is occupied. Three orbitals have two electrons each; the other two orbitals have one electron each. In addition, the one orbital of the $3s$ sublevel and the three orbitals of the $3p$ sublevel are filled for a total of nine occupied orbitals.

The correct choice is (E).

16. The electron configuration $1s^2 2s^2 2p^3$ indicates five valence electrons. The dot diagram that matches the correct distribution of five valence electrons is

$$\cdot \overset{\cdot\cdot}{\underset{\cdot}{\text{X}}} \cdot$$

The correct choice is (D).

17. The "weighted average atomic mass" is the value reported on most periodic tables and similar charts of information. It reflects the naturally-occurring distribution of the various isotopes of each element. For example, the distribution of chlorine is approximately 75% chlorine-35 and 25% chlorine-37, producing a weighted average atomic mass of 35.5 amu.

The correct choice is (E).

18. The spectrographic notation $3p^4$ refers to the fourth electron in the p sublevel of the third energy level. The p sublevel is the second available sublevel. (The first is the s sublevel.) The corresponding set of quantum numbers is 3, 1, 1, $+\frac{1}{2}$. The numeral 3 refers to the third principal energy level; the first numeral 1 refers to the second energy sublevel (0 is used for the first); the second numeral 1 refers to one of the three orbitals in the p sublevel (the numerals 0 and -1 could also be used); $+\frac{1}{2}$ refers to one of two possible spins (the other is $-\frac{1}{2}$).

The correct choice is (C).

19. There are two possible isomers for the complex ion, $[Co(H_2O)_4(NH_3)_2]^{2+}$. Each of six ligands is located at one vertex of an octahedron around Co^{2+} at the central position. The NH_3 groups can be located in either *cis* or *trans* positions as shown below.

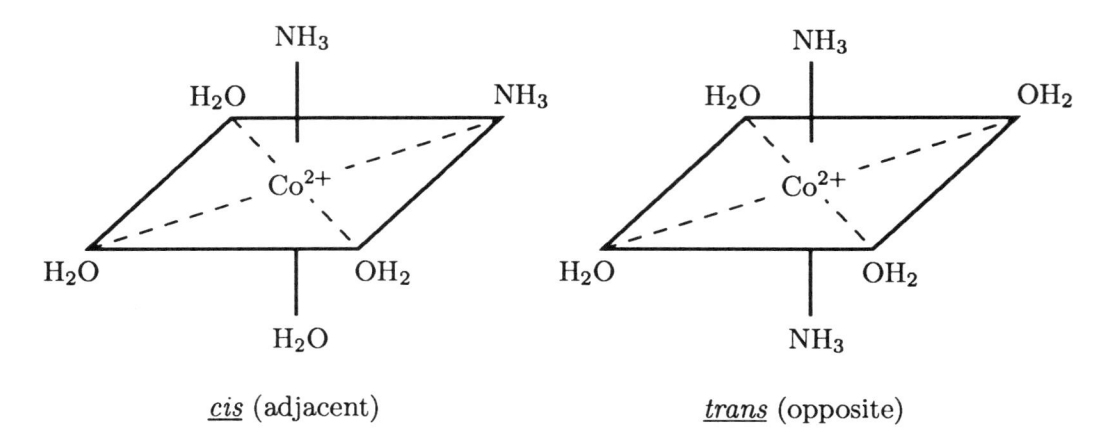

cis (adjacent)   *trans* (opposite)

The correct choice is (A).

20. The structural formula for CH_3COCH_3 below

shows 10 bonds: 9 *sigma* bonds and one *pi* bond.

The correct choice is (D).

21. The structural formula for CH_3COCH_3 in question 20 shows 3 *sigma* bonds around the central carbon atom. This corresponds to a bond angle of 120°.

The correct choice is (D).

22. Tellurium is a member of group 16 with six valence electrons like oxygen and sulfur. It is most likely to share two pairs of electrons to form H_2Te.

The correct choice is (C).

23. The symbols ^1_1H, ^2_1H and ^3_1H, represent three different nuclides that have one proton each but zero, one and two neutrons, respectively. Such nuclides with the same number of protons (same Z) but different numbers of neutrons (different A) are called isotopes.

The correct choice is (B).

24. The greatest difference between first and second ionization energies for a given element occurs when the first electron comes from one energy level (the valence shell) and the second electron comes from the next lower energy level which is an inner energy level. This electron from an inner energy level is subject to a much greater force of attraction than the valence electron. Thus, in order for a Group 1 element such as K to lose two electrons, one electron from an inner energy level must be used in addition to an electron from the valence shell. Each of the other elements has at least two valence electrons.

The correct choice is (D).

25. Low dipole moment is associated with weak forces between molecules. Such weak forces explain why some substances are gases at ordinary conditions. Of the compounds listed, only NH_3 is a gas at ordinary conditions.

The correct choice is (B).

26. The molecular geometry of the PF_5 molecule is best explained by dsp^3 hybridization which calls for an expanded octet of electrons (actually 5 electron pairs rather than 4) distributed to the five vertices of a trigonal bipyramid. The resulting F-P-F bond angles include 90° angles between axial and equatorial F atoms and 120° angles between adjacent equatorial F atoms. The octahedral shape is associated with d^2sp^3 hybridization.

The correct choice is (A).

27. The Law of Multiple Proportions calls for a fixed mass of one of the elements found in such a pair of compounds. In compound I, 76.5 grams of chromium combines with 23.5 grams of oxygen. Thus, 76.5/23.5 grams chromium per **ONE** gram of oxygen and, for compound II, 68.4/31.6 grams chromium per **ONE** gram of oxygen. (An equally correct choice would have been, for compound I, 23.5/76.5 grams per **ONE** gram of chromium and for compound II, 31.6/68.4 grams oxygen per **ONE** gram of chromium. However, that choice was not offered.

The correct choice is (A).

28. Balancing nuclear equations calls for referring to the sum of the subscripts and the sum of the superscripts. In this case, on the left, the sum of the superscripts equals 240 and the sum of the subscripts equals 93. Thus, the missing term must have a superscript of 240 and a subscript of 94. Note that each different subscript corresponds to one specific chemical symbol.

    The correct choice is (B).

29. Calcium carbonate is an ionic solid with cations and anions at the lattice points. These ions are Ca^{2+} and CO_3^{2-}. Only choice (B) offers ions found in $CaCO_3$. Of the ions offered in choice (D), the C^{4+} ion does not exist and the O^{2-} is not found in $CaCO_3$.

    The correct choice is (B).

30. Alpha particles are positively charged. A beam of alpha particles will be attracted toward the negative plate.

    The correct choice is (D).

31. At the same temperature, molecules have the same average kinetic energy; thus,

    $$KE_1 = KE_2 \quad \text{or} \quad \tfrac{1}{2}m_1v_1^2 = \tfrac{1}{2}m_2v_2^2$$

    where m_1 and v_1 refer to SO_2 molecules and m_2 and v_2 refer to SO_3 molecules. The values for m_1 and m_2 are molecular masses 64 and 80, respectively. The values for v_1 and v_2 are the unknown average molecular velocities. Substituting values where known and rearranging algebraically gives

    $$\tfrac{1}{2}(64)(v_1)^2 = \tfrac{1}{2}(80)(v_2)^2$$

    $$\frac{v_1}{v_2} = \frac{\sqrt{80}}{\sqrt{64}}$$

    The correct choice is (E).

32. A good way to solve many "which expression" problems is to label the values provided, then use those labeled values in the appropriate quantitative relationship. In this case

    $$\frac{1.85 \text{ grams}}{1 \text{ liter}} \times \frac{22.4 \text{ L (at STP)}}{1 \text{ mol}}$$

    This corresponds to choice (A). The other choices include various "attractive" components of common gas laws problems such as 273 $\underline{K}$ (standard temperature), 760 $\underline{mmHg}$ (standard pressure) and $0.0821 \underline{\frac{L \cdot atm}{mol \cdot K}}$ (R, the gas constant). Labeling the values in the other choices will verify that each is incorrect.

    The correct choice is (A).

Sample Examination I   133

33. In the context of the gas laws, the piston is used to contain a system in which pressure and volume are the most likely variables. However, temperature and number of molecules can also be changed, if specified. In this problem, temperature (T) and pressure (P) are held constant. The independent variable is volume (V). Intuitively, one could conclude that adding "more of the same gas" causes an increase in volume. Use of the general gas law $PV = nRT$ or $V = n\frac{RT}{P}$, where R, T, and P are constant, also shows that V (the dependent variable) increases as n (the independent variable) increases. The other given information, "constant temperature" and "same gas" indicates that average molecular velocity also remains the same. For additional mental exercise, try changing another (independent) variable, then consider the effect on a second, hence dependent, variable.

The correct choice is (E).

34. "Sealed identical flasks" immediately specifies equal volume for all three samples in this problem. The samples also contain the same number of molecules, 0.100 mol. Since Kr molecules are the heaviest of the three, the Kr sample has the greatest mass and, at equal volumes, the greatest density. Thus, only I and II are correct.

The correct choice is (C).

35. This is a liquid ⇌ vapor (gas) equilibrium system. As such, both the forward (evaporation) and reverse (condensation) reactions are occurring, eventually reaching the same rate at equilibrium. The presence of NaCl has no effect on the relationship between the opposing rates at equilibrium.

The correct choice is (A).

36. In the van der Waals equation of state for real gases

$$\left((P + \frac{n^2 a}{V^2}\right)(V - nb) = nRT$$

The effect of the $\underline{a}$ coefficient is to increase the pressure term to a value greater than the observed pressure. Where forces of attraction between molecules exist, the pressure exerted by the gas does not reach the "ideal" value; thus, a correction factor, the $\underline{a}$ coefficient, is applied.

The correct choice is (D).

37. When sodium chloride (or any nonvolatile solute) is added to water, the freezing point of the solution becomes lower than that of pure water (statement I). The presence of such a solute also decreases the vapor pressure of the solution compared to that of water (statement II). Addition of solid solutes to water generally produces a solution of greater density than pure water. Additional solute increases the mass of the system with little change in volume. Statement III is not correct.

The correct choice is (C).

38. The normal boiling point is identified by the temperature at the intersection of the 1 atmosphere line and the liquid/gas boundary. At elevations higher than sea level, the pressure is somewhat less than 1 atmosphere; thus, this boiling point is somewhat less than the normal boiling point.

    The correct choice is (B).

39. At 15°C, the liquid/vapor boundary is well below the 0.5 atm value (statement I). At and below 0.2 atm, no temperature values are found in the liquid phase. Therefore, at any pressure below 0.2 atm, sublimation, the process of direct change from solid to gas phase, occurs with no liquid phase observed (statement II). At 15°C for example, as conditions change from lower to higher pressure, the solid will eventually form, indicating that the solid phase is more dense than the liquid phase (statement III). Thus all three statements are correct.

    The correct choice is (E).

40. Water, as well as any other substance that can pass through a membrane, moves from a region of higher concentration to a region of lower concentration. In this case, since water is more "concentrated" in the cell, the cell will lose water and become shriveled.

    The correct choice is (B).

41. To behave as a Lewis base, a species must have at least one electron pair available to be shared. It is also useful to recall that any Bronsted-Lowry base is also a Lewis base. All of the species stated, except NH_4^+, have at least one unshared electron pair.

    The correct choice is (B).

42. Amphoteric behavior calls for reaction with acid or base. More specifically, an amphoteric compound can behave as a proton donor or a proton acceptor, depending on the nature of the other substances in the system. Thus, observations I and II support the claim of amphoteric behavior. Behavior in the presence of NaCl (observation III) is not related to amphoteric properties.

    The correct choice is (B).

43. Heating to dryness over a burner flame requires a very durable vessel such as a crucible (usually porcelain). The watch glass can be used only for slower evaporation at much lower temperatures. The thistle tube (usually glass) is a special funnel used to add liquid to a closed flask. The Buchner funnel (often porcelain) is used to support the filter paper in a vacuum filtration process. An Erlenmeyer flask (glass or plastic) is a general purpose flask, especially convenient for swirling mixtures in solution.

    The correct choice is (A).

44. As this transition proceeds, Pb^0 is oxidized to Pb^{2+}. In the anode (oxidation) chamber, $[Pb^{2+}]$ increases. Electrons flow through the external circuit away from the anode and toward the cathode. Positive ions move through the salt bridge toward the cathode.

The correct choice is (A).

45. Using the labeling strategy described in question 32 for the terms derived from the information given, the change in mass can be calculated from the expression below:

$$2.0 \text{ hr} \times \frac{3,600 \text{ sec}}{1 \text{ hr}} \times \frac{0.150 \text{ coul}}{1 \text{ sec}} \times \frac{1 \text{ mol e}^-}{96,500 \text{ coul}} \times \frac{1 \text{ mol Pb}}{2 \text{ mol e}^-} \times \frac{207 \text{ g Pb}}{1 \text{ mol Pb}}$$

With the labels "cancelled", this becomes

$$2.0 \text{ hr} \times \frac{3,600 \text{ sec}}{1 \text{ hr}} \times \frac{0.150 \text{ coul}}{1 \text{ sec}} \times \frac{1 \text{ mol e}^-}{96,500 \text{ coul}} \times \frac{1 \text{ mol Pb}}{2 \text{ mol e}^-} \times \frac{207 \text{ g Pb}}{1 \text{ mol Pb}}$$

simplified as

$$\frac{3,600 \times 0.150 \times 207}{96,500} \text{ g Pb}$$

The correct choice is (D).

46. In any electrochemical cell, two opposing half-reactions occur. In this case, Fe^{3+} is the stronger oxidizing agent. Therefore, the reduction half-reaction is

$$Fe^{3+} + e^- \to Fe^{2+} \qquad E° = 0.77 \text{ volts}$$

and the oxidation half-reaction is

$$Pb^0 \to Pb^{2+} + 2e^- \qquad E° = 0.13 \text{ volts}$$

In order to determine the cell voltage, the $E°$ values for the half-reactions are added together. Note that reversing a half-reaction gives the opposite sign to the $E°$ value. Note also that the number of electrons in a half-reaction is NOT used in the calculation of the cell voltage. (The logic here could be expressed as one Fe^{3+} ion "pulls" one electron with the same electromotive force that two Fe^{3+} ions "pull" two electrons.)

The correct choice is (A).

136 Sample Examination I

47. Note that Pb^{2+} is a product in this cell. Diluting the product will cause the reaction (using le Chatelier's principle) to shift to the right; that is, to aquire a higher positive voltage. The Nernst equation should be used to obtain a quantitative answer.

$$E = E° - \frac{0.059}{n} \log Q = E° - \frac{0.059}{n} \log \frac{[Pb^{2+}][Fe^{2+}]}{[Fe^{3+}]}$$

Substituting

$$E = 0.90 - \frac{0.059}{2} \log \frac{[0.010][1.0]}{[1.0]}$$

$$E = 0.90 - \frac{0.059}{2} \times (-2)$$

$$E = 0.90 + 0.06$$

The correct choice is (B).

48. Converting the information "0.75 mole fraction in methanol" gives the terms

$$\frac{3 \text{ mol methanol}}{4 \text{ mol (solute + solvent)}} \quad \text{and} \quad \frac{3 \text{ mol methanol}}{1 \text{ mol water}}$$

$$6 \text{ mol water} \times \frac{3 \text{ mol methanol}}{1 \text{ mol water}} = 18 \text{ mol methanol}$$

The correct choice is (E).

49. The dissolving of NH_3 in water is best described by the equation

$$NH_3 + H_2O \rightleftharpoons NH_4^+ + OH^-$$

This is net transfer of a proton from H_2O to NH_3.

The correct choice is (A).

50. Sulfuric acid ionizes to form H_3O^+, HSO_4^- and SO_4^{2-} ions in water solution. In addition, OH^- ions are found in any water solution, even one that has a high concentration of H_3O^+. OH^- ions are found in lowest concentration. The first ionization (nearly 100%) of H_2SO_4 produces H_3O^+ and HSO_4^-. The second ionization (a weak ionization) produces additional H_3O^+ and SO_4^{2-}. Thus, the ions listed in order of increasing concentration is OH^-, SO_4^{2-}, HSO_4^-, H_3O^+.

The correct choice is (A).

51. The heat of formation of water is a negative value, no matter what phase of water is specified. When the product is water in the liquid phase, the value of ΔH_f is negative but has a smaller absolute value than the corresponding value for the formation of solid water (ice). More energy will be given off when the product is in the solid phase.

The correct choice is (B).

52. The relationship between $\Delta G°$ and $E°$ is given by

$$\Delta G° = -n\mathcal{F}E°$$

where n is the number of moles of electrons transferred, $\mathcal{F}$ is the value of the faraday (96,500 coulomb/mole of electrons) and $E°$ is the cell voltage (1 volt = 1 joule/coulomb).

Substituting values

$$\Delta G° = -2 \text{ mol electrons} \times \frac{96,500 \text{ coulomb}}{1 \text{ mol electrons}} \times \frac{1.5 \text{ joule}}{\text{coulomb}}$$

By approximation arithmetic

$$\Delta G° = -2 \times \text{about } 100,000 \times 1.5 = \text{about } -300,000 \text{ joules or about } -300 \text{ kJ}$$

The correct choice is (E).

53. To compare the choices, it is most efficient to evaluate each in terms of number of Cl atoms. The "exact" number is not needed since the question asks for "greatest". There is 1 mol Cl atoms in 0.50 mol Cl_2O. There is 3 mol Cl atoms in 1.5 mol Cl_2. In 50 L ClF_3, there is between 2 and 3 mol of Cl atoms (22.4 liters provides 1 mole). Where mass is given, the molar mass must be determined (or at least approximated). Eighty grams of ClF (molar mass: 35 + 19 = 54) contains more than 1 but less than 2 mol Cl atoms; 80 grams of ClO_2 (molar mass: 35 + 16 + 16 = 67) contains slightly more than 1 mol of Cl atoms. Choice (B) at 3 mol Cl atoms is the greatest.

The correct choice is (B).

54. Calculation of exact percent oxygen by mass is not needed since the question asks for "greatest". It is most efficient to identify a constant amount (mass or moles) of nitrogen for each compound, then compare the corresponding amounts of oxygen. When 2 mol N is chosen, choice (A) becomes N_2O_2 and choice (B) becomes N_2O_4. Thus, it is apparent that N_2O_5 offers the greatest percent (or amount) of oxygen by mass.

The correct choice is (E).

55. As with question 32, a good way to solve the "which expression" problems is to label the values provided, then use those labeled values in the appropriate quantitative relationship. In this case

$$15.0 \text{ g Na}_2\text{O}_2 \times \frac{1 \text{ mol Na}_2\text{O}_2}{78 \text{ g Na}_2\text{O}_2} \times \frac{1 \text{ mol O}_2}{2 \text{ mol Na}_2\text{O}_2} \times \frac{32 \text{ g O}_2}{1 \text{ mol O}_2}$$

as in choice (B). The other choices are various incorrect arrangements of information from the problem.

The correct choice is (B).

56. Addition of an equal volume of solution causes [HNO$_2$] to decrease to 0.5 M. Addition of NO$_2^-$ ions shifts the equilibrium to the left causing more H$^+$ to become bonded to NO$_2^-$, forming HNO$_2$ molecules. The effect of dilution on ionization is negligibly small compared to the addition of NO$_2^-$. Thus, the total number of ions, including Na$^+$, in solution increases and the percent of HNO$_2$ molecules available that are ionized decreases.

The correct choice is (A).

57. As more water is added to a solution of HNO$_2$, the equilibrium shifts to provide more ions in solution. Thus, the total number of ions increases and the percent of available HNO$_2$ molecules that are ionized increases.

The correct choice is (D).

58. With increasing ionization, [H$^+$] in solution increases and K_a increases. The functions, pH and pK_a, are negative log functions. When [H$^+$] increases, pH decreases. Similarly, when K_a increases, pK_a decreases.

The correct choice is (D).

59. BaF$_2$ dissolves according to the equation

$$\text{BaF}_{2(s)} \rightleftharpoons \text{Ba}^{2+}{}_{(aq)} + 2\text{F}^-{}_{(aq)} \qquad K_{sp} = [\text{Ba}^{2+}][\text{F}^-]^2$$

The molar solubility is given as 7×10^{-4}. Thus, in a saturated solution,

$$[\text{Ba}^{2+}] = 7 \times 10^{-4} \quad \text{and} \quad [\text{F}^-] = 2 \times 7 \times 10^{-4}$$

Substituting

$$K_{sp} = (7 \times 10^{-4})(2 \times 7 \times 10^{-4})^2 = (7 \times 10^{-4})(1.4 \times 10^{-3})^2$$

The correct choice is (D).

60. In a saturated solution

$$[\text{Ba}^{2+}][\text{SO}_4^{2-}] = 1 \times 10^{-10}$$

$$[\text{Ba}^{2+}] = [\text{SO}_4^{2-}] = 1 \times 10^{-5}$$

In order for $[\text{SO}_4^{2-}]$ to decrease to 5×10^{-10}, $[\text{Ba}^{2+}]$ must increase. From the K_{sp}

$$[\text{Ba}^{2+}] = \frac{1 \times 10^{-10}}{[\text{SO}_4^{2-}]} = \frac{1 \times 10^{-10}}{5 \times 10^{-10}} = 0.2$$

The amount of Ba^{2+} originally present in one liter is negligibly small compared to 0.2 mol needed. Therefore the amount to be added is more than 6×10^{-3} mol BaCl_2 (choice (E)). (In this problem, "negligibly small" (1×10^{-5} mol) means that 0.2 is nearly the same as $0.2 + .00001$ and, at one significant figure, they are, indeed, the same.)

The correct choice is (E).

61. Adding inert gas to a gas phase reaction at constant volume has no effect on the rate of reaction. In choice (B), "inert" means that no competing reaction or catalysis occurs. "Constant volume" specifies that no dilution occurs.

The correct choice is (B).

62. As time increases for any reaction, the concentration of reactants decreases; hence, the rate of reaction decreases. With no temperature change specified, the rate constant, k, for any reaction remains the same, no matter how much time has elapsed.

The correct choice is (A).

63. The rate law for a reaction includes only the reactant species up to and including the slow step. Intermediates are not included in rate laws. Thus, the rate law is given by

$$\text{RATE} = k[\text{NO}][\text{NO}][\text{H}_2] = k[\text{NO}]^2[\text{H}_2]$$

The correct choice is (B).

64. The overall reaction is given by the sum of all the steps in the mechanism.

$$NO_{(g)} + NO_{(g)} \rightarrow N_2O_{2(g)}$$

$$N_2O_{2(g)} + H_{2(g)} \rightarrow N_2O_{(g)} + H_2O_{(g)}$$

$$N_2O_{(g)} + H_{2(g)} \rightarrow N_{2(g)} + H_2O_{(g)}$$

Note that intermediates, $N_2O_{2(g)}$ and $N_2O_{(g)}$ do not appear in the overall reaction.

$$2NO_{(g)} + 2H_{2(g)} \rightarrow N_{2(g)} + 2H_2O_{(g)}$$

The correct choice is (B).

65. Since MnO_2 is not consumed, it must be a catalyst. Action as a surface catalyst explains the behavior.

The correct choice is (A).

66. In the dissolving process process described, the enthalpy change (ΔH) is positive (endothermic implies increasing enthalpy) and the entropy change (ΔS) is positive (increasing disorder). The dissolving of many salts illustrates such a process.

The correct choice is (D).

67. In general, reactions proceed at a relatively slow rate when strong bonds between atoms within molecules must be broken (choice (E)). Enthalpy change (choice (A)) during a reaction is not necessarily related to reaction rate. Low energy of activation, the presence of a catalyst and high concentration of reactants are associated with rapid reaction rates.

The correct choice is (E).

68. In general, systems exhibit an increase in entropy whenever the number of moles of particles in the condensed phases decreases and the number of moles of particles in gas phase increases or whenever melting takes place. Of the choices offered, only the conversion of $Mg_{(s)}$ and $O_{2(g)}$ to $MgO_{(s)}$ exhibits a decrease in entropy.

The correct choice is (D).

69. Consideration of le Chatelier's principle will give the correct answer. Each of the changes, removal of $H_{2(g)}$, addition of $H_2O_{(g)}$, increase temperature of the system, and increase total pressure of the system will shift the equilibrium to the right increasing the yield of $CO_{(g)}$. (Note that one mole of gas is converted to two moles of gas.) However, while increase in surface area of the carbon may have an effect on the time required to reach equilibrium, it will have no effect on the yield.

The correct choice is (E).

70. A decrease in entropy is associated with an increase in order within the sample. In the formation of a crystalline solid from a supersaturated solution (choice (E)), a highly ordered phase is produced. In each of the other choices, there is an increase in entropy (randomness or disorder).

The correct choice is (E).

71. After filling the buret to the zero mark, the worker should have drained some of the solution from the buret to fill the tip and then refilled to zero or taken a new starting reading. Since some of the NaOH solution was used to fill the tip (and not to neutralize the acid), the concentration of the acid will be reported too large. Statement III describes a mistake.

It is true that phenolphthalein does not change until [H$^+$] reaches approximately 10^{-9} and pH = 9. However, this is not an unsatisfactory indicator of the endpoint for a titration using a strong acid/strong base reaction. A very small quantity of the base from the buret – even a drop or two – will cause the pH to change by a large quantity at the point of neutralization moving beyond pH of 9 further into the basic range. Statement I does not describe a mistake.

The worker was assigned to find the concentration of the acid as originaly supplied, not after the dilution carried out in this procedure. That dilution will have no effect on the quantity of acid to be neutralized or on the original concentration. Statement II does not describe a mistake.

The correct choice is (C).

72. Ions of transition elements are the cations that are most likely to be found in colored solutions. In general, such appearance of color is associated with the partially filled d-orbitals found in transiiton elements. Note that zinc is often not included as a transition element since its d-sublevel is filled.

The correct choice is (C).

73. The active ingredient in chlorine bleach is NaClO, sodium hypochlorite. This compound is also used as a sanitizer for swimming pools. Table salt (NaCl), lye (NaOH) and sodium bicarbonate (NaHCO$_3$) are other common household substances. Sodium peroxide, Na$_2$O$_2$, is not a common household product.

The correct choice is (C).

74. Amino acids are organic molecules with the general formula

$$H_2N - \underset{\underset{H}{|}}{\overset{\overset{R}{|}}{C}} - COOH$$

where R refers to one of about 20 known substituents. Thus, every amino acid contains carbon, oxygen, hydrogen and nitrogen. Of the elements offered, only phosphorus is not found as an essential component of all amino acids.

The correct choice is (E).

75. Adding 0.030 mol NH_3 to excess acid as in response I or to excess base as in response II will cause little change in pH. In response I, a small portion of the acid will be neutralized but not enough to change the pH appreciably. Adding NH_3 to the base, as in response II, will not cause any appreciable increase in $[OH^-]$ since, with the $[OH^-]$ originally at 3.0 M, little additional ionization of NH_3 will occur. However, in the case of the solution of NaCl (response III), the pH is approximately 7. The addition of NH_3 will produce enough OH^- ions to move the pH well into the basic range. The original solution could not have been NaCl.

The correct choice is (C).

Sample Examination I   143

Section II - Free-Response

See general directions and list of *Equations and Constants* on pages ii-iv.

Section II   Total Time – 90 Minutes
(Multiple-Choice Questions are found in Section I.)

Part A: Question 76
and
Question 77 or Question 78
Time: 40 Minutes

Access to calculators, periodic table, lists of standard reduction potentials,
and *Equations and Constants*

(2000 Examination directions) Clearly show the method used and steps involved in arriving at your answers. It is to your advantage to do this, because you may earn partial credit if you do and you will receive little or no credit if you do not. Attention should be paid to significant figures. Be sure to write all your answers to the questions on the lined pages following each question in the booklet with the pink cover. Do not write your answers on the green insert.

76. <u>Overall strategy</u>: Recognize that this system represents the ionization of a weak acid. A relatively small fraction of the dissolved acid molecules are dissociated into ions. The mass action expression, when set equal to the equilibrium constant, gives the quantitative relationship between concentrations of molecules and ions at equilibrium.

   (A)   <u>Strategy</u>: Substitute the known values in the mass action expression as above. The equilibrium (ionization) constant specifies the quantitative relationship.

   $$K_a = 4.0 \times 10^{-4} = \frac{[H^+][NO_2^-]}{[HNO_2]}$$

   $[H^+] = [NO_2] = x$; $[HNO_2] = 0.50 - x$ where x is negligibly small compared to 0.50, therefore, $[HNO_2] = 0.50$ can be justified as a reasonable approximation

   $$K_a = 4.0 \times 10^{-4} = \frac{x \cdot x}{0.50}$$

   $x^2 = 2.0 \times 10^{-4}$

   $x = 1.4 \times 10^{-2} = [H^+]$

   Use the definition of pH as found in the list of *Equations and Constants*.

   $pH = -\log [H^+] = -\log 1.4 \times 10^{-2} = 1.85$

(B) <u>Strategy</u>: The percent ionization is given by the number of ions formed, expressed as a fraction of the number of molecules available to ionize. The number of molecules dissolved in 1.0 liter of 0.50 M solution of HNO_2 is 0.50 mol. As calculated above, the number of H^+ ions present is equal to the number of dissolved molecules that have ionized. The fraction below gives the percent ionization.

$$\frac{0.014}{0.50} = 0.028 \times 100 = 2.8\%$$

(C) <u>Strategy</u>: Addition of a strong acid to a solution of a weak acid increases the number of collisions between hydrated protons and the anion of the weak acid. This favors the formation of more molecules of the weak acid, i.e. the reverse of the ionization reaction. A solution of 1.0 M HCl is nearly 100% ionized into H^+ and Cl^- ions. Addition of $HCl_{(aq)}$ to $HNO_{2(aq)}$ will shift the ionization equilibrium "to the left" to favor formation of HNO_2 molecules. After mixing the two solutions, the volume becomes 0.100 L. The mass action expression above applies to the new equilibrium.

0.020 L of 1.0 M HCl contains 0.020 mol H^+

0.080 L of 0.50 M HNO_2 contains 0.040 mol HNO_2

$$[H^+] = \frac{0.020 \text{ mol}}{0.100 \text{ L}} = 0.20; \quad [HNO_2] = \frac{0.040 \text{ mol}}{0.100 \text{ L}} = 0.40$$

Substituting known values in the mass action expression:

$$K_a = 4.0 \times 10^{-4} = \frac{[H^+][NO_2^-]}{[HNO_2]}$$

$$K_a = 4.0 \times 10^{-4} = \frac{0.20\,[NO_2^-]}{0.40}$$

$$[NO_2^-] = 8.0 \times 10^{-4}$$

Another way to think about this equilibrium system:

- What $[NO_2^-]$ is present at equilibrium when $[H^+] = 0.20$ and $[HNO_2] = 0.40$?

(D) <u>Strategy</u>: Consider the chemical reaction associated with the preparation of a buffer as described in the problem. When a buffer is prepared by adding OH^- to the solution of a weak acid, each OH^- ion accepts a proton from an acid molecule. Due to this donation of protons, for every mole of OH^- added, one mole of the conjugate base is formed. In this case, one mol NO_2^- ion is formed for each mol of OH^- added.

The pH of the solution is specified as 3.25. The unknown $[H^+]$ can be calculated from the definition of pH as found in the list of *Equations and Constants*.

$$pH = -\log[H^+]$$

$$[H^+] = 10^{-3.25} = 5.6 \times 10^{-4}$$

The chart below helps to summarize the chemical reaction (proton transfer) where x = mol OH^- added in 0.10 liter of solution.

	HNO_2	H^+	NO_2^-
available	0.050	—	—
Δ mol	$-x$	—	$+x$
mol at equil.	$0.050 - x$		x
equil. [ ]	$\dfrac{0.050 - x}{0.100}$	5.6×10^{-4} (given)	$\dfrac{x}{0.100}$

Use these terms in the mass action expression:

$$K_a = 4.0 \times 10^{-4} = \frac{[H^+][NO_2^-]}{[HNO_2]}$$

$$[H^+] = 5.6 \times 10^{-4}; \quad [HNO_2] = \frac{0.050 - x}{0.100 \text{ L}}; \quad [NO_2^-] = \frac{x}{0.100 \text{ L}}$$

$$K_a = 4.0 \times 10^{-4} = \frac{5.6 \times 10^{-4} \cdot \dfrac{x}{0.100}}{\dfrac{0.050 - x}{0.100}}$$

$$\frac{4.0 \times 10^{-4}}{5.6 \times 10^{-4}} = \frac{x}{0.050 - x}$$

$$0.714 = \frac{x}{0.050 - x}$$

$$x = 0.0357 - 0.714x$$

$$1.71x = 0.0357$$

$$x = 0.021 \text{ mol NaOH to be added}$$

146 Sample Examination I

Answer either question 77 or question 78 below.
(2000 examination directions) Only one of these two questions will be graded. If you start both questions, be sure to cross out the question you do not want graded.

The Section II score weighting for the question that you choose is 20 percent.

77. Overall strategy: As with all electrochemical devices, oxidation occurs at the anode. In an electrochemical cell, electrons flow through the external circuit from anode to cathode. Conservation of charge is maintained by ion migration through the porous barrier.

   (A) Strategy: Note that oxidation occurs at the anode for every electrochemical cell. Refer to the list of half-reactions to obtain those that pertain to this electrochemical cell.

   $$\text{anode}: \quad Cd^0 \rightarrow Cd^{2+} + 2e^-$$
   $$\text{cathode}: \quad Ag^+ + e^- \rightarrow Ag^0$$

   (B) Strategy: Use the half-reactions from above. Add the E° values for each half-reaction to obtain the overall E° value. Even though the reduction half-reaction is multiplied by 2, the value for E° is not. Note that the tendency of one Ag^+ to gain one e^- is the same as the tendency of two Ag^+ to gain two e^-.

   $$Cd^0 \rightarrow Cd^{2+} + 2e^- \quad\quad E^0 = 0.40 \text{ volts}$$
   $$2(Ag^+ + e^- \rightarrow Ag^0) \quad\quad E^0 = 0.80 \text{ volts}$$
   $$\mathbf{Cd^0 + 2Ag^+ \rightarrow Cd^{2+} + 2Ag^0} \quad E^0 = 1.20 \text{ volts (overall reaction)}$$

   (C) Strategy: Find the equation from the list of *Equations and Constants* that gives the relationship between E° and K_{eq}.

   $$\log K_{eq} = \frac{nE^\circ}{0.0592}$$

   $$\log K_{eq} = \frac{2 \times 1.20}{0.0592} = 40.54$$

   $$K_{eq} = 10^{40.54} = \mathbf{3.47 \times 10^{40}}$$

(D) Strategy: Find the equation from the list of *Equations and Constants* that gives the relationship between E at non-standard conditions and E°. The relationship is often referred to as the Nernst Equation.

$$E_{cell} = E°_{cell} - \frac{RT}{nF} \ln Q = E°_{cell} - \frac{0.0592}{n} \log Q$$

$$E_{cell} = 1.20 \text{ volts} - \frac{0.0592}{n} \log \frac{[Cd^{2+}]}{[Ag^+]^2} = 1.20 \text{ volts} - \frac{0.0592}{2} \log \frac{(1.0)}{(1.6 \times 10^{-10})^2}$$

$$E_{cell} = 1.20 \text{ volts} - 0.58 \text{ volts} = \mathbf{0.62 \text{ volts}}$$

Positive voltage is a measure of the net tendency of the forward reaction to occur. The lower voltage calculated above is consistent with a prediction based on Le Chatelier's principle, where decreased concentration of reactants [Ag$^+$] accounts for a decrease in tendency for the forward reaction to occur. This favoring of reactants corresponds to a decrease in voltage.

78. **Overall strategy:** In these separate samples of gases, no chemical change is under consideration. The problem addresses several comparisons of numbers of molecules, volume occupied and molecular velocity. Refer to the list of *Equations and Constants* to find applicable versions of the Ideal Gas Law and Graham's Law.

(A) **Strategy:** Calculate the number of sulfur atoms in each sample, then calculate the specified ratio where sulfur from H$_2$S is found in the numerator and sulfur from SO$_2$ in the denominator. This placement as numerator and denominator is the relationship stated in the problem.

$$10.0 \text{ g H}_2\text{S} \times \frac{1 \text{ mol H}_2\text{S}}{34.0 \text{ g H}_2\text{S}} \times \frac{1 \text{ mol S atoms}}{1 \text{ mol H}_2\text{S}} = 0.294 \text{ mol S atoms}$$

$$10.0 \text{ g SO}_2 \times \frac{1 \text{ mol SO}_2}{64.0 \text{ g SO}_2} \times \frac{1 \text{ mol S atoms}}{1 \text{ mol SO}_2} = 0.156 \text{ mol S atoms}$$

calculate the ratio $\dfrac{0.294 \text{ mol S atoms (in H}_2\text{S)}}{0.156 \text{ mol S atoms (in SO}_2)} = \mathbf{1.88}$

(B) **Strategy:** Use the Ideal Gas Law as found in the list of *Equations and Constants* to find volume of the gas at specified conditions.

$$V = \frac{0.294 \text{ mol H}_2\text{S} \times 0.0821 \text{ L} \cdot \text{atm} \cdot \text{mol}^{-1} \cdot \text{K}^{-1} \times 298 \text{ K}}{745 \text{ mm Hg} \times \dfrac{1 \text{ atm}}{760 \text{ mm Hg}}}$$

$$V = \mathbf{7.34 \text{ L}}$$

(C) **Strategy:** At the same temperatures, the kinetic energies of the two gases are the same. Use the definition of kinetic energy per molecule as found on the list of *Equations and Constants* to calculate the ratio of molecular velocities. This is one way of expressing Graham's Law.

$$\frac{1}{2} m_{\text{H}_2\text{S}} (v_{\text{H}_2\text{S}})^2 = \frac{1}{2} m_{\text{SO}_2} (v_{\text{SO}_2})^2$$

Solve for the assigned ratio and substitute known molecular masses. Note the inverse relationship.

$$\frac{(v_{\text{H}_2\text{S}})^2}{(v_{\text{SO}_2})^2} = \frac{\frac{1}{2} m_{\text{SO}_2}}{\frac{1}{2} m_{\text{H}_2\text{S}}} = \frac{64}{34}$$

$$\frac{(v_{\text{H}_2\text{S}})}{(v_{\text{SO}_2})} = \frac{\sqrt{64}}{\sqrt{34}} = \frac{\mathbf{1.37}}{\mathbf{1}}$$

(D) Strategy: This is an application Graham's Law. Total distance traveled is 100 cm; time of travel is the same for both species; ratio of velocities, hence distance traveled, is calculated above; the molecule with greater velocity (the lower mass molecule, H_2S) travels a greater portion of the 100 cm distance.

Total distance: $d_{H_2S} + d_{SO_2} = 100$ cm

Relationship between distances: $d_{H_2S} = 1.37 \, d_{SO_2}$

$1.37 \, d_{SO_2} + d_{SO_2} = 100$ cm

$2.37 \, d_{SO_2} = 100$ cm

$d_{SO_2} = \mathbf{42.2 \text{ cm}}$

Part B: Questions 79, 80, 81
and
Question 82 or Question 83
Time: 50 Minutes

Access to periodic table, lists of standard reduction potentials
and *Equations and Constants*
No access to calculators

Answer question 79 below. The Section II score weighting for this question is 15 percent.

79. <u>Overall strategy</u>: The list of ten reaction categories below is a useful method to organize information about chemical reactions. Note that some reactions may be classified in more than one category.

   <u>Redox</u> (Reactions that illustrate oxidation/reduction)
   1. Synthesis (Direct Combination)
   2. Decomposition (Analysis)
   3. Single Replacement
   4. Simple combustion (Burning)
   5. Redox by commonly-used "agents"

   <u>Non-redox</u> **(Reactions where no changes in oxidation numbers occur)**
   6. Double Replacement (often with precipitation or formation of water or gas)
   7. Qualitative Analysis (reactions associated with commonly used procedures)
   8. Acid-Base Reactions (Arrhenius, Bronsted-Lowry, Lewis)
   9. Complexation

   Organic Reactions (Reaction involving the compounds of carbon)
   10. Reactions that illustrate chemical properties of organic compounds

   ---

   (A) A zinc strip is placed in a solution of copper(II) chloride.

   Redox: single replacement **$Zn + Cu^{2+} \rightarrow Zn^{2+} + Cu$**

   (B) A piece of solid copper metal is covered with powdered sulfur in a crucible and heated until the sulfur melts around the copper.

   Redox: synthesis **$Cu + S \rightarrow Cu_2S$** (perhaps allow CuS)

   (C) Solid potassium chlorate is heated in a test tube.

   Redox: decomposition **$KClO_3 \rightarrow KCl + O_2$**

(D) Excess hydrochloric acid is added to a solution of sodium hydrogen sulfite.

Nonredox: acid-base $H^+ + HSO_3^- \rightarrow H_2O + SO_2$

(Note: H_2SO_3 is not generally accepted as a substance whose presence can be confirmed; H_2SO_3 probably not allowed.)

(E) A solution of mercury (I) nitrate is added to a solution of potassium chloride.

Non-redox: double replacement, precipitation $Hg_2^{2+} + Cl^- \rightarrow Hg_2Cl_2$

(F) A solution of excess 3M ammonia is added to a solution of chromium (III) nitrate.

Nonredox: complexation $Cr^{3+} + NH_3 \rightarrow Cr(NH_3)_6^{3+}$

("excess" implies other coordinations that include some H_2O are not likely to form)

(G) Excess sodium hydroxide pellets are added to an aqueous suspension of aluminum hydroxide.

Nonredox: acid-base reaction $Al(OH)_3 + NaOH \rightarrow AlO_2^- + H_2O$

or

$Al(OH)_3 + OH^- \rightarrow Al(OH)_4^-$

other species allowed such as $Al(OH)_6^{3-}$

illustrates amphoteric behavior of $Al(OH)_3$

(NaOH provided as non-dissociated solid; "excess" implies maximum proton donation to OH^-)

(H) Propene is added to a flask containing liquid bromine.

Organic: addition $C_3H_6 + Br_2 \rightarrow C_3H_6Br_2$

unsaturated hydrocarbon plus a halogen

(2000 Examination directions) Your responses to the rest of the questions in this part of the examination will be graded on the basis of the accuracy and relevance of the information cited. Explanations should be clear and well organized. Examples and equations may be included in your responses where approrpriate. Specific answers are preferable to broad, diffuse responses.

Answer both Question 80 and Question 81 below.
(2000 examination directions) Both questions will be graded.

The Section II score weighting for these questions is 30 percent (15 percent each).

80. Overall strategy: Refer to the Periodic Table. Locate each of the elements specified below in its family (group) and period.

   (A) Strategy: Recall that an oxidizing agent gains electrons and becomes reduced.

   Among the halogens, as atomic number increases, oxidizing strength decreases. Halogens act as oxidizing agents when they gain electrons in their outer energy levels. When the outer energy level is closer to the nucleus, the attraction for the added electron is greater. The smaller the atomic number, the closer the outer energy level is to the nucleus.

   (B) Strategy: Recall that a reducing agent loses electrons to become oxidized.

   Among the alkali metals, as atomic number increases, reducing strength increases. An alkali metal acts as a reducing agent when it loses an electron from its outer energy level. The greater the atomic number, the farther the outer energy level is from the nucleus. When the outer energy level is farther from the nucleus, the attraction between the nucleus and the outer electron is lower.

   (C) Strategy: The "best example" of an ionic solid is the compound in which the bond between the metal and the nometal has the greatest ionic character.

   Among the oxides of the elements of the Third Period, sodium oxide is the best example of an ionic solid. Of the elements in Period 3, Na, with the lowest ionization energy, loses its valence electron and becomes a positive ion most readily. Because of this, the bond between the sodium and oxygen will have the greatest ionic character. (Transfer of electron from metal to nonmetal is most nearly complete.)

(D) Strategy: When hydrides of metals dissolve in water, they act as proton acceptors to form molecules of $H_{2(g)}$. Hydrides of nonmetals, such as HCl, dissolve in water by donating protons to form the soluble H_3O^+ ion.

The hydride of sodium, NaH, is most likely to dissolve in water, accompanied by the formation of gas.

$2NaH_{(s)} + 2H_2O \rightarrow 2Na^+{}_{(aq)} + H_{2(g)} + 2OH^-{}_{(aq)}$

154 Sample Examination I

81. Overall strategy: The problem described is the dissolving of a very soluble salt in water. Because this is an exothermic process, energy is released and the temperature of the system increases as the dissolving proceeds. In the list of *Equations and Constants*, find the definitions of molarity (M) and molality (m) for the problems related to solution concentration.

   (A) Strategy: Apply the principle that energy is released when bonds form and energy is absorbed as bonds are broken.

   In the dissolving of $CaCl_2$, energy (lattice energy) is absorbed as ionic attractions are overcome between Ca^{2+} cations and Cl^- anions. Hydration of the ions occurs. Energy (hydration energy) is given off as the ions become hydrated by the formation of bonds between water molecules and the ions. In addition, a small amount of energy is required to separate the water molecules to provide space for the hydrating ions. Because the dissolving is a net exothermic process, more energy is released as bonds form than is absorbed as bonds are broken.

   (B) (1) Strategy: Use the definition of molarity (M).

   From the definition, determine that 0.50 mol $CaCl_2$ available must be dissolved in sufficient water to produce 0.50 L of 1.0 M solution. Obtain a volumetric flask or similar device about half-filled with water. Add the assigned quantity of solute, 0.50 mol $CaCl_2$. Add sufficient water to fill to the 500 mL mark. **The volume of solution produced is 500 mL.** Its mass will be something less than 555 grams because less than 500 mL of water is used.

   (2) Strategy: Use the definition of molality (m).

   From the definition, determine that 0.50 mol $CaCl_2$ available must be dissolved in 0.50 kg water to produce 0.555 kg of solution. Using a beaker and balance (or 500 mL volumetric flask, graduated cylinder or similar device) to measure 500 g (or 500 mL) water into a suitable vessel. Add the assigned quantity of solute, 0.50 mol $CaCl_2$ (55.5 g). **The mass of solution produced is 555 g.** Its volume will be something more than 500 mL since an amount of solute is added to 500 g (500 mL) of water.

   (C) Strategy: Dissolve $CaCl_2$ in water. Observe change in temperature.

   The mass of $CaCl_2$ (solute) and the mass of water (solvent) must be recorded. As the measured quantity of anhydrous $CaCl_2$ is dissolved in the measured quantity (mass) of water, the temperature change must be determined. The temperature of the solvent before dissolving and the temperature of the solution after dissolving must be recorded.

Answer either question 82 or question 83 below.
(2000 examination directions) Only one of these two questions will be graded. If you start both questions, be sure to cross out the question you do not want graded.

The Section II score weighting for the question that you choose is 20 percent.

82. <u>Overall strategy</u>: When a liquid hydrocarbon fuel burns in air or in oxygen, the products are usually water and carbon dioxide, both as gases. Such a reaction is exothermic – energy is released. This reaction is also accompanied by an increase in entropy because the products are in a more random or disordered state than the reactants. Refer to the list of *Equations and Constants* for the equations that give definitions of ΔS and ΔG.

   (A) <u>Strategy</u>: The reactants include one complex molecular substance in the liquid phase. The other reactant is in the gas phase.

   The sign of ΔS for this reaction is positive. All the products are relatively simple molecules in the gas phase. The reaction starts with 12.5 moles of total gas per mole of octane. As the reaction proceeds, the number of gas molecules becomes 17 per mole of original octane. This increase in the number of moles of gas accounts for a corresponding increase in entropy, that is, disorder or randomness.

   (B) <u>Strategy</u>: The reaction is specified as spontaneous at 298 kelvins. Negative values for ΔG are associated with all spontaneous reactions.

   The sign of ΔG for this reaction is negative. Because energy is released in this reaction, ΔH is known to be negative. Because entropy increases, ΔS is positive. All reactions with that set of thermodynamic parameters are spontaneous at all temperatures. This conclusion is also consistent with the relationship between these three parameters as specified in the equation $\Delta G = \Delta H - T\Delta S$, where ΔG must be negative because ΔH is negative and $|T\Delta H|$ is positive, where $|T\Delta H|$ refers to the absolute value of $T\Delta H$ (Note that Kelvin temperature is always a positive value. Therefore, the sign on $T\Delta S$ is always determined by the sign of ΔS.)

   (C) <u>Strategy</u>: When CO is produced rather than CO_2, less energy is released. Note the difference in the heat of formation of each oxide.

   The amount of energy released would decrease. For each mole of CO produced in place of CO_2, the energy difference is about 280 kJ; that is, about 280 kJ of energy is still stored in the reactants.

   (D) <u>Strategy</u>: Values for ΔH and ΔS are relatively constant over a wide range in temperature.

   The change in magnitude would be greatest for ΔG. At higher temperatures, the contribution of the entropy change, $T\Delta S$, to the value of ΔG as shown in the equation, $\Delta G = \Delta H - T\Delta S$, is increased.

83. <u>Overall strategy</u>: Reaction coordinate diagrams are used to describe energy changes as a reaction proceeds. The reaction coordinate axis (x-axis) is sometimes referred to as "time" or "progress of the reaction" which is directly proportional to time.

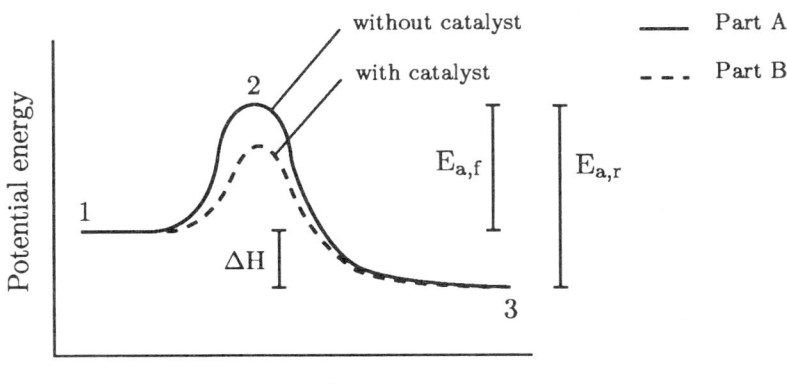

(A) <u>Strategy</u>: The relative position of the three components and corresponding intervals specified in part (A) should illustrate an exothermic reaction.

Potential energies identified above	Intervals identified above
1 – PE$_{reactants}$	ΔH
2 – PE$_{activated\ complex}$	E$_{a,f}$
3 – PE$_{product}$	E$_{a,r}$

(B) <u>Strategy</u>: On that same diagram, the relative position of the three components specified in part (A) should indicate a lower potential energy for the activated complex and the same values for potential energies of reactants and products; therefore, net heat of reaction is also the same.

(C) <u>Strategy</u>: When temperature increases, the rates of both forward and reverse reactions increase. However, the rate of the reaction with the higher activation energy increases more than the rate of the reaction with the lower activation energy.

When the temperature increases, the ratio, k$_f$/k$_r$ decreases. The rate constant for the reverse reaction, k$_r$, is associated with the reaction that has the higher energy of activation. Because of this, with the increase in temperature, both k$_f$ and k$_r$ increase, but k$_r$ increases more.

Sample Examination II

Section I - Multiple-Choice

1. Phosphorus is the element from this list whose oxide, P_4O_{10}, is a molecular solid at ordinary conditions. The oxide of silicon, SiO_2 (quartz), is a network solid. The oxides of nitrogen, N_2O, NO_2, etc. are gases at ordinary conditions. The oxide of magnesium, MgO, is an ionic solid. The oxides of bromine are not solid at ordinary conditions.

   The correct choice is (B).

2. Nitrogen is the element from this list with the lowest melting point. It is a gas at ordinary conditions. The other elements are liquid (Br_2) or solids (Si, P_4 and Mg) at ordinary conditions.

   The correct choice is (C).

3. Magnesium, a metal, is the element from this list that is the best conductor of electricity. Silicon is a semiconductor. The other elements are nonconductors.

   The correct choice is (D).

4. Phosphorus is the element from this list that is a molecular solid at ordinary conditions. Its formula is P_4. Silicon is a network solid. Nitrogen is a diatomic molecular gas. Magnesium is a metallic solid. Bromine is a molecular liquid.

   The correct choice is (B).

5. Magnesium is the element from this list whose oxide is an ionic solid. See question 1 for identification of other oxides.

   The correct choice is (D).

6. The formula for the covalently bonded molecule is CO_2. No other choices are molecules.

   The correct choice is (C).

7. The cation that exhibits sp^3 hybridization is NH_4^+ found in $(NH_4)_2CO_3$. Perchlorate, ClO_4^-, also exhibits sp^3 hybridization, but it is an anion.

   The correct choice is (A).

158   Sample Examination II

8. The anion that contains resonance bonds is CO_3^{2-}, found in $(NH_4)_2CO_3$.

   The correct choice is (A).

9. The only cation listed that will precipitate with PO_4^{3-} is Ca^{2+}, forming the insoluble salt, $Ca_3(PO_4)_2$.

   The correct choice is (D).

10. The only formula that contains an atom with the oxidation number of +7 is $NaClO_4$. The oxidation numbers in this formula are $\overset{+1\ +7\ -2}{NaClO_4}$

    The correct choice is (E).

Questions 11-16: The nature of any functional group in molecule determines the category.

11.
$$\begin{array}{c} | \quad | \quad | \\ -C-C-C- \\ | \quad | \quad | \\ OH \end{array}$$

The —OH group on a secondary carbon identifies this as a secondary alcohol. A secondary carbon atom is a carbon atom that is bonded to two other carbon atoms.

The correct choice is (A).

12.
$$\begin{array}{c} O \\ | \quad \| \quad | \quad | \\ -C-C-C-C- \\ | | \quad | \\ O \\ \| \end{array}$$

The functional group $-\overset{O}{\underset{\|}{C}}-$ identifies this as a ketone.

The correct choice is (D).

Sample Examination II 159

13.
$$-\overset{|}{\underset{|}{C}}-\overset{|}{\underset{|}{C}}-\overset{\overset{O}{\|}}{C}-OH$$

The functional group $-\overset{\overset{O}{\|}}{C}-OH$ identifies this as an organic acid.

The correct choice is (C).

14.
$$-\overset{|}{\underset{|}{C}}-\overset{|}{\underset{|}{C}}-\overset{|}{\underset{\underset{OH}{|}}{C}}-\overset{|}{\underset{|}{C}}-$$

As with the molecule in question 11, the −OH group on a secondary carbon identifies this as a secondary alcohol. A secondary carbon atom is a carbon atom that is bonded to two other carbon atoms.

The correct choice is (A).

15.
$$-\overset{|}{\underset{|}{C}}-\overset{\overset{O}{\|}}{C}-O-\overset{|}{\underset{|}{C}}-$$

The functional group $-\overset{\overset{O}{\|}}{C}-O-$ identifies this compound as an ester.

The correct choice is (E).

16.

[benzene ring]$-\overset{\overset{O}{\|}}{C}-OH$

As with the molecule in question 13, the functional group $-\overset{\overset{O}{\|}}{C}-OH$ identifies this compound as an organic acid.

The correct choice is (C).

17. Polarity of molecules is associated with nonsymmetrical distribution of electrons. Only PF_5 has a symmetrical distribution of its electron cloud (dsp^3 hybridization with trigonal bipyramidal shape) accounting for its nonpolar properties. H_2S is V-shaped (bent). PCl_3 and NH_3 are trigonal pyramidal. HNO_3 has a planar shape distorted by the presence of H^+.

The correct choice is (D).

18. In XeF_4, there are 12 electrons to be accommodated. See the Lewis structure below. The hybridization that accounts for this octahedral distribution is d^2sp^3.

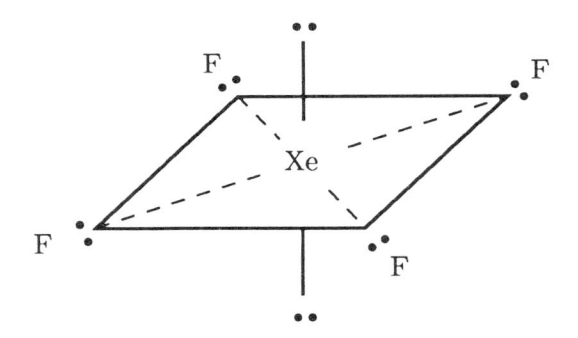

The correct choice is (E).

19. The colors of these pairs of solutions are given below.

   (A) $ZnSO_4$ and $CaCl_2$ (both colorless)

   (B) $CoCl_2$ and $CrCl_3$ (pink and blue)

   (C) K_2CrO_4 and $Na_2Cr_2O_7$ (yellow and orange)

   (D) $Ni(NO_3)_2$ and $CuBr_2$ (green and blue)

   (E) $AlCl_3$ and $KMnO_4$ (colorless and purple)

The only pair with the same color is choice (A) $ZnSO_4$ and $CaCl_2$.

The correct choice is (A).

20. The electron capacity of the third energy level is 18. This atom has only 8 electrons in that level. Thus, its third energy level is occupied but incomplete. The second principal energy level is filled with 8 electrons. Each of the s sublevels, 2s, 3s, and 4s is filled with 2 electrons.

The correct choice is (E).

21. As a Group 15 element, arsenic is most likely to have an oxidation number of +5. The only pair of formulas in which both members include arsenic with that oxidation number is $HAsO_3$ and $H_4As_2O_7$.

The correct choice is (E).

22. The formula for potassium hexachloroferrate(II) is K_4FeCl_6. With six Cl^- ion ligands attached to one Fe^{2+} (ferrous) ion, four K^+ ions are needed to maintain conservation of charge. The formula for the anion is $FeCl_6^{4-}$. Its charge is 4^-.

The correct choice is (D).

23. Of the five elements listed, two exhibit more than one oxidation state (ionic charge). Iron can be Fe^{2+} and Fe^{3+}. Tin can be Sn^{2+} and Sn^{4+}.

The correct choice is (B).

24. The bond angles associated with each hybridization are given below.

  (A) sp linear geometry – 180°

  (B) sp^2 trigonal planar geometry – 120°

  (C) sp^3 tetrahedral geometry – 109+°

  (D) dsp^3 trigonal bipyramidal geometry – 90° and 120°

  (E) d^2sp^3 octahedral geometry – 90°

The correct choice is (B).

25. According to Dalton's Law, in a mixture of gases, the total pressure is equal to the sum of the partial pressures. In equation form,

$$P_T = P_1 + P_2 + P_3 + \ldots$$

where P_T is the total pressure and each term, $P_1, P_2, P_3, \ldots$, is the partial pressure of one of the components of the mixture. The partial pressure for each gas can be obtained using the ideal gas law

$$P_1 = \frac{n_1 RT}{V}$$

For NO,

$$P = \frac{0.20 \times 0.0821 \times 273}{3} \text{ atm}$$

For NO$_2$,

$$P = \frac{0.10 \times 0.0821 \times 273}{3} \text{ atm}$$

For the mixture, the above equations can be solved separately and the results added. Or they can be added before solving as

$$P = \frac{(0.20 + 0.10) \times 0.0821 \times 273}{3} \text{ atm}$$

$$P = \frac{0.30 \times 0.0821 \times 273}{3} \text{ atm}$$

To locate the results in a "range of values", approximation arithmetic is satisfactory.

$$P = (0.10 \times \text{about } .08 \times \text{about } 300) \text{ atm}$$

$$P = (0.10 \times \text{about } 8 \times \text{about } 3) \text{ atm} = \text{about } 2.4 \text{ atm}$$

The correct choice is (A).

26. Of the descriptions of the system provided, only I and II are correct. The mixture contains 0.20 mol NO but only 0.10 mol NO$_2$. The partial pressure of NO is greater than the partial pressure of NO$_2$ because the number of molecules of NO is greater than the number of molecules of NO$_2$. Since the number of nitrogen atoms is 0.30 mol and the number of oxygen atoms is 0.40 mol, the third statement is not correct.

The correct choice is (D).

27. This equation should be completed based on the sum of the superscripts and the sum of the subscripts. The symbol for the alpha particle is $^4_2$He.

$$^{214}_{84}\text{Po} \rightarrow {}^4_2\text{He} + .?.$$

The superscript for the missing term is equal to 210 = (214 − 4). The subscript (atomic number) is equal to 82 = (84 − 2). Since the atomic number 82 matches the symbol, Pb, the missing term is $^{210}_{82}$Pb.

The correct choice is (B).

28. In any gas phase system, all the gas molecules do not travel at the same speed. Thus choice (A) is not true. All other statements are included in the kinetic molecular theory.

The correct choice is (A).

29. In the van der Waals equation of state for real gases

$$\left(P + \frac{n^2 a}{V^2}\right)(V - nb) = nRT$$

the actual volume of the molecules is the property that is most closely related to the value for the b coefficient. The a coefficient is most closely related to the forces of attraction between molecules. Note that, according to the kinetic molecular theory, ideal gas molecules do not occupy any space nor do they have any forces of attraction. Since real gases do occupy space and do have forces of attraction between molecules, the general gas law needs the minor "adjustments" to the pressure and volume terms as found in the van der Waals equation.

The correct choice is (B).

30. High vapor pressure is associated with weak molecular forces. High values for all of the other properties – viscosity, boiling point, melting point, critical temperature – are associated with strong molecular forces.

The correct choice is (D).

31. One sample of CO_2 is held at 10 atm and heated from −60°C to 30°C. A second sample of CO_2 is held at 1 atm and heated over the same range. In the first sample, melting occurs at some temperature greater than −56°C. Statement II is not true. In the second sample, since the sample is gas at the original conditions, no melting can occur. Statement I is true. The boiling point for the first sample is greater than the boiling point (actually, the sublimation temperature) for the second sample because the external pressure is greater for the first sample. Statement III is true.

The correct choice is (D).

32. If the pressure at the triple point is greater than 1 atm, then the liquid phase cannot exist until some pressure greater than 1 atm is provided. In other words, the only phase change that occurs at pressure less than 1 atm is sublimation. The other statements provided do not give information related to sublimation.

The correct choice is (A).

33. As any radionuclide decays, its rate of nuclear decay in grams per day decreases simply because, with each succeeding half-life period, half as many nuclei remain to undergo decay. However, the half-life period for any radionuclide is constant. As with all examples of first order kinetics, the half-life period is unrelated to the quantity of reactant present.

The correct choice is (D).

34. Since the formula mass of PH_3 is 34, its density is expected to be given by the expression $\frac{34 g}{22.4 L}$ at 1 atm and 273 K. At non-standard conditions, the volume is no longer 22.4 liters. To determine the density at nonstandard conditions, it is most efficient to "adjust" the volume of 22.4 liter to non-standard conditions. (Using this logic, it is not necessary to remember some principle for density at non-standard conditions.) The density expression becomes

$$\frac{34 \text{ g}}{22.4 \text{ L} \times \frac{760 \text{ mmHg}}{740 \text{ mmHg}} \times \frac{293 \text{ K}}{273 \text{ K}}}$$

Simplified as

$$\frac{34 \times 740 \times 273}{22.4 \times 760 \times 293}$$

The correct choice is (C).

35. The equation

$$\tfrac{1}{2}N_{2(g)} + 2H_{2(g)} + \tfrac{1}{2}Cl_{(g)} \rightarrow NH_4Cl_{(s)}$$

gives the reaction for the formation of $NH_4Cl_{(s)}$ from its elements in their standard states at 298 K and 1 atm of pressure. This corresponds to the definition for standard heat (or enthalpy) of formation.

The correct choice is (E).

36. Using the information given, the values of $\Delta H°$ for the dissolving process must be determined. The equation for dissolving is

$$NaCl_{(s)} \rightleftharpoons NaCl_{(aq)}$$

The value for $\Delta H°_{dissolve}$ is given by

$$\Delta H°_{dissolve} = \Delta H°_{f,\, NaCl_{(aq)}} - \Delta H°_{f,\, NaCl_{(s)}}$$

$$= -407 \text{ kJ/mol} - (-410) \text{ kJ/mol}$$

$$= +3 \text{ kJ/mol (slightly endothermic)}$$

Similarly the value for $\Delta G°_{dissolve}$ is given by

$$\Delta G°_{dissolve} = \Delta G°_{f,\, NaCl_{(aq)}} - \Delta G°_{f,\, NaCl_{(s)}}$$

$$= -393 \text{ kJ/mol} - (-384) \text{ kJ/mol}$$

$$= -9 \text{ kJ/mol (spontaneous at standard conditions)}$$

The correct choice is (A).

37. To determine the temperature effect on ΔG, the equation

$$\Delta G = \Delta H - T\Delta S$$

must be considered. Since ΔS is positive for the dissolving process, the term $-T\Delta S$ is negative and tends to increase spontaneity (negative values for ΔG). As $T\Delta S$ becomes larger, the absolute value of ΔG becomes larger causing ΔG to acquire a lower negative value.

The correct choice is (A).

38. Of the solutes listed, only CH₃OH is volatile. Its boiling point is less than that of water. At 0.10 m, the boiling point of the solution will be slightly less than that of pure water. The boiling points for the other solutions will be greater than 100°C with the boiling point of (NH₄)₃PO₄ being the highest since there will be 0.40 moles of dissolved particles per kg water.

The correct choice is (C).

39. The solution specified contains 75 g water/25 g H₂SO₄. Using this fact

$$600 \text{ g water} \times \frac{25 \text{ g H}_2\text{SO}_4}{75 \text{ g water}} = 200 \text{ g H}_2\text{SO}_4$$

The correct choice is (B).

40. In neutralization reactions such as this, 1 mol H₂SO₄ donates 2 mol H⁺. The unknown concentration of the H₂SO₄ solution is given by

$$\frac{0.015 \text{ L NaOH soln}}{0.030 \text{ L H}_2\text{SO}_4 \text{ soln}} \times \frac{0.30 \text{ mol NaOH}}{1 \text{ L NaOH soln}} \times \frac{1 \text{ mol H}_2\text{SO}_4}{2 \text{ mol NaOH}} = \frac{0.075 \text{ mol H}_2\text{SO}_4}{1 \text{ L H}_2\text{SO}_4 \text{ soln}}$$

The correct choice is (A).

41. In CaCO₃, the CO₃²⁻ ion accepts a proton to become soluble as HCO₃⁻

$$\text{CaCO}_{3(s)} + \text{H}_3\text{O}^+_{(aq)} \rightarrow \text{Ca}^{2+}_{(aq)} + \text{H}_2\text{O} + \text{HCO}_3^-_{(aq)}$$

The correct choice is (B).

42. Using a labeled expression to solve this problem

$$50 \text{ g C}_2\text{H}_5\text{OH} \times \frac{1 \text{ mol C}_2\text{H}_5\text{OH}}{46 \text{ g C}_2\text{H}_5\text{OH}} \times \frac{3 \text{ mol O}_2}{1 \text{ mol C}_2\text{H}_5\text{OH}} \times \frac{22.4 \text{ L O}_2 \text{ at 1 atm and 273 K}}{1 \text{ mol O}_2}$$

Simplified as

$$\frac{50 \times 3 \times 22.4}{46} \text{ L O}_2 \text{ (at 1 atm and 273 K)}$$

The correct choice is (E).

43. According to the Bronsted-Lowry theory of acid-base behavior, HPO_4^{2-} is classified as amphoteric because it can both accept and donate protons (choice E). The other statements are true but unrelated to amphoterism. Note that the terms amphoteric and amphiprotic are sometimes used interchangeably.

The correct choice is (E).

44. In this limiting reactant problem, it is efficient to ask two questions. If all the Al is consumed, what quantity of Cl_2 is required? If all the Cl_2 is consumed, what quantity of Al is required? Comparing these required amounts to the available amounts will give the necessary information to proceed to the final answer. If all the Al is consumed, then 0.60 mol Cl_2 is required. (The mole ratio is 2 mol Al/3 mol Cl_2.) If all the Cl_2 is consumed, then 0.50 mol Al is required. Comparing the required quantities to the available quantities leads to the conclusion that there is sufficient Cl_2 to consume all the Al but that there is insufficient Al to consume all the Cl_2. Some Cl_2 must remain uncombined. If 0.40 mol Al is consumed, then the maximum amount of $AlCl_3$ produced is 0.40 mol and 0.15 mol Cl_2 remains unreacted.

The correct choice is (B).

45. To meet the criterion for this answer, the total atomic mass of the halogen component must be less than the mass of the metal. Listing the atomic masses:

Ag	I	Ba	F_2	Ca	Cl_2	Fe	Br_2	Pb	Cl_2
108	127	137	19 + 19	40	35 + 35	56	80 + 80	207	35 + 35

wherever the mass of the halogen is less than the mass of the metal, the percent halogen by mass is less than 50%. Thus, no actual calculations are needed. The halogen contribution is less than 50% for BaF_2 and $PbCl_2$.

The correct choice is (B).

46. The amount of Cl^- ion available is given by

$$0.100 \text{ L} \times \frac{0.20 \text{ mol } Cl^-}{1 \text{ L NaCl soln}} + 0.100 \text{ L} \times \frac{0.20 \text{ mol } Cl^-}{1 \text{ L } CaCl_2 \text{ soln}}$$

The mixture contains 0.040 mol Cl^- in 200 mL of solution. The concentration of Cl^- is

$$\frac{0.040 \text{ mol}}{.200 \text{ L}} \quad \text{or} \quad \frac{0.20 \text{ mol}}{1 \text{ L}}$$

Note that, because both solutions had the same $[Cl^-]$ before mixing, no dilution occurs.

The correct choice is (C).

47. According to Raoult's Law

$$P_T = mf_A P°_A + mf_B P°_B + \ldots \left(\text{or } \mathcal{X}_A P°_A + \mathcal{X}_B P°_B + \ldots \right)$$

Substituting the known values from this problem

$$P_T = (0.20 \times 300 \text{ mmHg}) + (0.80 \times 500 \text{ mmHg})$$

The correct choice is (E).

48. The best net ionic reaction for the reaction between solid calcium sulfite and a solution of phosphoric acid is

$$3CaSO_3 + 2H_3PO_4 \rightarrow Ca_3(PO_4)_2 + 3H_2O + 3SO_2$$

even though no ions are explicitly represented in this equation. $CaSO_3$ is provided as a solid, hence not dissociated. H_3PO_4 is a weak acid and is best represented as a molecular substance. $Ca_3(PO_4)_2$ is a nearly insoluble solid. The double replacement product, H_2SO_3, (if, indeed, it is ever formed) breaks down immediately to H_2O and SO_2.

The correct choice is (E).

49. The half-reactions are

$$H_2S_{(aq)} + 3H_2O \rightarrow SO_3^{2-}{}_{(aq)} + 8H^+{}_{(aq)} + 6e^-$$

$$2IO_3^-{}_{(aq)} + 12H^+{}_{(aq)} + 10e^- \rightarrow I_{2(aq)} + 6H_2O$$

To maintain conservation of electrons, the necessary multipliers are 5 and 3

$$5\left(H_2S_{(aq)} + 3H_2O \rightarrow SO_3^{2-}{}_{(aq)} + 8H^+{}_{(aq)} + 6e^-\right)$$

$$3\left(2IO_3^-{}_{(aq)} + 12H^+{}_{(aq)} + 10e^- \rightarrow I_{2(aq)} + 6H_2O\right)$$

When added together and simplified, the overall reaction becomes

$$5H_2S_{(aq)} + 6IO_3^-{}_{(aq)} \rightarrow 3I_{2(aq)} + 5SO_3^{2-}{}_{(aq)} + 3H_2O + 4H^+{}_{(aq)}$$

and the coefficient for H^+ is 4.

The correct choice is (A).

50. From the list provided, the species that is least likely to behave as a Lewis base is BF$_3$. Since it has no unshared electron pairs on the central atom, it has no capacity to "donate" a share in a pair of electrons (or to accept a proton).

The correct choice is (C).

51. When the ionic species present are HPO$_4^{2-}$ and PO$_4^{3-}$, the equilibrium to be evaluated is

$$HPO_4^{2-} \rightleftharpoons PO_4^{3-} + H^+ \qquad pK_a = 12.3$$

$$K_a = \frac{[H^+][PO_4^{3-}]}{[HPO_4^{2-}]}$$

Since [HPO$_4^{2-}$] = [PO$_4^{3-}$], then [H$^+$] = K$_a$ and pH = pK$_a$ = 12.3

The correct choice is (E).

52. In this problem, the equilibrium pressures must be determined, then substituted into the correct mass action expression to determine the value for K$_p$.

	P$_{H_2}$	P$_{I_2}$	P$_{HI}$
available	1.25	1.75	—
change	−0.25	−0.25	+0.50
at equib	1.00	1.50	0.50

(information given in the problem stated in bold-faced type)

Based on the equation given, the mass action expression is

$$K_p = \frac{(P_{HI})^2}{(P_{H_2})(P_{I_2})}$$

With correct substitution, it becomes

$$K_p = \frac{(0.50)^2}{(1.00)(1.50)}$$

The correct choice is (D).

170 Sample Examination II

53. The HSO₄⁻ ion dissociates in water solution according to the equation

$$HSO_4^- \rightleftharpoons H^+ + SO_4^{2-}$$

Among the weak acids, it is relatively strong. At 0.10 M, its pH will be closest, among those listed, to 3. (If it were 100% ionized as a strong acid, its pH would be 1.)

The correct choice is (B).

54. Even though no value is given for K or ΔG, H₃O⁺ should be readily identified as a strong acid. Similarly, for the reverse reaction, NH₃ is unlikely to donate protons to water. In fact, NH₃ is a weak acceptor of protons from water. Thus, the equilibrium strongly favors the products. The proton transfer occurs because the H-NH₂ bond is **stronger** than the H-H₂O bond, not weaker as claimed in choice (C). The other statements are correct.

The correct choice is (C).

55. In this solubility equilibrium

$$K_{sp} = [Pb^{2+}][I^-]^2$$

If x is the molar solubility of PbI$_{2(s)}$, then $[Pb^{2+}] = x$ and $[I^-] = 2x$ (see dissociation equation).

$$6.5 \times 10^{-9} = (x)(2x)^2 = 4x^3$$

$$x^3 = \frac{6.5}{4} \times 10^{-9}$$

By approximation arithmetic

$$x = \sqrt[3]{\frac{6.5}{4}} \times \sqrt[3]{10^{-9}}$$

$$x = \text{about 1 (and less than 2)} \times 10^{-3}$$

The correct choice is (B).

56. As specified by the formula Cr(NO₃)₃, the charge on Cr is 3⁺. Therefore 3 moles of electrons are needed to produce one mole of chromium metal. To produce 0.15 mol chromium metal from Cr³⁺ in water solution requires 0.45 mol of electrons; that is, 0.45 faradays. The concentration of Cr³⁺ does not affect the quantity of electricity required.

The correct choice is (D).

57.
$$Ag^+ + e^- \rightarrow Ag^0 \qquad E° = 0.80 \text{ volts}$$
$$Cd \rightarrow Cd^{2+} + 2e^- \qquad E° = 0.40 \text{ volts}$$

In order to determine the voltage for an electrochemical cell, the redox half-reactions are identified and their voltages added. In this case, the net E° value is given by 0.80 volts + 0.40 volts. Note that the cadmium half-reaction must be written as an oxidation half-reaction; thus the sign of its voltage becomes positive.

The correct choice is (A).

58. When the equilibrium constant for a redox reaction is large, the value for E° is positive and the value for $\Delta G°$ is negative. Both indicate a spontaneous reaction to form products from reactants at standard conditions.

The correct choice is (B).

59. The Nernst equation is used to determine voltage at non-standard concentrations.

$$E = E° - \frac{0.059}{6} \log Q = 0.90 \text{ v} - \frac{0.059}{6} \log \frac{[Al^{3+}]^2}{[Zn^{2+}]^3}$$

$$E = 0.90 \text{ v} - \frac{0.059}{6} \log \frac{[10^{-2}]^2}{[10^{-2}]^3}$$

$$E = 0.90 \text{ v} - \left(\frac{0.059}{6} \times 2\right) = 0.90 \text{ v} - 0.02 \text{ v}$$

The voltage decreases by about 0.02 volts. Confirm this by using le Chatelier's principle which predicts that the reaction will shift to favor reactants because the dilution effect is greater for the reactants.

The correct choice is (B).

60. Since there are more molecules present due to the addition of $H_{2(g)}$, the total pressure will increase. According to le Chatelier's principle, this addition of H_2 will shift the equilibrium to favor formation of products. Thus, the number of NH_3 molecules increases.

The correct choice is (A).

61. When a catalyst is added to a reaction system, a new mechanism with a new and lower energy of activation takes over. Thus, statement I is not correct. However, the enthalpy (heat) of reaction and free energy of reaction remain the same (Statements II and III).

The correct choice is (C).

62. In this equilibrium system, as with any equilibrium system

$$2NO_{(g)} + Cl_{2(g)} \rightleftharpoons 2NOCl_{(g)}$$

the concentration of all components, including NOCl remains constant (Statement I). Because they have the same coefficient in the balanced chemical equation, the rate of formation of NO is equal to the rate of loss of NOCl (Statement III). The rate of loss of Cl_2 is equal to half the rate of formation of NOCl since two mol of NOCl form for every one mol Cl_2 lost. Thus, statement II is not correct.

The correct choice is (C).

63. The correct overall reaction is obtained by adding the steps of the mechanism together and collecting similar terms.

$$Cl_{2(g)} \rightleftharpoons 2Cl_{(g)} \qquad \text{fast equilibrium}$$

$$Cl_{(g)} + CHCl_{3(g)} \rightarrow HCl_{(g)} + CCl_{3(g)} \qquad \text{slow}$$

$$CCl_{3(g)} + Cl_{(g)} \rightarrow CCl_{4(g)} \qquad \text{fast}$$

Added together

$$Cl_2 + Cl + CHCl_3 + CCl_3 + Cl \rightarrow 2Cl + HCl + CCl_3 + CCl_4$$

When the intermediates are cancelled out, the overall reaction becomes

$$Cl_{2(g)} + CHCl_{3(g)} \rightarrow HCl_{(g)} + CCl_{4(g)}$$

The correct choice is (B).

64. Referring to the slow step, then working backward through the mechanism will establish the rate law. From the slow step:

$$\text{RATE} = k_1[Cl][CHCl_3]$$

Since Cl is not a reactant, it cannot appear in the rate law. From the fast equilibrium in step one:

$$[Cl] = k_2[Cl_2]^{\frac{1}{2}}$$

Substituting in the rate law

$$\text{RATE} = k_1 \times k_2[Cl_2]^{\frac{1}{2}}[CHCl_3]$$

Or simply, since $k_1 \times k_2$ = some other k

$$\text{RATE} = k[Cl_2]^{\frac{1}{2}}[CHCl_3]$$

The correct choice is (C).

65. The K_{sp} values for these two salts have different formulas because these salts have different dissociation equations.

$$\text{For } ZnC_2O_4: \qquad K_{sp} = [Zn^{2+}][C_2O_4^{2-}] = 2.7 \times 10^{-8}$$

$$\text{For } PbF_2: \qquad K_{sp} = [Pb^{2+}][F^-]^2 = 2.7 \times 10^{-8}$$

Thus, the molar solubility of $ZnC_2O_4 = (2.7 \times 10^{-8})^{\frac{1}{2}}$, about 1.5×10^{-4}

while the molar solubility of PbF_2 (call it x) $= \left(\dfrac{2.7}{4} \times 10^{-8}\right)^{\frac{1}{3}}$

By estimation arithmetic

$$x = \sqrt[3]{\dfrac{27}{4}} \times \sqrt[3]{10^{-9}} = \sqrt[3]{\dfrac{27}{4}} \times 10^{-3}$$

$$= \text{a little less than } 2 \times 10^{-3}$$

Thus, the molar solubility of PbF_2 is greater.

The correct choice is (B).

66. In this equilibrium system (or any other system at equilibrium),

$$\Delta G = \text{zero}$$

$$\text{Rate}_{forward} = \text{Rate}_{reverse}$$

Therefore statements II and III are correct. The equilibrium constants, K_p and K_c for a gas system, are equal only when the number of moles of gas is the same for products as for reactants. Thus, statement I is not correct.

The correct choice is (D).

67. Determination of the rate law can be made from data for the initial rates of several trials of the same reaction. This requires the comparison of the original concentrations of reactants and the corresponding effects on the initial rate. Comparing trials I, II, and III shows that increase in rate is directly proportional to the pressure of H_2. Comparing trials IV, V and VI shows that increase in rate is a second order function of the pressure of NO; that is, the rate is proportional to $(P_{NO})^2$.

The correct choice is (D).

68. The worker needed 0.50 kg water, which was measured correctly. The worker needed 0.50 mol ethanol, 23 grams. By measuring 23 mL of ethanol, the worker appeared to assume that the density of ethanol is the same as that of water. The mass of 23 mL of ethanol will be about 18 g, much less than the assigned amount. The concentration of the resulting solution will be less than the assigned 1.0 molal.

    The correct choice is (E).

69. Using the principle below (Hess's Law)

    $$\Delta H° = \sum \Delta H°_{f,PROD} - \sum \Delta H°_{f,REACT}$$

    $$\Delta H° = \left(\left(4 \times (-400)\right) + \left(2 \times (-300)\right)\right) - \left(2 \times (200)\right)$$

    $$\Delta H° = -2600 \text{ kJ}$$

    Since the equation includes 2 mol ethyne,

    $$\Delta H°_{comb} = -1300 \text{ kJ/mol}$$

    The correct choice is (B).

70. Agricultural fertilizers most often include nitrogen, potassium and phosphorus compounds that are soluble on water. Of the substances listed, ammonium nitrate is used most often. Use of barium phosphate as a source of phosphorus would be unsuitable since barium, a heavy metal, is dangerous and expensive.

    The correct choice is (E).

71. When ammonium chloride dissolves in water, a spontaneous (ΔG negative) endothermic (ΔH positive) process occurs. Ammonium chloride is an ionic solid. When it dissolves in water, a more random (disordered) system results. ΔS is positive.

    The correct choice is (D).

72. This is a typical dehydration of a hydrated salt. During the heating process and unknown to the worker, some of the material being heated was accidentally spilled. This occurred during the part of the procedure where water was being removed. This loss of material will be included in the observations as if it were loss of water. Since it occurred after the mass of the hydrated salt was measured, it has no effect on that observation. The mass of the hydrated salt will be reported correctly. However, the mass of dehydrated salt will be reported too small since some of it was spilled. The mass of the spill will be included as mass of water lost. Thus, the percent water in the hydrated salt will be reported too large.

    The correct choice is (C).

73. $KMnO_4$ is a commonly used oxidizing agent. In acid solution, its reduction product is Mn^{2+}. The oxidation product of Fe^{2+} is Fe^{3+}.

The correct choice is (A).

74. The infamous barium enema contains a barium compound ($BaSO_4$) that blocks the passage of x-rays. When present in the intestinal tract, it helps to produce x-ray images that are more accurate and easier to interpret.

The correct choice is (A).

75. Arsenic is used in n-type semiconductors because it has five, rather than four, valence electrons. These electrons are available to provide for controllable transport of charge.

The correct choice is (A).

176 Sample Examination II

Section II - Free-Response

See general directions and list of *Equations and Constants* on pages ii-iv.

Section II Total Time – 90 Minutes
(Multiple-Choice Questions are found in Section I.)

Part A: Question 76
and
Question 77 or Question 78
Time: 40 Minutes

Access to calculators, periodic table, lists of standard reduction potentials,
and *Equations and Constants*

(2000 Examination directions) Clearly show the method used and steps involved in arriving at your answers. It is to your advantage to do this, because you may earn partial credit if you do and you will receive little or no credit if you do not. Attention should be paid to significant figures. Be sure to write all your answers to the questions on the lined pages following each question in the booklet with the pink cover. Do not write your answers on the green insert.

76. <u>Overall strategy</u>: Recognize that this system represents a homogeneous gas phase equilibrium. With K_p at a value less than 1.00, there is relatively little NO at equilibrium. The mass action expression set equal to the equilibrium constant, K_p, gives the quantitative relationship between reactants and products at equilibrium. Note that K_p calls for concentration of gases expressed in units of pressure.

(A) <u>Strategy</u>: The format of the mass action expression can be found on the list of *Equations and Constants* in the Oxidation-Reduction section as Q (the symbol sometimes used for the general mass action expression).

$$K_p = 0.050 = \frac{(P_{NO})^2}{P_{N_2} \cdot P_{O_2}}$$

(B) <u>Strategy</u>: Substitute the known values in the mass action action. Solve for the unknown pressure.

$$K_p = 0.050 = \frac{(P_{NO})^2}{0.25 \cdot 0.25}$$

$(P_{NO})^2 = 0.050 \times 0.25 \times 0.25 = 3.1 \times 10^{-3}$ (take square root of both sides of equation)

$(P_{NO}) = 5.6 \times 10^{-2}$ atm

(C) Strategy: Use the Ideal Gas Law and the value for R as found in the list of *Equations and Constants*.

$PV = nRT$, where $P = 5.6 \times 10^{-2}$ atm, $V = 2.5$ L,
$T = 2,200$ K $+ 273$ K $= 2,473$ K, and
$R = 0.0821$ L atm mol^{-1} K^{-1}

$$n = \frac{PV}{RT} = \frac{5.6 \times 10^{-2} \text{ atm} \times 2.5 \text{ L}}{0.0821 \text{ L atm mol}^{-1} \text{ K}^{-1} \times 2,473 \text{ K}} = 6.9 \times 10^{-4} \text{ mol}$$

(D) Strategy: When 0.040 atm NO$_{(g)}$ is removed, the equilibrium of the system shifts to favor the formation of some NO$_{(g)}$ to replace that which is removed. The changes in pressure are summarized in the table below. Based on the stoichiometry of this reaction, one mole of N$_2$ and one mole of O$_2$ are consumed for every two moles of NO produced. The partial pressures of the two reactant gases at equilibrium are equal and the number of moles of NO formed is equal to twice the number of moles of either gas consumed.

	P_{N_2}	P_{O_2}	P_{NO}
available	0.25	0.25	$0.016 (= 0.056 - 0.040)$
chg. due to rx	$-x$	$-x$	$+2x$
at equil.	$0.25 - x$	$0.25 - x$	$0.016 + 2x$

$$K_p = 0.050 = \frac{(P_{NO})^2}{P_{N_2} \cdot P_{O_2}}$$

$$K_p = 0.050 = \frac{(0.016 + 2x)^2}{(0.25 - x) \cdot (0.25 - x)}$$

$$0.050 = \frac{(0.016 + 2x)^2}{(0.25 - x) \cdot (0.25 - x)} \quad \text{(take square root of both sides of equation)}$$

$$0.22 = \frac{(0.016 + 2x)}{0.25 - x}$$

$$0.056 - 0.22x = 0.016 + 2x$$

$$2.22x = 0.040$$

$$x = 0.018 \text{ atm}$$

Answer either question 77 or question 78 below.
(2000 examination directions) Only one of these two questions will be graded. If you start both questions, be sure to cross out the question you do not want graded.

The Section II score weighting for the question that you choose is 20 percent.

77. Overall strategy: Unlike many problems about weak acids, this problem does not address principles of chemical equilibrium. The problem calls for understanding and applying principles of solution preparation and the implications of partial ionization.

   (A) Strategy: In the list of *Equations and Constants* provided, find definition of molality as moles solute/kilogram of solvent. The molar mass of HF is 20.0 g. Quantities available are 40.0g (2 moles) of HF as solute and 2.00 kg water as solvent.

   $$0.200 \text{ mol} \times \frac{20.0 \text{ g HF}}{1 \text{ mol HF}} = \mathbf{4.00 \text{ g HF}}$$

   $$0.200 \text{ mol HF} \times \frac{1 \text{ kg water}}{0.100 \text{ mol HF}} = \mathbf{2.00 \text{ kg water}}$$

   To prepare the solution, 0.200 mol HF is needed to dissolve in 2.0 kg water. All of the water is used and 1.8 mol HF remains as excess.

   (B) Strategy: Calculate molality of HF molecules in solution, then find moles HF in 2.00 kg solvent.

   $$m_{HF} = 0.100 - x = 0.100 - 0.008 = 0.092 \text{ mol HF/kg solvent}$$

   In 2.00 kg solvent, **0.184 mol HF molecules**

   (C) Strategy: Percent ionization is the fraction of HF molecules dissociated into H^+ and F^- ions.

   Per kg solvent, of 0.100 mol HF added to solution, 0.008 mol HF dissociated.

   $$\text{Percent ionization} = \frac{\text{mol HF dissociated}}{\text{mol HF dissolved}} \times 100$$

   $$= \frac{0.008 \text{ mol HF dissociated}}{0.100 \text{ mol HF dissolved}} \times 100 = \mathbf{8\%}$$

(D) <u>Strategy</u>: Use the molal freezing point depression constant, K_f, as found in the list of *Equations and Constants* to determine molality of all particles dissolved in the solution.

Note that K_f is given as 1.86 K kg mol^{-1}. K, here, refers to kelvins. The label kg mol^{-1} is the inverse of molality, moles solute per kilogram of solvent.

$$0.201 \text{ K} \times \frac{1 \text{ m}}{1.86 \text{ K}} = \mathbf{0.108 \text{ m}}$$

(E) <u>Strategy</u>: The molality of all dissolved particles is equal to the sum of the molalities of H$^+$ ions, F$^-$ ions and HF molecules.

$$m_{H^+} + m_{F^-} + m_{HF} = 0.108$$

Per kg solvent, let x = mol HF dissociated = mol H$^+$ formed = mol F$^-$ formed

thus, $0.100 - x = m_{HF}$

$$x + x + (0.100 - x) = 0.108$$

$$x = 0.008 \text{ m}$$

For F$^-$: 0.0080 m

For HF: $0.100 - 0.008 = 0.092$ m

180 Sample Examination II

78. Overall strategy: The information provided is useful in the determination of the missing value and other thermodynamics parameters. Refer to the list of *Equations and Constants* for relevant information.

   (A) Strategy: Complete combustion in oxygen results in the formation of CO_2 and H_2O.

   $$CH_3COOH + 2O_2 \rightarrow 2CO_2 + 2H_2O$$

   (B) Strategy: From the tables of *Equations and Constants* provided with the exam, note that

   $$\Delta S° = \sum S°_{products} - \sum S°_{reactants}$$

   Substitute known values of S° as provided; then calculate unknown value.

   $$\Delta S° = \left[2(S°_{CO_2}) + 2(S°_{H_2O})\right] - \left[S°_{CH_3COOH} + 2(S°_{O_2})\right]$$

   $$\Delta S° = \left[2(213.6) + 2(69.96)\right] J\,K^{-1} - \left[159.81 + 2(205.0)\right] J\,K^{-1}$$

   $$\Delta S° = 567.12\ J\,K^{-1} - 569.81\ J\,K^{-1} = \mathbf{-2.69\ J\,K^{-1}}$$

   (C) Strategy: From the tables of *Equations and Constants* provided with the exam, note that

   $$\Delta H° = \sum \Delta H°_{f,products} - \sum \Delta H°_{f,reactants} \quad \text{(often known as Hess's Law)}$$

   Substitute known values for $\Delta H°_f$ as provided; then calculate unknown value. Since this is a combustion reaction, its standard enthalpy of reaction is known as the standard heat of combustion for acetic acid.

   $$\Delta H° = \left[2(\Delta H°_{f,\,CO_2}) + 2(\Delta H°_{f,\,H_2O})\right] - \left[\Delta H°_{f,\,CH_3COOH} + 2(\Delta H°_{f,\,O_2})\right]$$

   $$-874.5\ kJ = \left[2(-393.5) + 2(-285.83)\right] kJ - \left[\Delta H°_{f,\,CH_3COOH} + 2(0)\right] kJ$$

   $$-874.5\ kJ + \Delta H°_{f,\,CH_3COOH} = \left[2(-393.5) + 2(-285.83)\right] kJ$$

   $$\Delta H°_{f,\,CH_3COOH} = 874.5\ kJ + \left[(-787.0) + (-571.66)\right] kJ = \mathbf{-484.2\ kJ}$$

(D) Strategy: From the tables of *Equations and Constants*, find the definition of Gibbs free energy change, $\Delta G°$.

$$\Delta G° = \Delta H° - T\Delta S°$$

which, for this combustion reaction has the form

$$\Delta G°_{comb} = \Delta H°_{comb} - T\Delta S°_{comb}$$

The value for $\Delta H°_{comb}$ is given and $\Delta S°_{comb}$ was calculated in part (B). Temperature is specified as 298 K. Substituting these values gives

$$\Delta G°_{comb} = -874.5 \text{ kJ} - \left[298 \text{ K} \times (-2.69 \text{ J K}^{-1}) \times \frac{1 \text{ kJ}}{1,000 \text{ J}}\right]$$

$$\Delta G°_{comb} = -874.5 \text{ kJ} + 0.80 \text{ kJ}$$

$$\Delta G°_{comb} = \mathbf{-873.7 \text{ kJ}}$$

Part B: Questions 79, 80, 81
and
Question 82 or Question 83
Time: 50 Minutes

Access to periodic table, lists of standard reduction potentials
and *Equations and Constants*
No access to calculators

Answer question 79 below. The Section II score weighting for this question is 15 percent.

79. <u>Overall strategy</u>: The list of ten reaction categories below is a useful method to organize information about chemical reactions. Note that some reactions may be classified in more than one category.

    <u>Redox</u> **(Reactions that illustrate oxidation/reduction)**
    1. Synthesis (Direct Combination)
    2. Decomposition (Analysis)
    3. Single Replacement
    4. Simple combustion (Burning)
    5. Redox by commonly-used "agents"

    <u>Non-redox</u> **(Reactions where no changes in oxidation numbers occur)**
    6. Double Replacement (often with precipitation or formation of water or gas)
    7. Qualitative Analysis (reactions associated with commonly used procedures)
    8. Acid-Base Reactions (Arrhenius, Bronsted-Lowry, Lewis)
    9. Complexation

    Organic Reactions (Reaction involving the compounds of carbon)
    10. Reactions that illustrate chemical properties of organic compounds

    ---

    (A) Aluminum granules are placed in a warm solution of lead(II) nitrate.

    Redox: single replacement $Al + Pb^{2+} \rightarrow Al^{3+} + Pb$

    (B) Potassium metal is heated in a sample of chlorine gas.

    Redox: synthesis $K + Cl_2 \rightarrow KCl$

(C) A lump of manganese dioxide is added to a solution of hydrogen peroxide.

Redox: decomposition $H_2O_2 \xrightarrow{MnO_2} H_2O + O_2$

(Note: MnO_2 is a catalyst and not changed by this reaction)

(D) Excess 6M ammonia is added to a solution of zinc chloride.

Non-redox: complexation $Zn^{2+} + NH_3 \rightarrow Zn(NH_3)_4^{2+}$

(Excess implies full conversion to the complex ion.)

(E) Crystals of iron (II) sulfate are added to an acidified solution of potassium permanganate.

Redox: reducing agent commonly used
$FeSO_4 + MnO_4^- + H^+ \rightarrow Fe^{3+} + Mn^{2+} + SO_4^{2-} + H_2O$

(F) Hydrogen sulfide gas is burned in excess oxygen.

Redox: burning $H_2S + O_2 \rightarrow H_2O + SO_2$

(Excess implies that both products will be found as oxides.)

(G) Hydrogen sulfide gas is bubbled through a solution of manganese (II) chloride.

Nonredox: double replacement with precipitation $H_2S + Mn^{2+} \rightarrow MnS + H^+$

(H) Propane gas is heated in the presence of bromine vapor and a catalyst.

Organic: substitution $C_3H_8 + Br_2 \rightarrow C_3H_7Br + HBr$

(2000 Examination directions) Your responses to the rest of the questions in this part of the examination will be graded on the basis of the accuracy and relevance of the information cited. Explanations should be clear and well organized. Examples and equations may be included in your responses where approrpriate. Specific answers are preferable to broad, diffuse responses.

Answer both Question 80 and Question 81 below.
(2000 examination directions) Both questions will be graded.

The Section II score weighting for these questions is 30 percent (15 percent each).

80. Overall strategy: In general, Lewis electron dot structures are based on the distribution of the valence electrons of the bonded atoms and the application of the octet rule, wherever possible. An expanded "octet" allowing for five and six pairs of electrons can also be illustrated by Lewis dot structures. The valence shell electron pair repulsion model (VSEPR) in based upon choosing among several sets of hybrid atomic orbitals to account for the distribution of electron pairs. The resulting shapes are approximated by various polyhedrons such as the tetrahedron, the octahedron and several other similar structures. Note that all valence electrons need to be represented in the Lewis dot structure.

(A) Strategy: Note that P and S have five and six valence electrons, respectively.

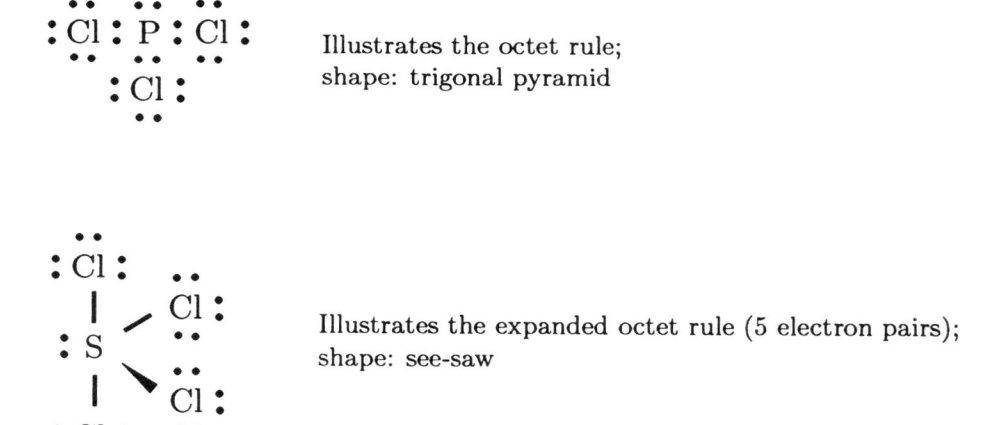

$:\ddot{C}l:\ddot{P}:\ddot{C}l:$
$\quad:\ddot{C}l:$

Illustrates the octet rule; shape: trigonal pyramid

$:\ddot{C}l:$
$\quad|\quad\nearrow\ddot{C}l:$
$:\ddot{S}$
$\quad|\quad\searrow\ddot{C}l:$
$:\ddot{C}l:$

Illustrates the expanded octet rule (5 electron pairs); shape: see-saw

(B) Strategy: Consider the implications of the octet rule and the role of expanded octets and odd-electron structure for each molecule.

PCl_3 - sp^3 hybrid orbitals with tetrahedral distribution of four electron pairs; three shared pairs and one unshared pair

SCl_4 - dsp^3 hybrid orbitals with trigonal bipyramidal distribution of five electron pairs sometimes called an expanded octet; four shared pairs and one unshared pair

(C) <u>Strategy</u>: Note that nitrogen has five valence electrons and oxygen has six. These 17 electrons cannot be arranged to meet the octet rule. NO₂ is sometimes known as an "odd-electron molecule". (NO is another example.) Sulfur has six valence electrons. In order to form covalent bonds with each of six fluorine atoms, six shared pairs of electrons must be included. This arrangement is sometimes called an expanded octet.

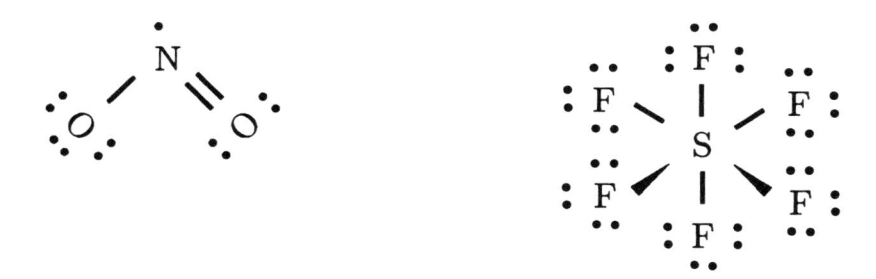

81. **Overall strategy:** When NaOH is added to CH_3COOH, the reaction

$$NaOH + CH_3COOH \rightarrow NaCH_3COO + H_2O$$

occurs. In net ionic form the equation becomes

$$OH^- + CH_3COOH \rightarrow CH_3COO^- + H_2O$$

Neutralization results when one mole NaOH has been added for every one mole of CH_3COOH present. Note that one product is CH_3COO^-, the conjugate base of CH_3COOH. As a relatively strong base, CH_3COO^- undergoes hydrolysis by accepting protons from water to form a basic solution.

(A) **Strategy:** In pH titration curve, the volume of $OH^-_{(aq)}$ added is plotted the x-axis shows and the corresponding pH values registered on the y-axis.

When a strong base is titrated against a weak acid, the pH of the reaction mixture begins in the acid range. As proton transfer occurs, the reaction mixture becomes less acid and the pH rises. At neutralization there is a rapid rise in pH. After neutralization occurs, addition of more base causes the pH of the solution to become constant in the basic range well above the value of 7.

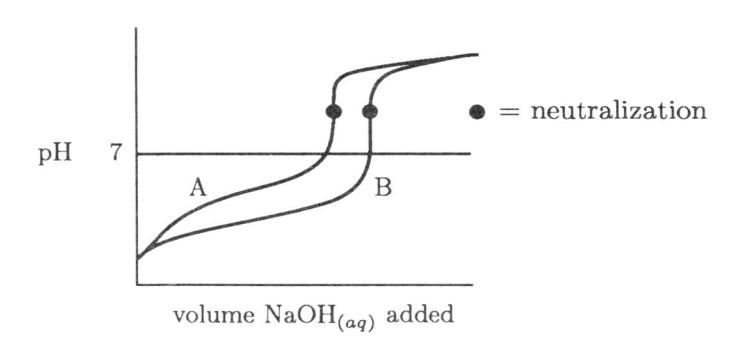

(B) **Strategy:** Recognize that neutralization of an additional amount of CH_3COOH calls for additional base. The pH at neutralization is not affected.

See curve labeled (B) above. Because $[CH_3COO^-]$ is the same, the pH value at neutralization is also the same.

(C) **Strategy:** CH_3COO^- is a product of this neutralization reaction as shown in equation above.

As the neutralization reaction proceeds, $[CH_3COO^-]$ increases. One mole of CH_3COO^- is produced for every mole of CH_3COOH neutralized.

(D) Strategy: For a neutralization reaction, the indicator must be chosen such that the pH range for its color change includes the pH at which neutralization occurs.

Methyl red is not suitable as an indicator for the neutralization of CH_3COOH by NaOH. This neutralization occurs when pH is greater than 7. One product of the neutralization of CH_3COOH is the CH_3COO^- ion. This anion undergoes hydolysis in water producing solutions that are basic according to the equilibrium reaction below:

$$CH_3COO^- + H_2O \rightleftharpoons CH_3COOH + OH^-$$

This accounts for the pH at neutralization to have a value greater than 7. The color of methyl red would change before neutralization had occurred.

Answer either question 82 or question 83 below.
(2000 examination directions) Only one of these two questions will be graded. If you start both questions, be sure to cross out the question you do not want graded.

The Section II score weighting for the question that you choose is 20 percent.

82. <u>Overall strategy</u>: According to the collision theory of reaction kinetics, a chemical reaction occurs when the reacting particles collide with sufficient energy to meet the energy of activation requirement, E_a, and with appropriate geometrical orientation to allow for the formation of the activated complex.

    (A) <u>Strategy</u>: With more molecules present at constant temperature and constant volume, $[H_2]$ increases.

    Rate of reaction increases. With higher concentration of H_2, there is greater frequency of collision between molecules of H_2 and I_2.

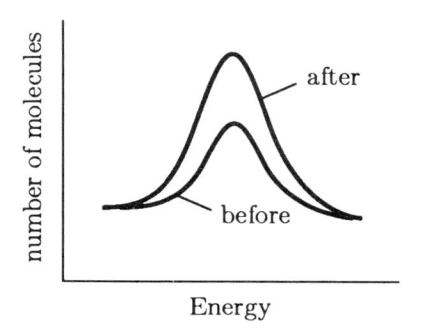

    (B) <u>Strategy</u>: Increase in volume results in a decrease in $[H_2]$.

    The rate of the reaction decreases. With lower concentration of H_2, there is a lower frequency of collisions between molecules of H_2 and I_2.

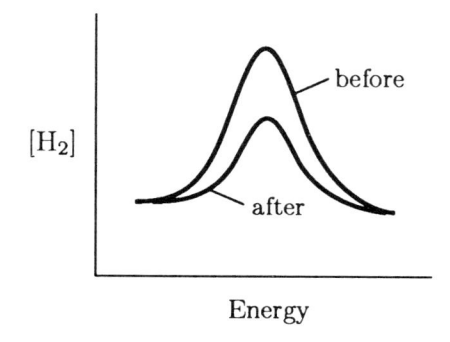

(C) <u>Strategy</u>: The diagram assigned is a reaction coordinate which shows progress of reaction (time) on the x-axis and potential energy on the y-axis. Reactants, activated complex and products are identified based upon progress of reaction and corresponding energy state. (The activated complex is an intermediate species in the reaction mechanism - a temporary structure formed when reactants first collide.)

The rate of the reaction increases. The addition of a catalyst provides a new reaction mechanism with a lower E_a requirement. With a lower E_a requirement, more molecules undergo chemical change upon collision.

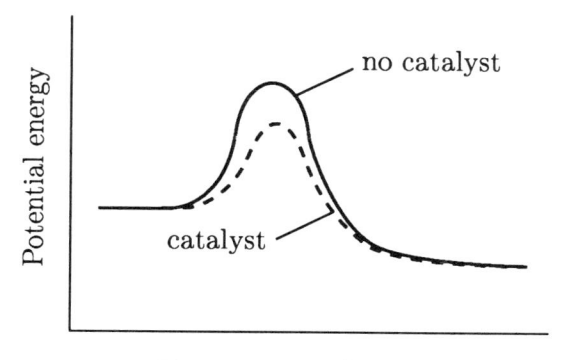

(D) <u>Strategy</u>: When temperature increases, the average kinetic energy of the molecules present increases. At higher kinetic energy, more molecules meet the E_a requirement.

The rate of the reaction increases. The number of molecules (area under the curve) remains constant. However, the number of molecules with energy greater than the E_a requirement increases causing the rate of reaction to increase.

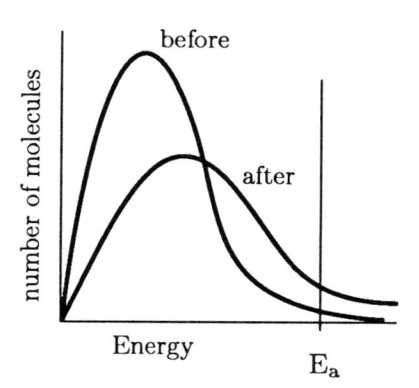

83. **Overall strategy:** Many properties are related to structure of the atom and corresponding location on the Periodic Table. Find potassium as the alkali metal (Group 1) in the fourth period.

   (A) **Strategy:** The nucleus of the K atom has 19 protons. The nucleus of Zn has 30 protons. The electrons by energy level are

   K: 2 8 8 1
   Zn: 2 8 18 2

   For both atoms, the outer electrons are in the fourth energy level. However, zinc has more protons, hence greater force of attraction for the valence electrons. Its electron cloud is pulled closer to the nucleus. The radius of the electron cloud of zinc is smaller.

   (B) **Strategy:** See electrons by energy level as above.

   The radius of the K^+ ion is smaller than the radius of the $K°$ atom. When the K^+ ion is formed from the $K°$ atom, one electron is lost. No electrons remain in the original valence energy level. The effective radius of this structure has decreased. In addition, a "shielding effect" is established in which inner (kernel) energy levels decrease the attraction of the positive nucleus for the outer energy level. The outer energy level of the K^+ ion is the third energy level. The outer energy level of the $K°$ atom is the fourth energy level. In the $K°$ atom, the three inner energy levels "shield" the outer fourth energy level.

   (C) **Strategy:** Recognize that Cl^- and K^+ are isoelectronic; i.e. they have the same electron structure. When species have the same electron structure, the one with greater nuclear charge has the smaller radius.

   With fewer protons and the same number of electrons, the electron cloud of Cl^- is greater. Because the electron/proton ratio for Cl^- is lower, the force of attraction between the positive nucleus and the negative electron cloud is lower.

(D) Strategy: The second ionization energy is the energy required to remove the second outermost electron from an atom after the outermost (highest energy) electron has been removed. This can also be described as the energy required to remove the highest energy electron from a +1 ion. The electrons by energy level are

K: 2 8 8 1
Ca: 2 8 8 2

In potassium, the second outermost electron is found in an inner energy level, the third energy level. In calcium, the second outermost electron is in the valence (fourth) energy level. Because the outermost electron in the K^+ ion is closer to the nucleus than the outermost electron in Ca^+, the attractive force is stronger in potassium. Less energy is required to remove the electron from calcium.

Sample Examination III

Section I - Multiple-Choice

1. Addition of dilute $HNO_{3(aq)}$ to the unknown solution would cause its pH to decrease as described unless neutralization of the added acid occurs. If the unknown solution contained OH^-, the OH^- would neutralize the acid as it was added. The change in pH would not occur as described.

    The correct choice is (E).

2. Adding NaOH solution to NH_4^+ in warm water solution causes the production of $NH_{3(g)}$. Since the presence of $NH_{3(g)}$ was not observed, NH_4^+ must be absent.

    The correct choice is (D).

3. When Na_2CO_3 solution is added to another solution containing Ca^{2+}, a white precipitate of $CaCO_3$ forms. Since no such precipitate was formed, Ca^{2+} was absent.

    The correct choice is (C).

4. When $FeCl_3$ solution is added to another solution containing OH^-, a reddish-brown precipitate of $Fe(OH)_3$ forms. Since no such precipitate was formed, OH^- is not present.

    The correct choice is (E).

5. When $AgNO_3$ solution is added to another solution containing Br^-, a yellow precipitate of AgBr forms. Since no such precipitate was formed, Br^- is not present. Note that AgCl is white.

    The correct choice is (A).

6. The number of occupied orbitals in Fe^0 is 15, given by energy level as

    $$1(s) + 4(s+3p) + 9(s+3p+5d) + 1(s) = 15$$

    When Fe^0 loses 3 electrons to become Fe^{3+}, only the $4s$ orbital becomes unoccupied. The number of occupied orbitals becomes 14.

    The correct choice is (A).

7. The name, pentaamminechlorocobalt(III) chloride, calls for five (penta) ammonia (ammine) ligands, one chloride ion (chloro) ligand, a cobalt 3^+ ion (as central atom) and enough chloride ions to maintain conservation of charge. This matches the formula in choice (C), $[Co(NH_3)_5Cl]Cl_2$. None of the other choices matches any reasonable coordination compound.

    The correct choice is (C).

8. In the dissolving of solid $CaCl_2$ in water, bonds between Ca^{2+} and Cl^- ions are broken. These ions are attracted to the polar water molecules forming an ion-dipole bond.

    The correct choice is (A).

Sample Examination III   193

9. A good way to solve this "which expression" problem is to label the terms and information provided in the problem, then use them in the appropriate quantitative relationship. The relationship between $\Delta G°$ and $E°$ is

$$\Delta G° = -n\mathcal{F}E°$$

where n = moles of electron transferred $\mathcal{F}$ = the value of the faraday (96,500 coulombs per mole of electrons) and $E°$ = the voltage for the cell, in this case 1.03 volts (joule/coulomb). Substituting the labeled values

$$\Delta G° = -2 \text{ mol e}^- \times \frac{96,500 \text{ coul}}{1 \text{ mol e}^-} \times \frac{1.03 \text{ joule}}{\text{coul}}$$

$$\Delta G° = -2 \times 96,500 \times 1.03 \text{ joules}$$

The correct choice is (A).

10. When any additional quantity of the oxidation product is added at the same concentration, there is no effect on the voltage. No change in concentration occurs. The cell remains at standard conditions.

The correct choice is (E).

11. Increasing the amount or the surface area of any electrode has no effect on the voltage. Note that the concentration of a solid cannot be changed.

The correct choice is (E).

12. The purpose of the salt bridge is to provide a path for the migration of ions in order to maintain conservation of charge in each half-cell. Wire of inert material such as platinum permits the movement of electrons, not ions. Replacing the salt bridge with a platinum wire would simply break the circuit. The voltage would become zero.

The correct choice is (C).

13. Addition of 0.010 mol $AgNO_{3(s)}$ to the beaker on the right would cause the concentration of the oxidizing agent (Ag^+) to increase. Consideration of the overall reaction

$$2Ag^+ + Ni \rightleftharpoons 2Ag + Ni^{2+} \qquad E° = 1.03 \text{ volts}$$

in terms of le Chatelier's principle indicates that the system will shift to favor formation of products and that the voltage will increase.

The correct choice is (A).

14. These sets of quantum numbers differ only in the third member, the m or m_ℓ quantum number. A difference in these numbers refers to the difference in orbitals within the same energy level and sublevel. Thus, these electrons have the same energy but occupy different orbitals.

    The correct choice is (A).

15. For "approximate fractional distribution", estimation arithmetic is satisfactory. The three possible molar masses result from the following combinations.

Formula	molar mass (amu)		
$^{35}Cl^{79}Br$	114	$3/4 \times 1/2 = 3/8$ about 3/4 of the Cl is 35 amu about 1/2 of the Br is 79 amu	
$^{35}Cl^{81}Br$	116	$3/4 \times 1/2 = 3/8$ about 3/4 of the Cl is 35 amu about 1/2 of the Br is 81 amu	} These two } possible } combinations of } isotopes with
$^{37}Cl^{79}Br$	116	$1/4 \times 1/2 = 1/8$ about 1/4 of the Cl is 37 amu about 1/2 of the Br is 79 amu	} molar mass } of 116 account } for half of all the } ClBr molecules
$^{37}Cl^{81}Br$	118	$1/4 \times 1/2 = 1/8$ about 1/4 of the Cl is 37 amu about 1/2 of the Br is 81 amu	

    The correct choice is (C).

16. Within a group of elements on the periodic table, as atomic number increases, several trends can be noted and explained. The number of valence electrons remains the same because each successive member of a group has the same electron configuration in its outer energy level. (Statement I is not true.) The radius of the most common ion increases, due to an increase in the number of energy levels with each successive member of a group. (Statement II is true.) The ionization energy decreases because, with each successive member, the outer electrons are further from the nucleus and, therefore, are subject to weaker forces of attraction. (Statement III is not true.)

    The correct choice is (B).

17. The bent molecule, YO$_2$, is a polar molecule with stronger intermolecular forces. Thus, the values for all three properties will be greater for YO$_2$, since those greater values are associated with stronger forces of attraction.

    The correct choice is (E).

18. In general, the melting points of ionic solids are higher than the melting points of molecular solids because attractions between ions with opposite charge are stronger than the forces of attraction between molecules. Note that in the melting of a molecular solid, the molecule itself is not separated into smaller components. The molecules are simply separated slightly from each other and acquire increased potential energy.

    The correct choice is (D).

19. The structural formulas for C$_2$H$_4$Cl$_2$ and C$_2$H$_2$Cl$_2$ give the best description of the bonds in these molecules.

$$\text{Cl} \overset{\sigma}{-} \underset{\underset{H}{|\sigma}}{\overset{\overset{H}{|\sigma}}{C}} \overset{\sigma}{-} \underset{\underset{H}{|\sigma}}{\overset{\overset{H}{|\sigma}}{C}} \overset{\sigma}{-} \text{Cl} \qquad \text{Cl} \overset{\sigma}{-} \underset{}{\overset{\overset{H}{|\sigma}}{C}} \overset{\sigma}{\underset{\pi}{=}} \underset{}{\overset{\overset{H}{|\sigma}}{C}} \overset{\sigma}{-} \text{Cl}$$

The molecule of C$_2$H$_2$Cl$_2$ contains two fewer *sigma* bonds, one more *pi* bond, but only one less shared pair of electrons.

The correct choice is (C).

20. The Lewis structure for PF$_3$ illustrates the octet rule.

$$\overset{\text{F}}{\underset{\text{F}}{\overset{|}{\underset{|}{\ddot{\text{P}} - \text{F}}}}}$$

With four valence shell electron pairs including three shared pairs, the electron distribution is tetrahedral and the molecular shape trigonal pyramidal.

The correct choice is (C).

Sample Examination III

21. The formulas for the five choices are given below.

    (A) potassium permanganate – $KMnO_4$
    (B) potassium acetate – KCH_3COO (or $KC_2H_3O_2$)
    (C) potassium oxalate – $K_2C_2O_4$
    (D) potassium perchlorate – $KClO_4$
    (E) potassium selenate – K_2SeO_4

    Only one, potassium acetate, has four different elements; the others have three different elements.

    The correct choice is (B).

22. An increase in the mean free path for molecules in a sample of gas calls for an increase in the space available to the gas molecules; that is, an increase in volume. Choices (A) and (B) specify constant volume. Increasing density (choice (C)) and increasing pressure (choice (E)) at constant temperature, can only be accomplished by decreasing the volume. Increasing temperature at constant temperature (choice (D)) can occur only when the volume increases. Thus, only choice (D) is correct. Note that the phrase "a sample of gas" implies that no molecules enter or leave the system; in effect, n (number of molecules) is constant.

    The correct choice is (D).

23. The molar mass of a gas is directly proportional to its density. At 1.50 g/L, the unknown gas is somewhat heavier than oxygen. Specifically

    $$\frac{32 \text{ g } O_2}{1 \text{ mol}} \times \frac{1.50 \text{ g unknown/L}}{1.25 \text{ g } O_2/L}$$

    The correct choice is (B).

24. During the vaporization of a liquid at its normal boiling point, attractive **forces between molecules** in the liquid are overcome as potential energy increases. The phrase "normal boiling point" confirms the condition that constant temperature (hence, average kinetic energy) is maintained. Note that bonds between atoms within molecules are not broken during vaporization at the normal boiling point.

    The correct choice is (E).

25. A p-type semiconductor permits transport of charge by providing spaces for movement of valence electrons. The valence shell of gallium has one less electron – hence a space – than the valence shell of silicon. Silicon with some gallium added is a p-type semiconductor.

    The correct choice is (C).

26. In a manner similar to question 29, the concentration of a solution that is 0.25 mole fraction in ethanol can be expressed

as
$$\frac{0.25 \text{ mol solute (ethanol)}}{1 \text{ mol}\bigl(\text{solute (ethanol)} + \text{solvent (water)}\bigr)}$$

or
$$\frac{0.25 \text{ mol solute (ethanol)}}{0.75 \text{ mol solvent (water)}}$$

To determine the number of moles of water needed

$$20 \text{ mol ethanol} \times \frac{0.75 \text{ mol water}}{0.25 \text{ mol ethanol}} = 60 \text{ mol water}$$

The correct choice is (C).

27. Since the dissolving of MX occurs, the value for ΔG must be negative ($\Delta G < 0$). From the relationship

$$\Delta G = \Delta H - T\Delta S$$

when ΔG is negative and ΔH is positive, $|T\Delta S|$ must be greater than ΔH $\bigl(|T\Delta S| > \Delta H\bigr)$.

The correct choice is (A).

28. To determine the number of moles of hemimellitic acid

$$0.420 \text{ g} \times \frac{1 \text{ mol}}{210 \text{ g}} = 0.0020 \text{ mol hemimellitic acid}$$

To determine the number of moles of OH$^-$, hence number of moles of protons

$$0.020 \text{ L} \times \frac{0.300 \text{ mol}}{1 \text{ L}} = 0.0060 \text{ mol OH}^- \text{ or } 0.0060 \text{ mol protons}$$

Putting these two facts together

$$\frac{0.0060 \text{ mol protons}}{0.002 \text{ mol hemimellitic acid}}$$

gives 3 mol protons/(one) mol hemimellitic acid.

The correct choice is (B).

198 Sample Examination III

29. Note that 25% by mass CH₃OH is the same as 75% by mass water. The most direct solution is given below:

$$100 \text{ g CH}_3\text{OH} \times \frac{75 \text{ g water}}{25 \text{ g CH}_3\text{OH}} = 300 \text{ g water}$$

The correct choice is (D).

30. Of the compounds listed, all are liquid at ordinary conditions. However, glycerine, $C_3H_5(OH)_3$ has the lowest vapor pressure due to extensive hydrogen bonding creating strong forces of attraction between molecules.

The correct choice is (E).

31. In a sample of "wet" gas, saturated with water vapor, the number of molecules of each gas, water and nitrogen is proportional to the partial pressure of each. Water vapor "contributes" 355 mmHg of the total 740 mmHg at the specified temperature. Thus, the fraction of water vapor molecules is

$$\frac{355}{740}$$

The correct choice is (A).

32. The usual properties of metals, such as conductivity and malleability, are best explained by the model that places cations (positive ions) in fixed geometric postions (a crystal lattice) surrounded by a diffuse cloud of electrons.

The correct choice is (D).

33. Strictly speaking, an ideal gas can never be liquified since it has no forces of attraction between molecules. With no forces of attraction, it has no critical temperature, the temperature above which it cannot be liquified, no matter what pressure is applied. Only statement (A) is consistent with the principles of the kinetic molecular theory.

The correct choice is (A).

34. Resonance, that is the delocalization of *pi* electrons, helps to explain equally distributed electron density and equal bond energies in SO_2, NO_3^-, and CO_3^{2-}. Resonance also helps to explain the higher C–C bond energy, hence lower reactivity, in C_6H_6. It does not explain the absence of three valence electrons in Al^{3+}.

The correct choice is (C).

Sample Examination III   199

35. The structural formula for SF₆ below

```
      F
   F  |  F
    \ | /
      S
    / | \
   F  |  F
      F
```

does not illustrate the octet rule. In order to account for six bonding pairs, an expanded octet (now 6, rather than 4, pairs) of electrons is proposed with those bonding pairs at the six vertices of a regular octahedron.

The correct choice is (C).

36. The most efficient way to solve this problem is to write a nuclear equation.

$$^{253}_{99}\text{Es} + ^{4}_{2}\text{He} \rightarrow ^{1}_{0}\text{n} + \,^{?}_{?}.$$

Then using the subscript and superscript values to determine the missing term

$$^{253}_{99}\text{Es} + ^{4}_{2}\text{He} \rightarrow ^{1}_{0}\text{n} + ^{256}_{101}\text{Md}$$

The correct choice is (D).

37. Since $H_2O_{(g)}$ and $H_{2(g)}$ occupy the same vessel at the same conditions, they have the same volume and temperature. The source of $H_2O_{(g)}$ is the liquid water in contact with the $H_{2(g)}$. The partial pressure of $H_2O_{(g)}$ is very small (about 25 mmHg) compared to the total pressure of 745 mmHg. Since nearly all of the pressure is due to the $H_{2(g)}$ gas, the number of $H_{2(g)}$ molecules must be much greater than the number of $H_2O_{(g)}$ molecules. At the same temperature, lighter $H_{2(g)}$ molecules have greater average molecular velocity than heavier $H_2O_{(g)}$ molecules.

The correct choice is (B).

38. A Lewis acid accepts a share in a pair of electrons, sometimes forming a coordination compound with a transition metal cation and a ligand such as SCN^-, as in choice (A).

The correct choice is (A).

39. To get the mass remaining in each crucible after dehydration, assume 100 grams (or any other mass)

$$\text{A:} \quad 100 \text{ g hydrate} \times \frac{208 \text{ g BaCl}_2}{244 \text{ g hydrate}}$$

$$\text{B:} \quad 100 \text{ g hydrate} \times \frac{160 \text{ g CuSO}_4}{250 \text{ g hydrate}}$$

The ratio of these two values is

$$\frac{\dfrac{208 \text{ g BaCl}_2}{244 \text{ g hydrate}}}{\dfrac{160 \text{ g CuSO}_4}{250 \text{ g hydrate}}}$$

and since, $244 \approx 250$, the ratio is closest to

$$\frac{208}{160}$$

The correct choice is (C).

40. Like water, pure ammonia undergoes self-ionization, donating and accepting a proton between NH_3 molecules as shown in the equation

$$NH_3 + NH_3 \rightleftharpoons NH_4^+ + NH_2^-$$

The correct choice is (D).

41. Since the normal boiling points of CH_3OH and H_2O are 65°C and 100°C, respectively, they have the same vapor pressure (760 mmHg, 1 atm) at those temperatures. Statement II is true. At those same temperatures, their average molecular velocities will not be the same since the average molecular velocity of CH_3OH (the heavier molecule) at 65°C is lower than that of water at 65°C and the average molecular velocity of H_2O will be even greater at 100°C. Statement I is not true. Since CH_3OH boils at a lower temperature than H_2O, its intermolecular forces must be weaker. Therefore, its heat of vaporization is also lower. Statement III is not true.

The correct choice is (B).

42. An amphoteric substance acts as either acid or base, depending upon the other substances present. In this context, testing $Zn(OH)_2$ with NaOH and HCl would be the only method of those offered to demonstrate amphoterism.

The correct choice is (D).

43. In this mixing procedure, [Ca^{2+}] decreases because it is diluted with the addition of NaCl solution. Similarly, [Na$^+$] decreases because it is diluted with the addition of the CaCl$_2$ solution. However, [Cl$^-$] remains the same because it had the same original concentration in both solutions. No dilution effect occurred.

The correct choice is (B).

44. All of these choices contain S in the +6 oxidation state. In a water solution with pH of 13.0, [OH$^-$] = 0.10. In such a basic environment, all the proton donors, including H$_2$SO$_4$ and HSO$_4^-$, would have lost their protons, leaving SO$_4^{2-}$ as the only possible species present. SO$_3$ dissolved in water forms H$_2$SO$_4$. H$_2$S$_2$O$_7$ is known as fuming sulfuric acid and is sometimes represented as H$_2$SO$_4 \cdot$ SO$_3$.

The correct choice is (E).

45. In an electrolysis reaction, electrons are "pumped in" to the negative electrode and "taken out" at the positive electrode by the external power supply. Negative ions are attracted to the positive electrode. In this case, I$^-$ ions are oxidized to I$_2$ at the positive anode. I$_2$, in the presence of I$^-$ ions in water solution, is found as the dark brown ion, I$_3^-$.

The correct choice is (A).

46. It is not necessary to calculate the values for percent oxygen by mass for each compound. The most efficient way to identify the oxide of manganese that contains the greatest percent oxygen by mass is to determine the number of oxygen atoms present for the same number of manganese atoms in each compound. Since the largest number of Mn atoms is 3, it is convenient to represent each formula based on 3 Mn atoms as shown below.

(A) MnO can be represented as Mn$_3$O$_3$

(B) MnO$_2$ can be represented as Mn$_3$O$_6$

(C) MnO$_3$ can be represented as Mn$_3$O$_9$

(D) Mn$_2$O$_3$ can be represented as Mn$_3$O$_{4.5}$

(E) Mn$_3$O$_4$ can be represented as Mn$_3$O$_4$

For the fixed amount of Mn (3 atoms), it is MnO$_3$ that has the greatest number of oxygen atoms (9), hence the greatest percent oxygen by mass.

The correct choice is (C).

47. The dissolving of calcium carbonate in hydrochloric acid (choice D) is the only reaction of those listed which is not a redox reaction. In choices (A) and (B), the metals are oxidized by the nonmetals. In choices (C) and (E), compounds are decomposed producing elemental oxygen.

The correct choice is (D).

48. In this limiting reactant problem, it is efficient to ask two questions. If all the Al is consumed, what quantity of Cl_2 is required? If all the Cl_2 is consumed what quantity of Al is required? Comparing the required amounts to the available amounts will give the necessary information to proceed to the final answer. If all the Al is consumed, then 0.90 mol Cl_2 is required. (The mole ratio is 2 mol Al/3 mol Cl_2.) If all the Cl_2 is consumed, then 0.50 mol Al is required. Comparing the required quantities to the available quantities leads to the conclusion that there is sufficient Al to consume all the Cl_2 but that there is insufficient Cl_2 to consume all the Al. Some Al must remain uncombined. If 0.75 mol Cl_2 is consumed, then the maximum amount of $AlCl_3$ produced is 0.50 mol and 0.10 mol Al remains unreacted.

The correct choice is (C).

49. In this reaction, the precipitate $Mg(OH)_2$ is formed, driving $[OH^-]$ to a very small value due to the excess quantity of Mg^{2+}. The volume of the mixture is 100 mL. It contains 0.010 mol NO_3^-. Therefore, $[NO_3^-] = 0.10$. No change in $[NO_3^-]$ occurs. The available quantity of Mg^{2+} was 0.0050 mol. Of that, 0.0025 mol Mg^{2+} reacted with (essentially) all of the available OH^- (0.0050 mol), leaving 0.0025 mol Mg^{2+} in 100 mL solution with $[Mg^{2+}] = 0.025$.

The correct choice is (D).

50. For dilute water solutions, the molal freezing point depression constant is $-1.86C°$/molality of dissolved particles. Since this substance is 20% dissociated, the molality of dissolved particles (including ions and molecules) is given by:

0.050 m (available) − 0.010 m (dissociated molecules)+
0.010 m (dissolved cations) + 0.010 m (dissolved anions)

= 0.060 molal in total dissolved particles

Therefore, $-(1.86 \times 0.060)$ °C is the predicted freezing point.

The correct choice is (B).

51. In this solution, the ratio of ions to molecules is

$$\frac{0.010 \text{ mol (cations)} + 0.010 \text{ mol (anions)}}{0.040 \text{ mol (molecules remaining after ionization)}}$$

or, simply, $\qquad \dfrac{0.020}{0.040} = \dfrac{1}{2}$

The correct choice is (C).

52. The ionization constant for this acid is given as

$$K_a = \frac{[A^+][B^-]}{[AB]}$$

Substituting the known values

$$K_a = \frac{0.010 \times 0.010}{0.040}$$

Note that for dilute solutions (especially at the precision of two significant figures), molality and molarity have the same numerical value. Note that choice (A) does not use the correct concentration of AB <u>molecules</u>.

The correct choice is (B).

53. The half-reactions are

oxidation: $\qquad Sn + 2H_2O \rightarrow SnO_2 + 4H^+ + 4e^-$

reduction: $\qquad 2H^+ + NO_3^- + e^- \rightarrow NO_2 + H_2O$

Choosing multipliers of 1 and 4, respectively, the equation becomes

$$1Sn + 4NO_3^- + 4H^+ \rightarrow 1SnO_2 + 4NO_2 + 2H_2O$$

Note that when the coefficients for the equation are to be added, the value "1" (appearing twice) must be included; thus, $1 + 4 + 4 + 1 + 4 + 2 = 16$

The correct choice is (B).

54. For any system at equilibrium, $\Delta G = 0$. Therefore the values of G for reactants and products are the same, as in Statement I. Also, for any system at equilibrium, the rate of the forward reaction is equal to the reverse reaction, as in Statement II. However, the concentrations of products and reactants are not necessarily equal at equilibrium. The large value of K_{eq} indicates that formation of products is strongly favored. Statement III is not true.

The correct choice is (C).

55. In this mixture, 1.0 mol H₃PO₄ will donate 1 mol H⁺ to 1.0 mol of the strongest base present, HPO_4^{2-}, forming 1.0 mol $H_2PO_4^-$. Thus, the quantity of $H_2PO_4^-$ becomes 2.0 mol. The dissociation equation is

$$H_2PO_4^- \rightleftharpoons H^+ + HPO_4^{2-} \qquad K_a = 8 \times 10^{-8}$$

To solve for [H⁺], substitute the known values in

$$K_a = \frac{[H^+][HPO_4^{2-}]}{[H_2PO_4^-]}$$

$$8 \times 10^{-8} = \frac{[H^+][HPO_4^{2-}]}{2.0}$$

Since $[H^+] = [HPO_4^{2-}]$

$$[H^+]^2 = 2.0 \times 8 \times 10^{-8} = 16 \times 10^{-8}$$

$$[H^+] = \sqrt{16} \times 10^{-4} = 4 \times 10^{-4}$$

Of the values given, 4×10^{-4} is closest to 5×10^{-4}.

The correct choice is (B).

56. In water solution, the CO_3^{2-} ion undergoes hydrolysis to produce a basic solution. However, CO_3^{2-} is not as strong as OH^-. The pH of 0.010 M OH^- is 13. At a concentration of 0.10, the pH of the CO_3^{2-} solution will be closer to 11 than 14. The acidic values of 1 and 3 and the neutral value 7 are not plausible.

The correct choice is (D).

57. The K_{sp} for Ag_2CrO_4 is given by

$$K_{sp} = [Ag^+]^2[CrO_4^{2-}]$$

The molar solubility is given as 1.3×10^{-4}. Therefore,

$$[Ag^+] = 2 \times 1.3 \times 10^{-4} \text{ and } [CrO_4^{2-}] = 1.3 \times 10^{-4}$$

Substituting the known values

$$K_{sp} = (2 \times 1.3 \times 10^{-4})^2 (1.3 \times 10^{-4}) = (2.6 \times 10^{-4})^2 (1.3 \times 10^{-4})$$

The correct choice is (B).

58. The contents of a 3.0 molal solution of H_2SO_4 are 1.00 kg H_2O for every 3.0 moles of H_2SO_4 (98 g/mol). The percent H_2SO_4 by mass is given by

$$\frac{(3 \times 98)\text{g } H_2SO_4 \times 100}{\left((3 \times 98) + 1000\right)\text{g solution}}$$

The correct choice is (E).

59. Warming the mixture is the best way to increase the rate at which the dissolving process occurs. This will also increase the rate of crystallization (the reverse reaction). Note that the question refers to the RATE of dissolving, not the solubility of NaI. Neither the addition of $NaI_{(s)}$ nor saturated $NaI_{(aq)}$ will have any effect on the rate of dissolving (or the rate of crystallization). Cooling the mixture will decrease the rates of both the forward and reverse reactions. Increasing the external pressure will have no effect on this system since there are no gas phase components.

The correct choice is (D).

60. The greatest difference in solubility in the silver and magnesium compounds of the anions listed is in their chlorides. AgCl is nearly insoluble; $MgCl_2$ is very soluble. $AgCH_3COO$ is often listed in tables as "slightly soluble" or with a K_{sp} of about 10^{-3}. AgCl is much less soluble (less than 0.01 g/L) than $AgCH_3COO$ (about 10 g/L). Therefore, Cl^- is a much better answer. Using NH_4^+, NO_3^- or H_3O^+ will not produce any precipitates suitable for effective separation.

The correct choice is (A).

61. Using the principle below (Hess's Law)

$$\Delta H^\circ = \sum \Delta H^\circ_{f,\text{PROD}} - \sum \Delta H^\circ_{f,\text{REACT}}$$

$$-700 = \left(-400 + \left(2 \times (-300)\right)\right) - \left((\Delta H^\circ_{f,CH_3OH})\right)$$

$$\Delta H^\circ_{f,CH_3OH} = -300 \text{ kJ/mol}$$

The correct choice is (C).

62. Of the choices given, only (D) has no effect on the rate of reaction described. Adding any kind of catalyst increases reaction rate. Adding a miscible liquid to a liquid phase reaction dilutes the reaction mixture and decreases the reaction rate. Adding excess base to a neutralization reaction for a nearly insoluble weak acid increases the rate at which this solid donates protons since there will be a higher concentration of proton acceptors. However, adding inert gas to a gas phase reaction at constant volume has no effect because, at constant volume, there is no dilution. Since the added gas is "inert", it takes no part in any reaction.

The correct choice is (D).

63. The best measure of stability of a compound is its value for ΔG_f°. A lower value for ΔG_f° indicates greater stability. Thus, ethene is more stable.

Solving the relationship for ΔS_f° will establish the sign for ΔS_f°:

$$\Delta G_f^\circ = \Delta H_f^\circ - T\Delta S_f^\circ$$

ethene: $68 \text{ kJ/mol} = 52 \text{ kJ/mol} - 298K \times \Delta S_f^\circ$

$$\Delta S_f^\circ = \frac{16 \text{ kJ/mol}}{-298K},$$

thus the sign of ΔS_f° is negative

ethyne: $209 \text{ kJ/mol} = 227 \text{ kJ/mol} - 298K \times \Delta S_f^\circ$

$$\Delta S_f^\circ = \frac{-16 \text{ kJ/mol}}{-298K},$$

thus the sign of ΔS_f° is positive

Both compounds have the same constituent elements, $C_{(s)}$ and $H_{2(g)}$. The fact that their signs for ΔS_f° are opposite is a measure of the entropy (disorder) of the compounds compared to the entropy of their constituent elements. $C_2H_{2(g)}$ has higher entropy than its elements. C_2H_4 has lower. The fact that they have the same numerical value has no special significance.

The correct choice is (D).

64. In order to determine ΔS_f° for the dissolving process, the values for ΔG° and ΔH° for that same process must be determined. Using Hess's Law as in question 61:

$$\Delta G_{dissolve}^\circ = \sum \Delta G_{f,PROD}^\circ - \sum \Delta G_{f,REACT}^0$$

$$\Delta G_{dissolve}^\circ = (-393) - (-384)$$

$$\Delta G_{dissolve}^\circ = -9 \text{ kJ/mol}$$

$$\Delta H_{dissolve}^\circ = \sum \Delta H_{f,PROD}^\circ - \sum \Delta H_{f,REACT}^\circ$$

$$\Delta H_{dissolve}^\circ = (-407) - (-410)$$

$$\Delta H_{dissolve}^\circ = 3 \text{ kJ/mol}$$

Then to determine $\Delta S_{dissolve}^\circ$, use the values determined above in the ΔG° relationship

$$\Delta G_{dissolve}^\circ = \Delta H_{dissolve}^\circ - T\Delta S_{dissolve}^\circ$$

$$-9 \text{ kJ/mol} = 3 \text{ kJ/mol} - 298K \times \Delta S_{dissolve}^\circ$$

$$\Delta S_{dissolve}^\circ = \frac{-12 \text{ kJ/mol}}{-298K} = \frac{12,000 \text{ joule}}{298 \text{ mol} \cdot K}$$

Approximating

$$\frac{12,000 \text{ joule}}{\text{about } 300 \text{ mol} \cdot K} = \text{about } 40 \text{ j/mol} \cdot K$$

which corresponds to the range in choice (A).

The correct choice is (A).

65. To determine the rate law, several trials of the same reaction can be used. The effect of differences in concentration of the reactants on the observed rate is used to establish the exponents of each term. Note that any one trial should have introduced only one difference as the independent variable. The observed rate is the dependent variable. Comparing trials 1 and 2, doubling [A] doubles the rate. The exponent for [A] is 1. (If that doubling of [A] had produced a quadrupling of the rate, the exponent for [A] would have been 2.) Comparing trials 2 and 3, doubling [B] also doubles the rate. The exponent for [B] is also 1. Comparing trials 2 and 3 shows that there is no effect on the rate when [C] is changed. (If the exponent for [C] were also one, changing [C] by a factor of 1.5 would have caused the rate to change by the same factor.)

The correct choice is (C).

66. As any trial of this reaction (and almost any other reaction) proceeds at constant temperature, the rate of reaction decreases because the concentrations of the reactant molecules decrease. Choices (A), (B) and (C) are incorrect. The reason given in (E) is incorrect since, at constant temperature and with no catalyst, there will be no change in effectiveness of collisions

    The correct choice is (D).

67. Isomers of 1-butanol must have the molecular formula C_4H_9OH (or $C_4H_{10}O$). Of the choices offered, only (B) includes both members with the correct molecular formula. The structural formulas for all four alcoholic isomers of C_4H_9OH are

    $$-\overset{|}{\underset{|}{C}}-\overset{|}{\underset{|}{C}}-\overset{|}{\underset{|}{C}}-\overset{|}{\underset{|}{C}}-OH \qquad \text{1-butanol}$$

    $$-\overset{|}{\underset{|}{C}}-\overset{|}{\underset{\underset{OH}{|}}{C}}-\overset{|}{\underset{|}{C}}-\overset{|}{\underset{|}{C}}- \qquad \text{2-butanol}$$

    $$-\overset{|}{\underset{|}{C}}-\overset{\overset{OH}{|}}{\underset{\underset{-C-}{\underset{|}{|}}}{C}}-\overset{|}{\underset{|}{C}}- \qquad \text{2-methyl-2-propanol}$$

    confirming the fact that they are isomers. A fourth isomer is

    $$-\overset{|}{\underset{|}{C}}-\overset{|}{\underset{\underset{-C-}{\underset{|}{|}}}{C}}-\overset{\overset{OH}{|}}{\underset{|}{C}}- \qquad \text{2-methyl-1-propanol}$$

    The correct choice is (B).

68. The best net ionic equation for the reaction of solid calcium phosphate with excess concentrated sulfuric acid is choice (A)

$$Ca_3(PO_4)_{2(s)} + 3H_2SO_4 \rightarrow 3CaSO_{4(s)} + 2H_3PO_4$$

even though no ions are represented explicitly in this equation. There is little water in concentrated sulfuric acid. Therefore, H_2SO_4 is best represented as molecular substance. H_3PO_4 is a weak acid and should always be represented as molecular, even at low concentrations in water. Since $CaSO_4$ is nearly insoluble in water, it, too, is best represented as a non-dissociated solid, even in the presence of water.

The correct choice is (A).

69. The correct name for the molecule

```
              Cl
         |    |    |    |    |
      —  C —  C —  C —  C —  C  —
         |    |    |    |
              Cl   Br   Br
```

is 2,2-dichloro-3,4-dibromopentane. The prefix, di, is used <u>twice</u> and the numeral, 4, is used <u>once</u>.

The correct choice is (D).

70. In the structural formula

[benzene ring with NO₂ groups at two adjacent positions]

the hexagon represents the benzene ring with six carbon atoms and one hydrogen atom at each vertex where no other atom or group of atoms is specified. Thus, the molecular formula is $C_6H_4N_2O_4$.

The correct choice is (D).

71. In this system, water evaporates from both beakers. At the same time, water vapor condenses in both samples according to the equilibrium

$$H_2O_{(\ell)} \rightleftharpoons H_2O_{(g)}$$

The rate of evaporation is greater for the pure water. Since there is a continuous source of $H_2O_{(g)}$, the rate of condensation in beaker B is always greater than the rate of evaporation. The solution becomes more dilute as water is added. Water is "moved" from beaker A to beaker B. The volume of liquid in beaker B has increased while the volume in beaker A has decreased.

The correct choice is (B).

72. The half-reactions in an alkaline battery are

anode: $$Zn_{(s)} \rightarrow Zn^{2+}_{(aq)} + 2e^-$$

cathode: $$2NH_4^+{}_{(aq)} + 2MnO_{2(s)} + 2e^- \rightarrow Mn_2O_{3(s)} + 2NH_{3(aq)} + H_2O_{(\ell)}$$

The anode is made of zinc metal.

The correct choice is (E).

73. When the dissolving of a solid is observed in a styrofoam cup calorimeter experiment, the change in volume of the solution as the solute dissolves is not measured. In general, it is negligibly small and has no effect on the energy change being observed. Temperature changes and masses of the components of the system must be precisely and accurately measured.

The correct choice is (E).

74. Since the sulfuric acid dissolves in water, ΔG_{soln} must be negative. Since the dissolving process is exothermic, ΔH_{soln} must be negative. Since this dissolving process changes the system to a more disordered condition, ΔS_{soln} must be positive.

The correct choice is (C).

75. The condition described corresponds to the placing of an open container of water, perhaps even an ordinary ice cube tray, in a low temperature freezer. The vapor pressure of water is negligibly small at 230 K. The liquid phase changes to solid, giving off energy. Both ΔG and ΔH are negative. Since the change produces a more ordered condition, ΔS is also negative. Thus, all three statements are correct.

The correct choice is (E).

Section II - Free-Response

See general directions and list of *Equations and Constants* on pages ii-iv.

Section II Total Time – 90 Minutes
(Multiple-Choice Questions are found in Section I.)

Part A: Question 76
and
Question 77 or Question 78
Time: 40 Minutes

Access to calculators, periodic table, lists of standard reduction potentials,
and *Equations and Constants*

(2000 Examination directions) Clearly show the method used and steps involved in arriving at your answers. It is to your advantage to do this, because you may earn partial credit if you do and you will receive little or no credit if you do not. Attention should be paid to significant figures. Be sure to write all your answers to the questions on the lined pages following each question in the booklet with the pink cover. Do not write your answers on the green insert.

76. <u>Overall strategy</u>: Recognize that this is a solubility equilibrium problem. The solute is an ionic solid and a weak base. The equilibrium constant is known as a solubility product constant, K_{sp}.

   (A) <u>Strategy</u>: Note that the reactant is the solid form of $Ca(OH)_2$. The products are the dissociated ions. The solid form does not appear in the mass action expression because its concentration does not vary.

   $Ca(OH)_2 \rightleftharpoons Ca^{2+} + 2OH^-$

   $K_{sp} = [Ca^{2+}][OH^-]^2$

   (B) <u>Strategy</u>: The solubility is given in grams per liter. Determine moles per liter for each of the dissociated ions. Note that two mol OH^- form for every mol $Ca(OH)_{2(s)}$ that dissolves.

   $$\frac{0.51 \text{ g } Ca(OH)_2}{1 \text{ L sol'n}} \times \frac{1 \text{ mol}}{74 \text{ g}} = \frac{6.9 \times 10^{-3} \text{ mol } Ca(OH)_2}{1 \text{ L sol'n}}$$

   Therefore, $[Ca^{2+}] = 6.9 \times 10^{-3}$ and
   $[OH^-] = 2 \times 6.9 \times 10^{-3} = 1.4 \times 10^{-2}$

   $K_{sp} = [Ca^{2+}][OH^-]^2 = 6.9 \times 10^{-3} \times (2 \times 6.0 \times 10^{-3})^2 = 1.3 \times 10^{-6}$

(C) Strategy: Find the definition of pH and the water equilibrium expression in the list of *Equations and Constants*.

$$pH = -\log[H^+] \text{ and } [H^+] \cdot [OH^-] = 1.0 \times 10^{-14}$$

$$[H^+] = \frac{1 \times 10^{-14}}{[OH^-]} = \frac{1.0 \times 10^{-14}}{1.4 \times 10^{-2}} = 7.14 \times 10^{-13}$$

$$pH = -\log 7.14 \times 10^{-13} = 12.15$$

(D) Strategy: Precipitation occurs if the ion product for the mixture in question is greater than K_{sp}. Calculate the ion product for the mixture and compare that value to the K_{sp}. Note that the final volume of the mixture is 0.100 L.

$$[Ca^{2+}] = \frac{0.040 \text{ L} \times 0.020 \text{ mol} \cdot L^{-1}}{0.100 \text{ L mixture}} = 0.0080 \text{ M}$$

$$[OH^-] = \frac{0.060 \text{ L} \times 0.015 \text{ mol} \cdot L^{-1}}{0.100 \text{ L mixture}} = 0.0090 \text{ M}$$

Ion product $= [Ca^{2+}][OH^-]^2 = 0.0080 \cdot (0.0090)^2 = 6.5 \times 10^{-7}$

$K_{sp} = 1.3 \times 10^{-6}$

The ion product is less than the K_{sp}, indicating that the solution has not reached its saturation point. No precipitation occurs.

Sample Examination III 213

Answer either question 77 or question 78 below.
(2000 examination directions) Only one of these two questions will be graded. If you start both questions, be sure to cross out the question you do not want graded.

The Section II score weighting for the question that you choose is 20 percent.

77. Overall strategy: When used a a fuel, butane burns in oxygen to form CO_2 and H_2O. Energy is released as the reaction proceeds.

   (A) Strategy: "Complete combustion" calls for the formation of CO_2 and H_2O when hydrocarbons burn. Incomplete combustion implies formation of CO or C as well as CO_2.

   $$2C_4H_{10(g)} + 13O_{2(g)} \rightarrow 8CO_{2(g)} + 10H_2O_{(l)}, \text{ or}$$

   $$C_4H_{10(g)} + \frac{13}{2}O_{2(g)} \rightarrow 4CO_{2(g)} + 5H_2O_{(l)}$$

   (B) Strategy: Find number of moles of $O_{2(g)}$ consumed, then use Ideal Gas law as provided in the list of *Equations and Constants* to calculate volume at specified conditions.

   $$10.0 \text{ g } C_4H_{10} \times \frac{1 \text{ mol } C_4H_{10}}{58 \text{ g } C_4H_{10}} \times \frac{13 \text{ mol } O_2}{2 \text{ mol } C_4H_{10}} = 1.12 \text{ mol } O_2$$

   $$V = \frac{1.12 \text{ mol } O_2 \times 0.0821 \text{ L} \cdot \text{atm} \cdot \text{mol}^{-1} \cdot \text{K}^{-1} \times 298 \text{ K}}{0.965 \text{ atm}}$$

   V = 27.9 L

(C) Strategy: From the list of *Equations and Constants* provided, find

$$\Delta H° = \sum \Delta H°_{f, \text{products}} - \sum \Delta H°_{f, \text{reactants}} \text{ (often known as Hess's Law)}$$

Use the values for $\Delta H°_f$ provided for all reactants and products to calculate $\Delta H°$.

$\Delta H°_{\text{comb}}$ for butane corresponds to $\Delta H°$ for this combustion reaction. Substituting the known values in Hess's Law, the unknown $\Delta H°_f$ can be calculated.

$$\Delta H°_{\text{comb}} = \left[8(\Delta H°_{f, CO_2}) + 10(\Delta H°_{f, H_2O})\right] - \left[2(\Delta H°_{f, C_4H_{10}}) + 13(\Delta H°_{f, O_2})\right]$$

$$2(-2,874.5) = \left[8(-393.5) + 10(-285.83)\right] - \left[2(\Delta H°_{f, C_4H_{10}}) + 13(0)\right]$$

$$\Delta H°_{f, C_4H_{10}} = \frac{[-3,148 - 2,858] - [2(-2,874.5)]}{2}$$

$$\Delta H°_{f, C_4H_{10}} = -128.5 \text{ kJ mol}^{-1}$$

(D) Strategy: Note that the energy from 1 mole of C_4H_{10} is used to increase the temperature of an unknown mass of water from 15.0°C to 70.0°C. First, identify the standard heat of combustion, $\Delta H°_{\text{comb}}$, as the amount of energy produced; then calculate the mass of water that could be heated by that amount of energy to the specified temperature.

$$\frac{2,874.5 \text{ kJ energy}}{55.0°C} \times \frac{1,000 \text{ J}}{1 \text{ kJ}} \times \frac{1 \text{ g} \cdot °C}{4.18 \text{ J}} \times \frac{1 \text{ kg}}{1,000 \text{ g}} = \mathbf{12.5 \text{ kg } H_2O}$$

Alternative set-up using information from list of *Equations and Constants*.

$q = m\,c\,\Delta T$ where $q = 2,874.5$ kJ (given in part (C))
$\Delta T = 55°C$
$c = 4.18$ kJ kg^{-1} °C^{-1}

$$m = \frac{q}{c\Delta T}$$

$$m = \frac{2,874.5 \text{ kJ}}{4.18 \text{ kJ kg}^{-1} \text{ °C}^{-1} \cdot 55°C}$$

$$\mathbf{m = 12.5 \text{ kg } H_2O}$$

78. **Overall strategy**: Recognize that the problem represents an application of the differential rate laws; that is, a series of experiments for which the initial concentrations and rates are known.

   (A) <u>Strategy</u>: Compare trials to look for change in one concentration, then find the corresponding change in initial rate of formation.

   Rate = k[NO]^2[Br$_2$]^1 or = k[NO]^2[Br]

   When [NO] doubled with [Br$_2$] constant (compare trials I and III), rate quadrupled. Hence, order in NO is 2.

   When [Br$_2$] doubled with [NO] constant (compare trials I and II], rate doubled. Hence order in Br$_2$ is 1.

   (B) <u>Strategy</u>: To calculate the rate constant, k, choose any trial and substitute its values in the rate law as determined in part (A).

   From Trial I, 1.20×10^{-3} M sec^{-1} = k(0.10 mol L^{-1})^2(0.100 mol L^{-1})^1

   $$k = \frac{1.20 \times 10^{-3} \text{ mol L}^{-1} \text{ sec}^{-1}}{(0.10 \text{ mol L}^{-1})^2 (0.100 \text{ mol L}^{-1})}$$

   k = 1.20 M^{-2} sec^{-1}

   (C) <u>Strategy</u>: Determine new concentrations and substitute in rate law determined in part (A); use same value for k because no temperature change is specified. Note that all concentrations are doubled when volume decreases to one-half original value. At these higher concentrations, rate is expected to be greater.

   [NO] becomes 0.400; [Br$_2$] becomes 0.200

   Rate = k[NO]^2[Br$_2$]

   Rate = 1.20 M^{-2} sec^{-1} (0.400)^2(0.200)

   Rate = 0.0384 M sec^{-1} or 3.84 × 10^{-2} mol L^{-1} sec^{-1}

(D) <u>Strategy</u>: Recognize that as [NO] has decreased to 0.150 M, [Br$_2$] has also changed. Based on the stoichiometry of the reaction, when [NO] has decreased by 0.150 M, then [Br$_2$] has decreased by 0.075 M to 0.025 M.

Applying the rate law as above,

Rate = k[NO]^2[Br$_2$] = 1.20 M^{-2} sec^{-1}(0.150)^2(0.025)

Rate = **6.75 × 10^{-4} M sec^{-1}**

Sample Examination III 217

Part B: Questions 79, 80, 81
and
Question 82 or Question 83
Time: 50 Minutes

Access to periodic table, lists of standard reduction potentials
and *Equations and Constants*
No access to calculators

Answer question 79 below. The Section II score weighting for this question is 15 percent.

79. <u>Overall strategy</u>: The list of ten reaction categories below is a useful method to organize information about chemical reactions. Note that some reactions may be classified in more than one category.

   <u>Redox</u> **(Reactions that illustrate oxidation/reduction)**
   1. Synthesis (Direct Combination)
   2. Decomposition (Analysis)
   3. Single Replacement
   4. Simple combustion (Burning)
   5. Redox by commonly-used "agents"

   <u>Non-redox</u> **(Reactions where no changes in oxidation numbers occur)**
   6. Double Replacement (often with precipitation or formation of water or gas)
   7. Qualitative Analysis (reactions associated with commonly used procedures)
   8. Acid-Base Reactions (Arrhenius, Bronsted-Lowry, Lewis)
   9. Complexation

   Organic Reactions (Reaction involving the compounds of carbon)
   10. Reactions that illustrate chemical properties of organic compounds

   ---

   (A) Liquid bromine is mixed with a solution of potassium iodide.

   Redox: single replacement $Br_2 + I^- \rightarrow I_2 + Br^-$

   (B) Magnesium metal is ignited in a sample of nitrogen gas.

   Redox: synthesis $Mg + N_2 \rightarrow Mg_3N_2$

   (C) Solid mercury (II) oxide is heated in a test tube.

   Redox: decomposition $HgO \rightarrow Hg + O_2$

(D) Molten magnesium chloride is electrolyzed using inert electrodes.

Redox: decomposition $MgCl_2 \rightarrow Mg + Cl_2$

(E) A few drops of dilute sulfuric acid are added to a solution of sodium chromate.

Non-redox: $CrO_4^{2-} + H^+ \rightarrow Cr_2O_7^{2-} + H_2O$

not included in listed categories; reaction frequently used in general chemistry lab

(F) A solution of sodium phosphate is added to a solution of iron (III) chloride.

Non-redox: double replacement with precipitation $Fe^{3+} + PO_4^{3-} \rightarrow FePO_4$

(G) Hydrochloric acid is added to an aqueous suspension of barium hydroxide.

Non-redox: acid-base reactions $Ba(OH)_2 + H^+ \rightarrow H_2O + Ba^{2+}$

(H) Acetic acid is mixed with 1-propanol in the presence of concentrated sulfuric acid.

Organic: (esterification)

$$CH_3COOH + C_3H_7OH \xrightarrow{H_2SO_4} CH_3COOC_3H_7 + H_2O$$

organic acid reacts with alcohol to produce ester and water. H_2SO_4 is a dehydrating agent.

(2000 Examination directions) Your responses to the rest of the questions in this part of the examination will be graded on the basis of the accuracy and relevance of the information cited. Explanations should be clear and well organized. Examples and equations may be included in your responses where approrpriate. Specific answers are preferable to broad, diffuse responses.

Answer both Question 80 and Question 81 below.
(2000 examination directions) Both questions will be graded.

The Section II score weighting for these questions is 30 percent (15 percent each).

80. <u>Overall strategy</u>: The pH of a buffer solution remains relatively constant when small amounts of acid or base are added. A buffer solution contains a proton acceptor and a proton donor which neutralize the added acid or base. Each buffer has a maximum capacity to neutralize such additions.

    (A) <u>Strategy</u>: Use definition of buffer solution. Describe behavior of its components.

    A buffer solution is a solution which resists change in pH when when either acid or base is added. The added acid or base is neutralized by the proton donor or acceptor that is present in the buffer solution.

    (B) <u>Strategy:</u> Lewis dot structures show the valence electrons of the constituent atoms and the arrangement of electron pairs distributed according to the octet rule.

    (C) <u>Strategy</u>: Flask (1) contains 0.15 mol CO_3^{2-} and 0.25 mol HCO_3^-. The added $KHSO_4$, an acid, donates potons to the strongest base present, CO_3^{2-}.

    The addition of 0.10 mol $KHSO_4$ causes $[CO_3^{2-}]$ to decrease and $[HCO_3^-]$ to increase as 0.10 mol H^+ is transferred from HSO_4^- to CO_3^{2-}, forming 0.10 mol additional HCO_3^-. Buffer capacity has not been exceeded because 0.050 mol CO_3^{2-} remains to act as a proton acceptor if more acid is added.

(D) Strategy: Flask (2) contains 0.15 mol CO_3^{2-} and 0.25 mol HCO_3^-. The added NaOH, a base, accepts protons from the strongest acid present, HCO_3^-.

The addition of 0.10 mol NaOH causes $[CO_3^{2-}]$ to increase and $[HCO_3^-]$ to decrease as 0.10 mol H^+ is transferred from HCO_3^- to OH^-, forming 0.10 mol additional CO_3^{2-}. Buffer capacity has not been exceeded because 0.15 mol HCO_3^- remains to act as a proton donor if more base is added.

At equilibrium

$$[HCO_3^-] = \frac{0.25 - 0.10}{0.500} = \frac{0.15}{0.500} \qquad [CO_3^-] = \frac{0.15 + 0.10}{0.500} = \frac{0.25}{0.500}$$

$[HCO_3^-] = 0.30 \text{ M} \qquad [CO_3^-] = 0.50$

Not that use of K_I and/or K_{II} is not required for these problems.

81. Overall strategy: The value of the faraday is determined by measuring the amount of electricity comsumed and the corresponding amount of $H_{2(g)}$ produced according to the half-reaction

$$2H^+ + 2e^- \to H_2$$

In the electrolysis experiment, inert electrodes are connected to a source of direct current and immersed in a solution of sulfuric acid. Gas tubes are set in place to collect the gases produced. The time of operation and the current (amperage) are measured. According to information found in the list of *Equations and Constants*, the faraday is expected to be 96,500 coulombs per mole of electrons.

(A) Strategy: Show labeled diagram that includes each of the items specified in the question, properly connected.

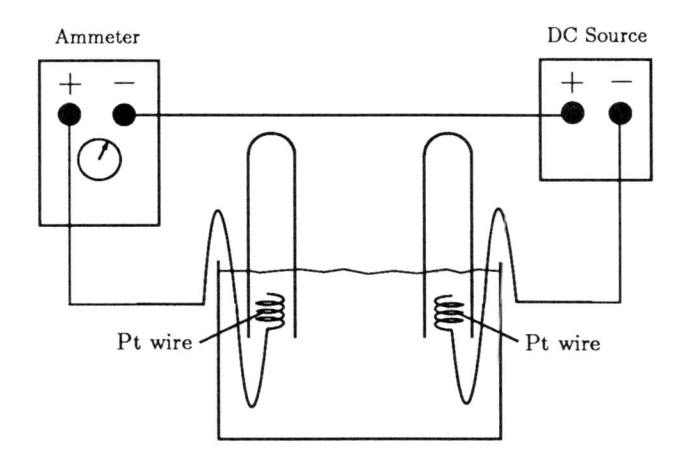

Sulfuric acid solution with two gas measuring tubes and two platinum wires.

(B) Strategy: Recall the decomposition reaction

$$2H_2O \to 2H_2 + O_2$$

The corresponding volume of oxygen is 45.0 mL. Two volumes of $H_{2(g)}$ are produced for every one volume of $O_{2(g)}$.

(C) Strategy: As shown on the list of *Equations and Constants*, electric current as measured by an ammeter is given as coulombs per second.

The measurement of time and current for the experiment allows for the calculation of number of coulombs of electricity transferred. Measurements required:

- number of seconds during which electrolysis was carried out (time)
- rates of current in amps (coulombs per second)

(D) <u>Strategy</u>: Consider the possibility that copper would undergo chemical change.

If copper were used instead of platinum, copper would be oxidized at the anode. Hydrogen gas would still be produced by reduction at the cathode. The purpose of the experiment could still be met, because the mass of copper oxidized (dissolved in solution as Cu^{2+}) would be chemically equivalent to the amount of hydrogen gas produced. The presence of copper would not affect the production of hydrogen gas.

Answer either question 82 or question 83 below.
(2000 examination directions) Only one of these two questions will be graded. If you start both questions, be sure to cross out the question you do not want graded.

The Section II score weighting for the question that you choose is 20 percent.

82. Overall strategy: Refer to the categories below. Recall the differences in the forces of attraction and the particles at the lattice points associated with each category

Categories of Solids

	1	2	3	4
	ionic solid	metallic solid	molecular solid	network (covalent solid)
(i) example	CaS (*calcium sulfide*)	**Mg magnesium**	CO_2 (*carbon dioxide*)	**C (diamond)**
(ii) particle at lattice point	Ca^{2+}; S^{2-} ions	Mg^{2+} *ions*	CO_2 molecule	C atoms
(iii) force between particles	**ionic bond**	**metallic bond**	*van der Waals forces*	*covalent bond (shared pair of electrons)*

82. Overall strategy: Note that each of the four categories is characterized by differences from the other three. These differences should be clearly addressed.

    1. ionic solid

        (i) **given** CaS *calcium sulfide*

        (ii) Ca^{2+} and S^{2-} ions found at the lattice points

        (iii) force of attraction: ionic bond (coulombic attraction between oppositely charged ions)

    2. metallic solid

        (i) magnesium (or any metal, including alloys)

        (ii) **given** Mg^{2+} *ions* (surrounded by a diffuse cloud of electron density)

        (iii) force of attraction: metallic bond - coulombic attraction between positive ions and negative electron cloud (diffuse cloud of electron density)

3. molecular solid

   (i) **given** CO_2 *carbon dioxide*

   (ii) CO_2 molecules found at the lattice points

   (iii) force of attraction: intermolecular forces (London forces or van der Waals forces)

4. network (covalent) solid

   (i) allow carbon ($C_{graphite}$ or $C_{diamond}$), quartz (SiO_2), silicon carbide (SiC)

   (ii) atoms such as C (or Si and O) found at the lattice points

   (iii) **given** *covalent bond* (electrons shared by adjacent atoms)

83. <u>Overall strategy</u>: The structure of organic molecules is based upon chains or rings of carbon atoms linked by covalent bonds. A name for each compound can be established based upon the IUPAC system.

(A) <u>Strategy</u>: Recognize that $C_2H_2Cl_2$ is a chlorinated alkene. Isomers have the same molecular formula but different structural formulas.

    1,1-dichloroethene   *cis*-1-2-dichloroethene   *trans*-1-2-dichloroethene

(B) <u>Strategy</u>: Recognize that 2-butene is a four-carbon alkene with one double bond and that the addition process occurs at the double bond site.

(C) <u>Strategy</u>: Recognize that $C_6H_4Br_2$ is an substituted aromatic hydrocarbon. It is closely related to the C_6H_6 molecule.

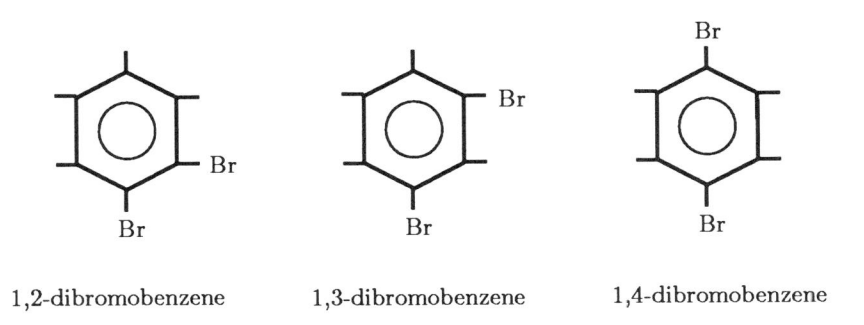

    1,2-dibromobenzene   1,3-dibromobenzene   1,4-dibromobenzene

(D) <u>Strategy</u>: Consider the difference in bonding between adjacent carbon atoms in these molecules.

<u>Strategy</u>: C_2H_4 is an unsaturated hydrocarbon. There is one double bond in each of its molecules. It reacts with bromine by addition across the double bond. C_6H_6 is an aromatic hydrocarbon. It behaves more like a saturated compound than an unsaturated compound. It does not react readily with electrophilic reagents like bromine. Each C-C bond in C_6H_6 is a resonance bond with a bond order of about 1.5.

NOTES

NOTES

NOTES

NOTES

NOTES